THE MINSTREL BOY

THOMAS MOORE
After Sir Martin Shee. P.R.A.

THE MINSTREL BOY

A PORTRAIT OF TOM MOORE

BY

L. A. G. STRONG

LONDON

HODDER AND STOUGHTON LIMITED

ST. PAUL'S HOUSE, WARWICK SQUARE, E.C.4

First published, 1937

Made and Printed in Great Britain for Hodder and Stoughton Limited,
by Butler & Tanner Ltd., Frome and London

TO W. B. YEATS

PREFACE

My acquaintance with Tom Moore began very early, when my grandmother sang me some of the *Melodies*, and my grandfather presently allowed me to balance on my legs the big green-bound volume with the brass clasp and the Maclise drawings. (I can still feel its back, cold and uneven, on my bare knees.) So the poet became a great figure in my mind, and I have been attracted to him ever since. For more than ten years I had thought of writing about him. Then I spoke of the idea to Mr W. B. Yeats, who encouraged me, and I began collecting material; but it is only now that I have had the time and the opportunity to begin.

I have tried less to write a history of Tom Moore than to draw his portrait, and to clear away some of the irrelevancies of criticism which have been heaped upon him. I am not afraid of partiality because, in life, affection does not blind me to a friend's faults, nor do they make me like him less: and I do not see why it should be different in literature.

To draw the portrait, I have made free use of Moore's Journal and Letters. A man's own way of telling what happened to him, and his comments upon it, reveal his character better than pages of description. So, on many occasions, I have let Moore tell his own story. His was a nature best expressed in intimacy, and his quick affections, his genius for friendship, give his own letters, and those written to or about him, a peculiar value.

The book makes no pretence to scholarship or completeness, though scholars have looked over my shoulder, and I have, by good luck and through the kindness of others, had access to a considerable amount of new material. My list of debts is long. The chief creditor is Mr Stephen Gwynn, whose *Moore*, in the *English Men of Letters* series, seems better every time I re-read it, and adds to my respect for his scholarship and insight. He has also helped me from time to time with fresh information.

Others whom I most gratefully thank are, in alphabetical order, Mr R. I. Best, the Librarian of the National Library of Ireland: Mr Edmund Blunden, who read my manuscript: Professor Edmund Curtis: Mrs Rosemary Edmonds: Mr R. Dudley Edwards, for information about the Penal Laws: Miss Letitia Emanuel, for translating Italian documents and for information about the College of Arcadia: Dr F. O'D. Fawcett, whose knowledge of Irish music has greatly helped me: Mr J. W. Hanna, the Librarian of Trinity College, Dublin, who brought to my attention a number of recently discovered letters and papers: the Earl of Ilchester, who very kindly sent me copies of Moore's letters in the Library at Holland House: Miss Barbara Lyall: Mr Seamus MacCall, Moore's most recent biographer, who very kindly communicated to me several points which he had discovered: Mrs Geoffrey Mander, who most generously allowed me to share in the results of her researches into the life of Mary Shelley: Miss Katherine Munro, whose historical knowledge supported me at many points: Miss Sylva Norman: Mr Frank O'Connor: Miss Monica Redlich, whose help, as always, was invaluable: Mr James Stephens: Professor W. F. P. Stockley, who allowed me to see an unpublished essay: Professor W. F. Trench: Mr Tom Turner: and Mr Laurence Whistler.

I am most grateful also to Moore's publishers, Messrs Longmans Green, and Messrs John Murray, for access to and leave to quote from their files: to Sir John Murray, for leave to quote from Byron's letters: and to Dr Williams' Trustees, for leave to quote a passage of Crabb Robinson.

CONTENTS

CHAPTER VII

CHAPTER VIII

PART TWO

HEYDAY

CHAPTER IX

CHAPTER X

CHAPTER XI

PART THREE

THE LAST YEARS

LIST OF ILLUSTRATIONS

*The portraits and sketches in this volume are reproduced by the kind permission
of the National Gallery, Dublin, and the Rischgitz International Art Agency.
The facsimile letter and accounts, by courtesy of Messrs. Longmans, Green and Co.*

PART ONE

AN INTRODUCTION

CHAPTER I

THE SCOPE OF MOORE'S LIFE

TOM MOORE was not a great man or a great poet, but he has many titles to attention. He was an admirable and a lovable human being, warm-hearted, honest, humorous, and kind. One particular job, on the borderline between poetry and music, he did as well as it has ever been done. He was a master of light verse, and, of his three biographies, one at least became a minor classic. He was the friend of Emmet, Byron, Scott, Canning, and Sydney Smith: a Prime Minister edited his memoirs: and he put Ireland back on the cultural map of Europe.

His contemporary fame was enormous. The greatest houses in the land were open to him, poor men ran to do him service, theatre audiences rose and cheered when he came in: but he kept a level head, and a precise knowledge of his own limitations. He was a famous talker in an age of famous talkers. His singing moved sophisticated men and women to tears. He was praised by Shelley, and hailed as a master by Poe. As late as the eighteen-fifties, he was confidently described as the greatest of lyric poets.

But there was more to him than that. Not by accident does a man become, and remain for close on a hundred years, the voice of his country: nor do songs born in the drawing-room reach and hold the thatched cabin. There was in Moore a stroke of passive genius, which enabled him to divine a spirit just about to be born among his countrymen, to surrender to it, and become its voice. Not its ideal voice:

> Comes a rather female song,
>   Sweet and sad; 'tis Tommy Moore
> Singing of Ierne's wrong. . . .

3

wrote Ralph Hodgson, and Moore himself deplored the softer
influences of his early years, which limited his expression to
elegance rather than to strength: but the sweet, plangent strains,
the nostalgia for Tara, woke in his countrymen a living sense
of their lost heritage, and, coupled with O'Connell's energy,
inspired them to regain it. Moore, too, was the first Irish man
of letters to be identified with his country. The others, from the
world's point of view, merely happened to be of Irish birth. But
Moore, almost from the beginning, was known as the singer and
champion of Ireland, and dragged his country with him into the
limelight. The short, cherubic figure with the bright eyes and
the curling hair, laughing with Byron, melting the young ladies
in the drawing-room, but inflexible in his protest against injustice and wrong, is among the chief architects of modern Ireland.
He walked on the sunny side of the road, but he was faithful.
Time and again, when patriotism and profit pulled in opposite
ways, he chose against his interest. Too easy-going, too frivolous
perhaps, to make his country's laws, he made its songs. For him,
chance and choice were one. The thing he liked doing was the
thing which best served his country. Instead of dying for Ireland
with Emmet and Fitzgerald, he lived to be her minstrel, and
to maintain her cause on more fronts than one.

> The Irish had long made the deuce of a clatter,
>   And wrangled and fought about MEUM and TUUM,
> Till England stepped in, and decided the matter
>   By kindly converting it all into SUUM.

"Our Irish rulers have always proceeded in proselytism on the
principle of a wedge with its wrong side foremost. The courteous address of Launcelot to the young Jewess, 'Be of good
cheer, for truly I think thou art damned,' seems to have been
the model on which the Protestant Church has founded all its
conciliatory advances to Catholics."

This forcible neatness comes as a surprise to many who think
of Moore only in terms of "The Last Rose of Summer". He

was a man of extraordinarily diverse gifts and sterling character, witty and accomplished, knowing his world, yet remaining simple as a boy. He married a penniless girl of sixteen, and remained her faithful lover till his death. He was universally popular, and that in spite of resolute independence and principles which he would never compromise. In one of the most interesting periods of English history, he knew almost everyone of literary and social importance, and kept a journal for thirty years, in which he recorded candidly his thoughts and his impressions of all whom he met.

It would be foolish to claim for Moore qualities which he did not possess. He had neither intensity nor real depth of character, he worried rather than agonized, he lacked a vision of evil. We can never give him the interest we give a Byron, a Coleridge, or a Shelley. Yet he stands strongly in his own right, as a sufficiently rare human and literary phenomenon, who has been and still is the subject of vigorous controversy. For many years now, in reaction from his excessive fame, he has been neglected and derided: but his record will bear inspection better than most.

CHAPTER II

HALCYON DAYS

Birth and parentage—Other relatives—The Moores' home
circle—Tom a gifted child—Malone's school—Samuel Whyte
—First theatricals—Music at home

AUNGIER STREET, Dublin, is a continuation of St George's Street,
which leads southwards out of Dame Street at a right angle: and
there, at No. 12, on the 27th of May 1779, Tom Moore was
born. His mother immediately had the fact commemorated by
having a crown-piece struck with an inscription of his name, the
place, and the date. The more orthodox method, that of register-
ing the child, was not open to her. Under the laws then existing,
state registration of birth was not possible for a Catholic.[1]

Tom's parents were of good middle-class stock, but in humble
circumstances. John Moore was a descendant of the O'Moores
who were dispossessed of their lands in Bloody Mary's reign and
driven into Kerry. Anastasia Codd came of an English Protestant
family who had fled to Ireland to escape the same queen's perse-
cutions, and was born in Wexford. John had a small wine-mer-
chant's business in Johnson Court, off Grafton Street. Anastasia's
father was a provision merchant. The pair were married in 1778,
and, with the money which his bride brought him, John set up
as a grocer in Aungier Street.

[1] The Established (Protestant) Church was theoretically held to comprehend everyone in the country, and no recognition was given to any other
communion whatever. Officially, therefore, a child would need to be regis-
tered in the Protestant Church of the parish. Catholics were naturally unwilling to do this: but, as the parish priests were beginning to keep unofficial
records of their own, Anastasia's action was not strictly necessary.

Anastasia's family had long since been Catholics, like her husband's. Outwardly at any rate, she was the better Catholic of the two, being devout to the point of superstition. John, who took things more lightly, was given to criticizing the priests, and lost few chances of getting in a dig at them.

Anastasia would begin to laugh: then, remembering herself, she would bite her lip and exclaim,

"I declare to God, Jack Moore, you ought to be ashamed of yourself."

But "Jack Moore" would go on chuckling unrepentantly in his corner.

When it came to a question of principle, however, he was inflexible, even to his own damage, as we shall see presently.

Anastasia Moore played a very important part in her son's life. Tom adored her, and her influence upon him was far stronger than his father's. She was under twenty years old when she married, and so was young enough to be a real companion to her children. John was a good many years her senior: she used to twit him good-naturedly with being "an old bachelor" before she came along and took him in hand. Affectionate, sociable, and gay, she loved parties, and kept open house, as far as her means allowed. Whatever other entertainment her guests found, there was at any rate no lack of talk and singing: for Anastasia was passionately fond of music. She sang well herself, in a clear, soft voice: and, as soon as they were old enough, she was urgent that Tom and his sister Catherine should have music lessons. She was socially ambitious, more for her children's sake than her own, and she devoted herself heart and soul to their welfare. Once she realized little Tom's abilities, she spared no effort to encourage him and make opportunities for his advancement. Above all, she and her husband were fond of one another, and the spirit in which the children grew up was one of good humour and affectionate harmony. Tom was born into an atmosphere that entirely suited his nature, an atmosphere which he reproduced in his own family, and carried with him to his life's end.

From the first, Anastasia strove to fit her boy for a higher walk of life than that to which he had been born. She could not stretch far, but she stretched as far as she could. High society for her was manifested in the shape of one Miss Dodd, "an elderly maiden lady": and to her, whenever possible, she sent little Tom, to learn polite usage. And Tom, young as he was, understood and seconded her efforts. He was not at all shy, being ready at any time to meet all and sundry. Years afterwards, he was to praise his mother's diligence. "To her constant attention to this object" (i.e., his social betterment), he wrote, "I owe both my taste for good company, and the facility I afterwards found in adapting myself to that sphere."

Miss Dodd, however, was by no means a stern preceptress: indeed, it probably never occurred to her that she was a preceptress at all. Tom loved his visits to her, particularly round about Christmas time, when he would stay for "three whole days" and be made much of by the lady and her friends. Once, when she had a large tea-party, he hid under the table with a musical box, waiting in delighted suspense for the moment when he could astonish the guests with a burst of unexpected music "from—they knew not where". Miss Dodd and he had plotted the surprise together. Tom never forgot the incident, nor the sense of power which he felt as he huddled down, waiting for his opportunity.

Of Tom's other relations—apart from his sisters—only two seem to have made a clear impression. One was his grandfather, Tom Codd, who lived at Wexford, in the Cornmarket. The child was taken down to see him, and brought back two or three pictures which became vague and legendary in his mind. One of them only was personal: the old man suffered from gout. The others concerned his surroundings. He had a provision shop, which little Tom recognized at once from its likeness to his own at home: and there was a good deal of machinery, the purpose of which he could not remember, but afterwards supposed to have something to do with weaving.

The other relation, whom he came to know well and to love, was his uncle Richard. Richard was his mother's brother, and lived with the Moores, sharing Tom's bedroom. We hear little of him, except that he was much older than Anastasia, a little older even than her husband: and that, when he died in 1809, his nephew was much grieved: "the first dear friend", he wrote, "it has ever been my fate to lose".

II

Tom was a precocious child, but only in ability. Throughout his childhood and boyhood, he had every excuse to be spoilt. Encouraged to perform in public, praised and petted by the ladies, a favourite with his schoolmasters, sought after and made much of by little girls, he took it all naturally, and his head was never turned. He had, all his life long, a simple pleasure in success, so natural, and at the same time so devoid of complacency, that it never made him enemies: and he was as readily delighted by another's success as by his own. Moore is a remarkable example of a man whose life from childhood was in one key. There was no conflict in his early days: perhaps not enough.

"My youth was in every respect a most happy one . . ." he wrote: and—

"I attribute very much to the cheerful and kindly circumstances which . . . surrounded my childhood, that spirit of enjoyment, and, I may venture to add, good temper, which has never, thank God, failed me to the present time." (July 1833.)

Even so, he realized the dangers of such halcyon days, and was able shrewdly to assess their effect upon his talent. When he was with Scott at Abbotsford in 1825, he saw forcibly how much the novelist had gained from his manly, open-air background, and his intimate knowledge of the cottagers and crofters. As they walked together, Moore turned impulsively to his host, and pointed to the contrast between all this and his own over-feminine upbringing.

"I said that the want of this manly training showed itself in my poetry, which would have perhaps had a far more vigorous character, if it had not been for the sort of *boudoir* education which I received."

All the same, the *boudoir* education had its austerities : Tom's mother would sometimes wake him up at two or three in the morning, and hear him his lessons, to make sure that he knew them. But love and affection were the only compulsions at Aungier Street, and the boy's cheerful and affectionate nature received its final impress.

The great weakness of Moore's poetry is that it lacks passion. He knew it. Sentiment, not passion, was his *forte*, and he said so plainly. In life, he shrank always from deep emotion, and could not bear to be present at his own child's deathbed. Yet there was nothing effeminate about him. Moore's "independence" was a favourite theme with his contemporaries, and the robust Scott named "a manly frankness" as the chief of his virtues.

It is a pretty puzzle, to determine how much the upbringing contributed, and how much the inheritance. Moore had his mother's emotional and sanguine temperament, and much of her moral earnestness, with a flavour of his father's humour. He was to show great strength and tenacity of character, and to attract the admiration of men whose admiration was not given easily. Whether the softness of his poetry sprang from the fundamental quality of his talent, or was an acquired idiom only, can probably never be answered.

III

The first gift that little Tom showed was for reciting, and
Anastasia, whose own tastes lay much in that direction, eagerly
developed it. Before he had reached his fourth birthday, she
taught him a set of political verses which severely censured
Grattan. The choice seems odd, as the child can hardly have
understood what they were about. It reflected, perhaps, the
ardour of Anastasia's own convictions, or, more probably, it
was intended to amuse the gathering of guests who came for
music and recreation to No. 12. Tom memorized easily, revealed
gifts as an actor, and was soon regularly on show in his mother's
drawing-room and at the houses of her friends. He would say
his piece, be much applauded, picked up, sat upon ladies' knees,
and receive tit-bits of cake and sips of sherry, while all congratulated his mother on her gifted child. Happily, it never seems to
have occurred to him that all this was anything out of the
ordinary, or that other children were not treated in the same
way. "I was", he says, in his own account of his childhood, "still
perfectly a child; nor had the least consciousness of being different from any other child in this respect."

The only tribute to his precociousness which he remembered
stuck in his mind because it amused him. He was staying with his
mother at the country-house of some friends named McClellan
—and it is characteristic of the social sense he was already de-
veloping that, despite their evident wealth, their carriage and
horses, they struck the child as "rather vulgar people". One of
the other guests, a Captain Mahony, impressed by Tom's alert-
ness, said laughingly to Anastasia that he must spend all his nights
with "the little people" on the hills close by. This became a
regular joke between him and Tom, and the Captain would
enquire of him, every morning at breakfast, what he had been
doing with his "little friends" the night before.

The only other friends whom Tom visited were a family of

the name of Dunn, who had a house at Dundrum. Here there were a number of children, and they all used to play together in a field close to the house, around the ruins of an old tumbledown castle. One day they decided to make Tom king of the castle. The boys bore him in triumph on their shoulders to the highest part of the ruin, where he was solemnly crowned by one of the little girls of the party. Years later, when he was in Dundrum, he looked in vain for the ruin, wondering if his memory was at fault: but one of the former Miss Dunns, now a sedate married lady, relieved him by telling him that the remains of the castle had been cleared away, and that she perfectly well remembered the day of his coronation.

Very soon, at any rate before his sixth birthday, Tom was sent to his first school. This establishment was only a few doors from the Moore home. The headmaster was an eccentric named T. S. Malone, who wore a cocked hat and spent most of the night in public-houses, being seldom in a condition to attend to his pupils until noon or afterwards, when he would compensate himself for his sore head by beating most of his class. Tom, however, seems to have been his favourite, and to have escaped the rougher side of his attentions. Mrs Moore, who always went out of her way to heap kindness and favours on all who might help her son, took pains to propitiate the curmudgeonly schoolmaster: and Tom, the youngest in the school, sitting up and piping out his lesson without a fault, managed to endear himself on his own account. Teachers are so grateful for a really intelligent boy that he has to be very unpleasant not to be liked, or at least left unmolested, by them: and the combination of youth and quickness softened the crapulous Malone. Tom profited, too, by such attention as Malone was able to give, and, on the 27th of July, 1785, he was awarded a silver medal, for "Reading History at a publick Examination".

The next year he was sent to the best school in Dublin. This was at 75 Grafton Street. The headmaster was Samuel Whyte, a man of some celebrity. Sheridan the dramatist had been his pupil close on thirty years before, and something of his fame had flowed back to Whyte and the school. Whether Sheridan had influenced him, or he Sheridan, Whyte was passionately interested in all to do with the stage, and had written a long poem entitled *The Theatre*. He also taught elocution, both to amateurs and professional actors. Whyte was delighted with Tom's gifts, and under his tuition they developed amazingly. A year from entering the school, Tom was performing in public, and was soon the star pupil. Elocution came first on his curriculum, but he learnt also English, Latin, and Greek.

His teacher in the classics was Donovan, a man of uncouth manner, but shrewd, honest, and kindhearted. Donovan was to teach him something else besides Latin and Greek: but, for the present, the boy learned so fast that he had a great deal of time left over for the subjects which interested him best.

Tom's first appearance on the stage was in March 1790, when he was not yet eleven. At a performance of *Jane Shore*, given at Lady Borrowes' private theatre in Kildare Street, the epilogue, "A Squeeze to St Paul's", was spoken by "Master Moore", with such success that everyone decided he must become an actor.

In December of the same year, he received as a prize an abridged Richardson, with the following inscription:

"The English Grammar School, No. 75 Grafton Street, Dublin. . . . At a general public examination, held on the 15th, 16th, and 17th days of December, 1790, Master Thomas Moore, having acquitted himself in a very distinguished manner in Castalia's Dialogues, is honoured with this premium. 4th Latin Class. W. W."

Besides such official performances, Tom was much encouraged by Whyte in private. The leading actors and actresses of the day came to Whyte's house, and he would often summon his favourite pupil, and make him show off his talents to the professionals.[1] Anastasia was off her head with delight, and Tom, revering actors as beings from a magical world, sat wide-eyed with admiration, and never learned to take their praises and petting as his right.

It says much for him that, in spite of his success at school and the way in which Whyte singled him out for favours, Tom was always popular with the other boys. The least sign of conceit would have brought immediate vengeance on his head; but his naturalness, and his ability to make the others laugh, saved him. No one seems to have been jealous, except the mothers of less favoured boys: and we are told of only one who expressed her feelings after a public performance. No doubt Anastasia was a match for her: and, if she complained to Whyte, she got little satisfaction.

IV

Tom's first rhymes were made so early that he could not re-member when he began. No trace of these nursery efforts sur-vives. The earliest verses we have are a foretaste of the bright commentary on current events, the metrical journalism, which he was to turn out in such quantities. When Tom was eleven, Dublin fell victim to the popular craze for "quizzing". A quiz was the toy which in our day has revived under the name of "yo-yo": and Grafton Street and Stephen's Green were full of men and women playing with the things as they walked along. Tom's couplet, which did more credit to his observation than to his ear, ran as follows:

> The ladies, too, when in the streets, or walking in the Green,
> Went "Quizzing" on, to show their shapes and graceful mien.

By this time the Moore family had increased,[2] and, for the summer months, the children were sent into lodgings at Sandy-

[1] He remembered particularly being called in to recite *Alexander's Feast* to Miss Campion.
[2] Tom was followed by two girls, Catherine and Ellen.

mount, which was at that time a mere village. There they bathed
and played with many other children, and at weekends their
parents came out to join them. Tom was very active: he bathed
and ran about and practised jumping, in imitation of Harlequin
in the pantomime. Harlequin he loved above all characters, principally because of his athletic prowess, and he practised assiduously to reproduce his feats, diving again and again over the rail
of a tent-bed until he achieved one of them to his satisfaction.
He had an admiring audience, composed mostly of little girls, to
whom he was a hero: and, again with a hint of precocity, he lost
his heart in more than one romance. Looking back, from later
life, he remarks on the validity of these first love affairs, which
"have a romance and a sweetness about them that never come
again". Moore always kept enough of the child about him to
remember childhood accurately, and, if the language he uses to
describe it seems a little over-ripe, it was an unusual childhood
he was remembering.

Another amusement of the holidays was acting. Just before
the end, there was a grand performance of O'Keefe's *The Poor
Soldier*. Tom was Patrick, the hero, "in a uniform far too large".
The part of Norah, the heroine, was played by a pretty little girl
called Fanny Ryan, and Tom threw into his scenes with her a
feeling beyond his years. At the end of the play, he spoke an
epilogue, written by himself, which shows a great advance upon
the "Quiz" verses. The Epilogue laments that the actors must
in a day or so return to school.

> Our Pantaloon that did so agèd look,
> Must now resume his youth, his task, his book,
> Our Harlequin who skipped, leap'd, danced and died,
> Must now stand trembling by his tutor's side.

When he came to the last two lines,

> Whate'er the course we're destined to pursue,
> Be sure our hearts will always be with you,

the pathos of the occasion was almost too much for him, and he had difficulty in not bursting into tears.

But the happy days were prolonged for some time after he went back to school. The weather was still summery, and the little Moores and many of the other children stayed on to get the last of the sun and sea air before returning to town. Every week-end, as long as they were there, Tom came out to join them, riding on his pony. His sisters and a number of other girls went in to meet him and escort him to the lodgings, dancing and laughing along by his side: and when the short hours were over, they went back with him part of the way, and stood waving after him till his pony was out of sight.

It is noteworthy, in the light of many a modern childhood, that all Moore's recollections of his early years were happy. Even when his mother woke him in the small hours to hear him his lessons, he sat up and repeated them "cheerfully"; though it is more than likely that his subsequent idleness at Trinity was in reaction from excess of zeal on Anastasia's part.

He relates one occasion at least on which he found her zeal a little awkward.

"On our days of public examination which were, if I recollect, twice a year, there was generally a large attendance of the parents and friends of the boys: and on the particular day I allude to, all the seats in the area of the room being occupied, my mother and a few other ladies were obliged to go up into one of the galleries that surrounded the school, and there sit or stand as they could. When the reading class to which I belonged, and of which I had attained the first place, was called up, some of the boys in it who were much older and nearly twice as tall as myself, not liking what they deemed the disgrace of having so little a fellow at the head of the class, when standing up before the audience all placed themselves above me. Though feeling that this was unjust, I adopted the plan which, according to Corneille, is that of 'l'honnête homme trompé', namely, 'ne dire mot',—and was submitting without a word to what I saw the master himself did not oppose, when to my surprise and, I must say, shame, I heard my mother's voice breaking the silence, and saw her stand forth in the opposite gallery, while every eye in the room was turned towards her, and in a firm, clear tone (though in reality she was ready to sink with the effort), address herself to the enthroned schoolmaster on the injustice she saw about to be perpetrated. It required, however, but very few words to rouse his attention to my wrongs. The big boys were obliged to descend from their usurped elevation, while I,—ashamed a little of the exhibition which I thought my mother had made of herself, took my due station at the head of the class."

All the same, Anastasia was very careful lest Tom's head should be turned by too much praise. When the artist Paulett Carey wanted to publish a drawing of the young prodigy in his *Sentimental and Masonic Magazine*, much to Tom's disappointment she refused.

v

With all this was growing up a love for music—"the only art for which, in my own opinion, I was born with a real natural love; my poetry, such as it is, having sprung out of my deep feeling for music". Children will often protect their best talent from premature development, and Tom, precocious and docile about everything else, was recalcitrant over his music. The Moores possessed an old harpsichord, which a customer had handed over in part payment of a debt, and Anastasia sought to make use of it. Accordingly she hired a young apprentice piano-tuner, first of all to put the instrument in order, and then to teach Catherine and Tom to play on it. Catherine took her lessons meekly, but Tom was not interested, and inveigled the youth into playing games with him instead: so that most of the time was spent in emulating Harlequin, vaulting over the chairs and tables in the

3

drawing-room. He would, however, return to the harpsichord when no one was by, and pick out tunes for himself with one finger. His mother heard him one day doing this and humming to himself, and discovered that he had a natural singing voice. Thereafter he had to sing at her parties: but, though willing enough to sing, he would not learn to play, and successfully resisted a second attempt to teach him a year or so later.

From this time onward, he contributed his share towards the musical parties which his mother held on every possible occasion. These he enjoyed mightily. There was little room in the Aungier Street house, but this worried nobody. The drawing-rooms at the front and back, which adjoined each other, were crowded out, and one could hardly hear oneself speak for the noise and laughter. Supper was laid in a tiny room off the back drawing-room, and the guests sat huddled together, scarce able to move, and getting more fun than ever out of their close quarters. When everyone had eaten—and the meal took a long time, owing to the smallness of the space and the number to be accommodated—the music would begin. Among the regular performers were Joe Kelly the actor, a big handsome man with a fine voice, and Wesley Doyle, the son of a well-known music teacher, whose voice Tom remembered as "very sweet and touching". Doyle was able to accompany himself and others on the piano, but Kelly did not know a note of music, was in fact almost illiterate. The two sang duets, which were always a great feature of the evenings. An officer of the Irish Brigade, by name Blake, would play on the Spanish guitar, at which he was an expert. Anastasia would then be called upon to sing, and Tom after her. One of her favourites was *How sweet in the woodlands*, and Tom would sing something of Dibdin, the composer of *Tom Bowling*, who was then at the height of his popularity.

When Tom was about fifteen, Mrs Moore realized a project she had had in mind for some time. Dissatisfied with the old harpsichord, she had been saving to buy a piano, and at last managed to find one to suit her purse. Tom would not play, though Wesley Doyle tried hard to teach him: but Catherine was more amenable, and one William Warren (soon promoted to "Billy") was engaged to teach her. In default of the piano, Tom, fired by the prowess of Blake, tried his hand at the guitar, but gave it up when he did not progress as fast as he had hoped.

CHAPTER III

GROWING PAINS

The Dublin of Moore's boyhood—Tom and his Confessor—
Politics—A meeting with Napper Tandy—A debating society
—First verses published—Entry into Trinity

THE Dublin in which Tom grew up was a city of violent con-
trasts. It was, in common opinion, the next capital in the Empire
after London, and had at first sight a great deal to recommend
it for that honour. The journey from London was a long business. When one had gone by coach to Park Gate, near Chester,
or to Holyhead, admiring the mountain scenery of North Wales,
there remained a sea journey which in fair weather took from
ten to twelve hours, and in bad weather could take days. Land-
ing at the South Wall, visitors would be shocked by the poor and
ragged creatures who swarmed down to get what they could,
and by the slums and hovels of Ringsend, along which they
drove the three miles to the city. Once fairly in, they were
invariably surprised by the city's magnificent architecture, particularly the noble squares and the Custom House. The wide
streets, too, came in for praise: but they were dirty, full of beggars, and, as to-day, they encouraged reckless driving. "Noddies"
and "Jingles", precursors of the outside car, drove hell-for-
leather on the cobbles and dirt, and the pedestrian had to get
out of their way as best he might. Heaps of refuse were allowed
to accumulate in the streets, to such an extent that vehicles were
sometimes overturned by them. St Stephen's Green was surrounded by a ditch into which any old rubbish and refuse would
be thrown.

The houses in the residential parts of the city, where life was quieter and the roads were better paved, dispensed lavish hospitality to the visitor, but it was generally noted that the standard of comfort was lower than that of London. Intellectually and artistically, the city was second to none. Books were not only read, they were bought, often at higher prices than London would pay. The theatre flourished. There were a number of playhouses, all in keen competition. Mrs Siddons, when she visited Dublin for a few nights in 1783, went away with a profit of over a thousand pounds. The other arts, and the sciences, were pursued with equal zest. The Royal Dublin Society had been running for fifty years, and the Royal Irish Academy, for the study of "science, polite literature, and antiquities", was founded in 1785. Trinity College was the nominal centre of intellectual life, though the dons were undistinguished, and entry, until a year before Tom needed it, was restricted to Protestants.

There was abundance of good talk in the city. The visitor, if at first appalled by the violent contrast between the well-to-do squares and the bitter poverty only just beyond them—contrast which a drive into the country would intensify—soon let his attention be diverted by the wit, the good nature, the loquacity, and the apparently boundless hospitality of the Dubliners. His uneasiness might be roused again, when he found that, despite the many busy industries, the silk looms, the glassware, and the distilleries, there was a good deal of unemployment. The linen trade, hitherto flourishing, had been hard hit by the outbreak of the American War of Independence: and the prosperity of the distilleries seemed in part to be effected at the expense of the poor, who, though apparently too destitute to buy food, managed somehow to make themselves drunk in astonishing numbers.

Politically, the city boiled with excitement. The Irish Volunteers had helped Grattan to realize his heart's desire, and in 1781, when Tom was two years old, Ireland had an Independent Parliament, which was for the next few years busy wrangling with Pitt over Free Trade. It fought England also on the Catholic question. Catholics still laboured under heavy handicaps, though the old penal laws, so cruel that they were condemned outright by no less a person than Dr Johnson, who could not be accused of prejudice in favour of the Irish, had been gradually relaxed. Mass was celebrated without concealment, and Catholics were allowed to own land and enter the army. They had no political status, however, and many of the professions were still barred to them. Too timid as a class to urge their own cause, they found their best champions among the Protestants, who saw that the country could never be united while Catholics were kept in such a state of inequality. Accordingly, in 1793, a further Act was passed, by virtue of which Tom was enabled to become a member of Trinity. But the party of reaction was strong, and, only a year later, Lord Fitzwilliam, who as Viceroy had expressed practical sympathy with the Catholics, was obliged to resign.

In the meantime, the Irish Volunteers had given place to the United Irishmen, a frankly revolutionary society founded in Belfast by Wolfe Tone. Inspired by the French Revolution, this society set itself to overthrow the English domination, armed its members, and organized drilling on a large scale up and down the country. Tone was an implacable enemy of England, and there was abundant discontent upon which he and his supporters could work.

In this atmosphere of excitement Tom grew from child to boy, and from boy to young man.

II

His character developed rapidly. Affectionate and biddable as he was, he showed at an early age considerable independence of mind. Anastasia had, of course, brought him up a strict Catholic. He attended mass regularly every Sunday, and, somewhere about his twelfth year, started going to confession. His confessor was Father O'Halloran, a benign and gentle old man, who at first appealed to him strongly. There was, moreover, the joy of a special breakfast afterwards, of beefsteak, eggs, and buttered toast, to mark the occasion and reconcile him to its solemnity. But Tom did not take kindly to confessing his sins. His chief objection was that Father O'Halloran, for all his gentleness, was virtually a stranger: and he found it "both painful and humiliating" to rake up before him six months' wrongdoing in thought and word and deed. The visits, infrequent as they were, became increasingly "irksome", and by the time he was seventeen he had stopped going altogether. This must have meant tearful scenes with Anastasia, but Tom probably found an ally in his father, who could not be ill pleased to see his son rebel.

Jack Moore had many Protestant friends. Neither he nor Anastasia ever allowed religion to interfere with their personal friendships. Their friends were of all sorts, and of all interests: but music and politics came first. The Moores, though they took no active part, were intensely interested in politics, and some of the most violent firebrands in the United Irishmen were in and out of Aungier Street.

Tom took to this political excitement as a duck to water. The picturesque always appealed to him: the way to his loyalty was through his emotions and his sense of poetry. In the general election of 1790, when Grattan and Fitzgerald were returned, enthusiastic crowds chaired them through the streets of Dublin. Aungier Street was on the route, and the Moores' window was full of heads. Tom waved a bunch of laurel so vigorously that he caught, or thought he caught, Grattan's eye, and was "prodigiously proud" in consequence.

A year or so later, he met the celebrated Napper Tandy, immortalized in *The Wearing of the Green*. A public dinner was given in Tandy's honour, and Tom's father took him along. Before the evening was out, he had the rare privilege of being taken on the great man's knee, where he sat proudly for several minutes. One of the toasts at the dinner made an indelible impression on his mind. It ran "May the breezes of France blow our Irish oak into verdure!" Tom thought it poetical: and, indeed, it has, especially in the word "verdure", something of his touch. As for its politics, he was, as he often said, "born a rebel", and everything around him helped to inspire him to an ardent nationalism.

On a December night in 1792, he saw for the first time the proscribed green uniform of the National Guard, its buttons engraved with "a cap of liberty surmounting the Irish harp". This was worn by Matthew Dowling, a clever drunken attorney, on a visit to the Moores' house. Actually to see, at his father's table, the uniform which had been forbidden by the tyrant! Tom gazed and gazed, and felt his heart swell within him.

All this time Donovan, his classical tutor, a fiery patriot, was instilling into him a sense of Ireland's wrongs and a hatred of her oppressors. The whole Moore circle held these views, but in Donovan they reached white heat. Finding his pupil apt, he devoted more and more time to them, letting them encroach upon school hours till they shared the time "pretty equally" with the classics. Music and love of Ireland—everything was pointing the way, and shaping the plastic mind for its life's work.

III

Tom's chief school friend was Beresford, son of Beresford Burston the lawyer, who had a fine house at Blackrock, where Tom spent a great part of his holidays. Burston, like many other Protestants, was a strong supporter of the Catholics, and here again the boy found food for his ideas. The lawyer was pleased with him, gave him encouragement, and, on at least one occasion, commended his verses as "doing him honour".

At home, the chief out-of-school occupation was the conduct

DUBLIN IN 1776
From an engraving

of a literary and debating society, which numbered exactly three. The members were Tom and the two clerks from the shop, Tom Ennis, shrewd and humorous, and Johnny Delaney, who was younger and had less personality. Tom shared a bedroom with the pair of them, but his corner of it was partitioned off by boarding, and had a very literary appearance. Furnished with a table, a chest of drawers, and a bookcase, it was plastered with inscriptions of his own making. Off the bedroom was a closet, and here, at dead of night, the society met, in its heyday as often as twice a week. For literature, each member produced riddles in verse, which all three had to guess: after which they discussed politics.

One night, Tom's verse riddle proved too hard for his associates, and the meeting broke up without having solved it. The tenacious Tom Ennis was particularly reluctant to give in, but, rub his head as he would, he could not get the answer. In the small hours of the morning, Tom was roused from sleep by loud cries of "A drum, a drum, a drum", and a thumping of fists against the wooden partition of his cubicle. The clerk had lain awake until the solution came to him.

Tom's parents, by the way, knew nothing of the society and its objects.

During his last year at school, Tom's range of studies was widened to admit two more languages, French and Italian. The former he learned from an *émigré* named La Fosse, whose intelligence he praises, and who in six months taught him quite a lot. Inspired by La Fosse, he tried his hand at French verse, and produced a *Conte* in imitation of La Fontaine, thirty or forty verses long. His tutor in Italian was Father Ennis.

He mentions both these men in speaking of the year 1793–4, but later, when he comes to "scattered recollections" of the interval between May 1798 and his first visit to London, he repeats his description of La Fosse. The point is important only as one of the very few uncertainties in Moore's own account of his early days. There seems little doubt that the *émigré* figured at both times, and that Moore overlooked the fact that he had described him already.

IV

All this time the verses were coming on steadily, and attracting more and more attention. Tom's first appearance in print was in October 1793. The journal he selected was the *Anthologia Hibernica*, a short-lived venture on the part of Mercier, the University bookseller. Tom had been reading it attentively for some months, and had noticed with particular admiration Samuel Rogers' *The Pleasures of Memory*.

One of the Moores' friends at the time was an old lady named Miss Hannah Byrne, who came a great deal to the house, and was on very good terms with Tom. She encouraged his talent, and the pair corresponded, as it were, in verse. A reply to one of Miss Byrne's metrical exhortations was one of the pieces he chose to contribute. She had charged Tom with writing too much about love. Addressing her as "Zelia", the young poet defended himself.

> 'Tis true my theme to love inclines,
> And wreathes of Cypria's myrtle twines;
> Quits all aspiring lofty views
> And chaunts what Nature's gifts infuse.
>
> Timid to try the mountain's height,
> Beneath she strays, retired from sight;
> Careless, culling amorous flowers,
> Or quaffing mirth in Bacchus' bowers.

The last verse ran:

> When first she raised her simplest lays
> In Cupid's never-ceasing praise,
> The God a faithful promise gave,
> That never should she feel Love's stings,
> Never to burning passion be a slave,
> But feel the purer joy thy friendship brings.

"Poor Hannah Byrne!" wrote Tom in his *Memoirs*. "Not even Sir Lucius O'Trigger's 'Dalia' [1] was a more uninspiring object than my *Z*alia was."

The second poem was *A Pastoral Ballad*, on well-worn lines, beginning

> Ah, Celia! when wilt thou be kind?

and tittuping amiably along for several stanzas.

> My gardens are crowded with flowers,
>   My vines are all loaded with grapes;
> Nature sports in my fountains and bowers,
>   And assumes her most beautiful shapes.
>
> The shepherds admire my lays,
>   When I pipe they all flock to the song;
> They deck me with laurels and bays,
>   And list to me all the day long.
>
> But their laurels and praises are vain,
>   They've no joy or delight for me now;
> For Celia despises the strain,
>   And that withers the wreath on my brow.

These elegant but unremarkable verses were submitted to the editor of the *Anthologia* with the following modest letter:

> AUNGIER STREET, SEPT. II, 1793.

SIR,

If the following attempts of a youthful muse seem worthy of a place in your Magazine, by inserting them you will much oblige a constant reader,

> TH–M–S M– –RE.

The constant reader was obliged on this and several further occasions. In February of the following year the *Anthologia* printed *A Paraphrase of Anacreon's Fifth Ode*

> Let's, with the gaily-clustering vine,
> The rose, Love's blushing flower, entwine! . . .

---

[1] The name under which Mrs Malaprop corresponded with Sir Lucius in Sheridan's *The Rivals*.

and, in March, an *Ode to Samuel Whyte*. Even the stage-struck schoolmaster, vain as he was, and accustomed to flowers of speech, may have blinked a little at the opening:

> Hail! heaven-taught votary of the laurell'd Nine!
> That in the groves of science strike their lyres:
> Thy strains which breathe an harmony divine,
> Sage Reason guides, and wild-eyed beauty fires. . . .

At any rate, he digested the praises, and was sufficiently well pleased to reprint the ode a year later as an ornament to his own *Poems on Various Subjects*: and it is worth remarking that, for all their floridity, the lines show a better ear and a firmer touch than anything Tom had written up to that time.

In June a further effort appeared—*To the Memory of Francis Perry.*

> Life's fading spark now gleams the last dim ray—
> 'Tis out—th'unfettered spirit wings its flight
> In happier climes to drink eternal day
> And mix with kindred souls in realms of light. . . .

It is a piece of empty versification, with nothing to commend it.

V

Tom's last year at school ended gloriously. He had done so well in classics under Donovan, in spite of the excursions into politics with which the hours were enlivened, that it was not thought necessary to move him to Dr Carr's Latin School, the usual preparation for entering Trinity.

He was entered upon the register on June 2nd, 1794. The Act of 1793 had not removed all disabilities from the Catholic student, and it was suggested to the Moores that, in order to be eligible for scholarships and monetary prizes, and the ultimate chance of a fellowship, Tom should be entered as a Protestant. The suggestion was firmly put aside. Jack Moore may have exercised his wit at the expense of the priesthood, and have been no great hand at the observances of his faith, but he was not the kind to change sides for a bribe; and, in any case, Anastasia would never have suffered such a thing. Tom himself declares that "such an idea could hold but a brief place in honest minds". Yet the awkward fact remains that, in the Register, is clearly inscribed "Thomas Moore, P.Prot.": P. standing for *Pensionarius*, or commoner, and Prot. for Protestant.

There are three possible explanations. The first is that, despite all appearances to the contrary, the Moores were hypocrites, and father, mother, and son acquiesced in a falsehood for Tom's advancement. Apart from the inherent improbability of this, the deception, if any, was not kept up; for Tom, though at first he worked well, did not, on account of being a Catholic, receive the financial rewards to which his success would otherwise have entitled him. We are left to suppose, therefore, that the Moores gave up their deceit, or were forced to give it up. It is far more likely that they never attempted it.

The second explanation is that the entry was a mistake on the part of somebody else. This is not very likely either. The third, and most probable, is that the entry was made deliberately by someone else on Tom's behalf, someone who hated to think of his not winning the due rewards of his gifts. The likeliest person here would be Samuel Whyte. The schoolmaster, proud of having taught Sheridan, foresaw as bright a future for his latest star, and did not mean to let the world forget that he had taught him. In the 1795 edition of his poems, besides printing Tom's Ode, he added a note to the effect that the author of it had "entered college at a very early age, with distinguished honour to himself as well as to his able and worthy preceptor". Whyte may well have been unable to bear the idea of his pupil's not gaining all the distinctions he could, and so doing his master additional credit: and, without the consent of Tom or his parents, may have taken the step of entering him as a Protestant.

It is the most probable explanation of an odd incident, and we may accept it without any desire to whitewash the Moore family. They do not, in plain fact, seem to have been the sort of people to consent to a subterfuge, much less to renege for their own gain: and, when Tom actually entered Trinity at the beginning of 1795, it was as a Catholic.

CHAPTER IV

TRINITY

A holiday at Blackrock—Tutors and examinations—The Kingdom of Dalkey Island—Friends at Trinity—Love affairs?

BEFORE he began his studies at Trinity, in January 1795, Tom had
a prolonged holiday. Most of it he spent at Blackrock with the
Burstons. He read Mrs Radcliffe's romances, listened to Beresford's sister playing on the harpsichord, and passed his days in a
dream of happiness. He had many reasons for satisfaction, one of
which was the fact that he no longer was Master Tommy Moore
of 12 Aungier Street, but Mr Thomas Moore, of Trinity College: and the sight of his name, so printed, among the list of
subscribers to the *Anthologia Hibernica*, gave him a thrill of pride.
But he did not need reasons. His happiness was irrational, natural,
its own justification. The present was delightful, the future
promised him fair. He was with friends, and free to do as he
pleased. What more could a young man want, especially a young
man so naturally cheerful, so responsive to friendship and
kindness?

So he spent wonderful days at Blackrock, among the trees and
by the sea, watching summer fade into autumn, feeling the after-
noons shorten, and coming in, as the light faded and the chill rose
from the fields, to the comfort of the house, the wood fire in the
grate, and the soft candles in the music room. He often dwelt on
these days in later life, sitting down to his piano to play the
Haydn sonata and one or two other pieces which recalled them
most vividly to his mind. Speaking of them in his *Memoirs*, he
lets fall a phrase which epitomizes, finally, his cardinal weakness
as a poet.

31

"If I were to single out the part of my life the most happy and the most *poetical* (for all was yet in fancy and in promise with me), it would be that interval of holidays."

The italicized word and the explanatory bracket tell almost everything we need know about Moore as a poet. To him, poetry was the language of fancy, not of fact. It existed, ornamentally, at a remove from life. His imagination was "chilled by the real scene". An "innocent child" was more "poetical" than a man. He dressed things up in verse, prettified them, adorned them with "fancy". Munster became "Mononia", and Wicklow had to yield the adjective "Lagenian". His verses abound with the equivalent of conceits. They are the product of fancy. Only in his best work, in the finest of the Irish Melodies, *which must be considered always with the airs to which they were written*, does he transcend his limitations and reach an evocative power which, its artistic sovereignty apart, has been one of the greatest forces in the rebuilding of his country.

II

With most men of real ability, the academic side of their university days is the least important. Moore's time at Trinity was exceedingly valuable, although academically he achieved very little. It introduced him to Irish music: it confirmed the temper of his mind: it taught him to get on well with the philistines: it gave him his friendship with Emmet, and all which that friendship meant to him afterwards. The only benefit his official studies brought was the impulse to translate *Anacreon*, the work that made his first credentials when he came over to try his luck in London.

His tutor was Robert Burrowes, a clergyman, a good scholar with a considerable reputation as a wit, who became Dean of Cork. Moore, in his *Memoir* of 1833, credits him with the authorship of the magnificent *The Night before Larry was stretched*: but

the anthologists have not followed his lead. Tom worked hard
at first, to please his mother, and "gained a premium" in the
examinations of his first year, albeit in a somewhat unorthodox
manner. The subject was a Latin Prose, and Tom, hearing that
Walker, the examiner, was a person of greater literary taste than
his colleagues, handed in a set of English verses.

The paper was read, Tom looking on with beating heart.
The examiner looked up.

"Did you write these yourself?"

"Yes, sir."

"Upon my word, the verses do you much credit, and I shall
lay them before the Board with a recommendation that you shall
have a premium for them."

And the premium was duly granted, a handsomely bound
copy of *The Travels of Anacharsis*, "*propter laudabilem in versibu
componendis progressum*".

The reluctance to submit Latin compositions seems to have
persisted, for, some time later, he missed a classical premium
owing to his refusal to send in a copy of Latin hexameters. Tom
and another undergraduate, named Ferral,[1] were so evenly
matched that the examiner, Usher, was unable to separate them.
Accordingly he took them to his rooms, and questioned them in
turn upon the set books, the *Orations* of Demosthenes and
Virgil's *Georgics*. He continued till dinner-time, when, being still
unable to separate them, he bade them return next morning. On
his way home, Tom decided that Usher must now be satisfied
with their ability to translate, and would therefore be likely to
question them on the historical background of the *Orations*. He
therefore went to a bookseller friend and borrowed two large
volumes, which, in spite of a musical party, he managed to
skim before he went to bed. Next morning Usher, as he had
foreseen, started asking questions about the Philippics. The

---

[1] There are two Ferrals on the register. This is almost certainly John, the
younger.

unlucky Ferral could answer nothing, and Tom won hands down.

It was characteristic that, after this piece of opportunism, he should throw away his success through an artistic scruple. One of the set tasks was a copy of Latin verses. Tom had never tried his hand at them before, and was afraid of bungling. Usher tried hard to persuade him, telling him bluntly that it was a mere matter of form, and that it did not matter how bad his verses were: but he would not budge, and Ferral received the prize. Tom did not mind in the least. He rated his own slickness at its true value.

It was the practice at that time to start certain lectures at the unearthly hour of six in the morning. Tom's Greek lectures took place at this hour, by candle-light. The lecturer, Magee, afterwards an Archbishop, used to put the undergraduates on one after another to translate. Tom did not attend regularly, but, when he did, he prepared his translation with great care, and was fastidious about his English. Magee put him on one morning, and was so amazed at the quality of his performance that he let him go on for four or five pages, before stopping him with compliments and expressions of regret at the necessity for "interrupting" him and putting on someone else in his place.

The only other attempt Tom made to distinguish himself as a scholar was when, partly on his own account and partly in response to the repeated exhortations of his mother, he tried for a scholarship. His lack of training in verse showed itself, and Dr Kearney winced more than once at a false quantity, but he took a high place. His only reward was honour and glory, for, as a Catholic, he could not receive any financial award.

On Tuesday, June 13th, 1797, Tom's name was placed first on a list of thirteen exhibitions awarded as a supplement to the list of scholars published on the previous day, Trinity Monday. Since the religious disability persisted, he again received nothing but the credit.

Apart from this, however, he contented himself with doing just as much curricular work as would save him from disgrace, and gave his attention to other things. The dons were not an inspiring lot, and this may have had something to do with it: but the easing-off was probably a natural and salutary reaction from the precocity of his earlier years, and the pressure put on him by his mother.

III

Outside the regulation studies, he found plenty to interest him and keep his pen amused. There was, for instance, the business of the King of Dalkey Island. Some of the sprightlier citizens of Dublin, in want of a diversion, decided to constitute a mock kingdom, with titles, offices, and all the appurtenances of court. At the time when Tom was involved, the reigning monarch was one Stephen Armitage, a pawnbroker, popular for his good spirits and his powers as a singer. Tom was brought into the circle by a friend of his, Mrs Battier, "Harriet, Countess of Laurel," who was King Stephen's poet laureate. She was "an odd, acute, warm-hearted and intrepid little woman" who wrote verse satires: and her example spurred Tom to make his first effort in this line. The anniversary of the pawnbroker's accession was celebrated, one Sunday in the summer, by a procession of barges on the river, and a visit to Dalkey Island, where the old ruined church served as a cathedral. There was a certain amount of ecclesiastical parody, and Tom's satire, among others, was sung as a hymn. Addressed to "King Stephen", it congratulated him upon not requiring to be protected from attempts at assassination, as, by popular report, was George the Third.

> Thou rid'st not, prisoned in a metal coach,
> To shield from thy anointed head
> Bullets of a kindred lead,
> Marbles, and stones, and such hard-hearted things.

It all reads rather dully now, but charades seldom bear reporting: and the joke must have seemed a good one, for it was kept up for several years.

Tom's chief friends during his early years at college were young Burston—the two were entered for Trinity together, and, later, for the Middle Temple—and a youth named Bond Hall. Both were hearty, cheerful young men, who took no interest whatever in the things nearest Tom's heart. They cried out loudly, if he as much as mentioned literature or the arts: and, evidently, they did him a great deal of good. That he left Trinity a good mixer must largely be put down to their credit. He had always been sociable, and met people of all kinds at his father's house; but they were drawn together by love of music, by interest in politics, or by some other enthusiasm. It was good for him to be with young men who had no interests beyond their own immediate pleasures. He had enough sense not to be harmed. Hall, who was gay and witty, held him on that account. From Burston he gradually drifted away. They had no ideas in common, and only the habit of schoolboy friendship kept them together.

Another friend was Hugh George Macklin, older than Tom, and a member of the Historical Society. Here there was some common ground, for Macklin wrote verses: but he was a boastful fellow, re-christened "Hugo Grotius Braggadocio" by the rest, and Tom was ever afterwards critical of boasters.

More important was John Wilson Croker, who afterwards became Secretary to the Admiralty. Croker entered Trinity in 1796, and at once showed signs of brilliance. This friendship, though the two did not very often meet, lasted till Moore's death. There was an interval of coldness soon after Moore's departure from Dublin, when he took Croker to be the author of some anonymous criticisms of his work and character: but, on Croker's denial of this, Moore wrote him a cordial and sincere apology, and the friendship was resumed.

IV

It was only likely that healthy, cheerful, and idle young men should pay attention to women, and, under the influence of Hall and Burston, one might reasonably expect Tom to have had adventures. Evidently he had: he admits as much: but he gives no details. For all his candour, Tom could be very unrevealing when he chose, confessing just enough to obscure the facts. He introduces the subject, only to be vague about it, but we may remember that he was writing many years afterwards, with the example of Byron fresh before him, and that a long and happy married life intervened between then and the far-off days when he had addressed his poems to Cara, Fanny, Rosa, Julia, Cloris, and the rest. Not that the poems need be taken seriously. They are full of kisses, and reclinings on the breast, but the ladies might as well all be imaginary. There are a great many of them, and they are summed up fairly enough in *The Catalogue*.

> "Come, tell me," says Rosa, as kissing and kist,
>   One day she reclin'd on my breast;
> "Come, tell me the number, repeat me the list
>   Of the nymphs you have lov'd and carest."—
> Oh Rosa! 'twas only my fancy that roved,
>   My heart at the moment was free;
> But I'll tell thee, my girl, how many I've loved,
>   And the number shall finish with thee.
>
> My tutor was Kitty; in infancy wild
>   She taught me the way to be blest;
> She taught me to love her, I lov'd like a child,
>   But Kitty could fancy the rest.
> This lesson of dear and enrapturing lore
>   I have never forgot, I allow:
> I have had it *by rote* very often before,
>   But never *by heart* until now.
>
> Pretty Martha was next, and my soul was all flame,
>   But my head was so full of romance
> That I fancied her into some chivalry dame,
>   And I was her knight of the lance.

But Martha was not of this fanciful school,
    And she laugh'd at her poor little knight;
While I thought her a goddess, she thought me a fool,
    And I'll swear *she* was most in the right.

My soul was now calm, till, by Cloris's looks,
    Again I was tempted to rove;
But Cloris, I found, was so learned in books
    That she gave me more logic than love.
So I left this young Sappho, and hasten'd to fly
    To those sweeter logicians in bliss,
Who argue the point with a soul-telling eye,
    And convince us at once with a kiss.

Oh! Susan was then all the world unto me,
    But Susan was piously given;
And the worst of it was, we could never agree
    On the road that was shortest to Heaven.
"Oh, Susan!" I've said, in the moments of mirth,
    "What's devotion to thee or to me?
I devoutly believe there's a heaven on earth,
    And believe that that heaven's in *thee*!"

A few of the verses headed *To* . . . sound a deeper note, and
Moore himself confesses that they rose from some perturbation
in his spirit. Speaking of the political excitements of his Trinity
days, he adds:

"I was also in another direction feeling thrown in the way of
impressions and temptations, to any of which my time of life,
vivacity of fancy, and excitable temperament, rendered me
peculiarly susceptible."

The reading which he did for his projected translation of
Anacreon, browsing about among the old books in Marsh's
library, was not all prompted by love of scholarship.

"The line of study that at this time chiefly attracted me was
that which accorded most, not only with the task on which I was
engaged, but unluckily also with one of the feelings then most
dominant over my mind."

"One of the feelings": does this refer to any special episode, or
to a state of mind? Moore throughout his life had great success

with women. He admits frankly to preferring their company to that of men,[1] adding that, during his Trinity days at any rate, the preference kept him out of the "coarse dissipations" in which so many of his contemporaries engaged. Yet in all his time in London, and the years when he was at the height of his fame in society, there is no evidence of an affair with anyone.[2] Once he was married, the disposition of his mind, and his power to turn everything into fancy, may well have kept his loves "poetical" and ideal. A young man feels differently, and, idealistic though he must have been, there was probably more than fancy behind the lines he wrote to Bessy. Certainly hers was

> . . . not my earliest vow;
> Though few the years I yet have told,
> Canst thou believe I've lived till now.
> With loveless heart or senses cold?
>
> No—other nymphs to joy and pain
> This wild and wandering heart hath mov'd.
> With some it sported, wild and vain,
> While some it dearly, truly lov'd .

He refers elsewhere to "the foolishly-loved that are dead", and writes, in a letter to Lady Donegal, dated October 25th, 1814, "There are already three whom I (at least fancied I) loved, now cold in the earth."

It all amounts to very little. The "wild and wandering heart" was probably not so wild, and did not wander far. Unlike his later namesake, Moore may have kissed and not told. It was not only his celebrity which in later life made him such a success with women: and, as a young man, he had already most of the personal attributes which won that success. He was lively and amusing, he sang, he considered his company. The readiness "to please and to be pleased", which Scott put high in his catalogue

---

[1] Yet, with the exception of Mary Godfrey and Lady Donegal, his closest friends were all men.

[2] Several of his countrymen have tried very hard to find one.

of Moore's attractions, more than atoned for his lack of inches. He had an affectionate disposition, was easily moved, and ready to fancy himself in love. He was capable of warm attachments, and, especially in his addresses to Bessy, would have tended to magnify anything that had happened to him, and make high romance of it. But his ornate language cuts both ways, and there is a note, particularly in the *Memoirs*, which suggests that there had been something on which he did not care to look back.

We may conclude, after discounting the verse conventions of his time, and realizing that he was one who, in certain directions, made an ounce of experience yield a ton of consequence, that he had a number of flirtations, fell more or less in love on several occasions, and had an episode or two which he was anxious to forget. It seems unimportant, at this distance, to speculate whether an undergraduate had the sort of experience which traditionally belongs to his years; but Moore was a devoted husband, and, unless his contemporaries have engaged in a unanimous and highly uncharacteristic feat of suppression, a man of chaste life; and that at a period and in a society which would have thought none the worse of him had he taken the opportunities which his singing and his celebrity gave him.[1] He was, too, a man who retained to old age the characteristics of his boyhood, and so, in any account of him, the detailed story of his early years is valuable.

V

Meanwhile, everything was going very happily at Aungier Street. Billy Warren, Catherine's music teacher, had become an intimate friend, and was in the house at all times. Catherine's music lessons were communal affairs, and Tom, standing by the piano, and taking in what went on, gradually learned enough to be able to pick out tunes, and to accompany his own singing,

[1] See Appendix A.

without any direct teaching. He also began, tentatively, to compose tunes on his own.

Some time in 1796, he wrote a masque, which was performed privately in the front drawing-room. It was about a lady who, owing to the machinations of an unkind spirit, was haunted by a phantom, which reassuringly turned out to be a real and agreeable young man. Catherine played the lady, a friend named Sally Masterson the spirit, and Tom was the phantom. The only fragment of this piece which survived was a song entitled *Delusive Dream*, for which Warren wrote the music, and which Tom himself used often to sing in later years, with great applause.

CHAPTER V

ERIN GO BRAGH

Edward Hudson—Introduction to Irish music—Robert Emmet
—Tom's letter in *The Press*—Emmet's rebuke—Chancellor
Fitzgibbon holds an Inquisition—Tom acquitted—Death of
Emmet—"She is far from the land"—Charges against Moore
as patriot

IT was at Trinity that Tom received the impress which was for
ever to link music with love of country in his mind, and make
one the expression of the other. That impress he owed to two
men, Edward Hudson and Robert Emmet.

Emmet and Hudson were themselves close friends, and at the
heart of the political activity that was stirring the university.
Their influences on Moore were indissoluble. Hudson was the
musician; Emmet, in Moore's presence, proclaimed the aid that
music might give him and his cause. Tom himself gives two
accounts of those exciting days, in his *Memoirs*, and in his *Life of
Lord Edward Fitzgerald*. There are slight discrepancies between
the two, but only in matters of detail; and, as elsewhere, Tom is
sometimes a year out in his dates. But the main facts are abundantly clear.

Edward Hudson was an exceedingly good-looking young
man of high artistic gifts, the chief of which was for music. He
was a skilled flautist, and was passionately interested in the native
Irish airs, which he collected, and transcribed for the flute. He
was also an ardent politician. At the time when Tom made his
acquaintance, he was twenty-two or three. Tom and he spent
many hours together, playing through air after air, and then, in a
transport of romantic patriotism, talking over Ireland's wrongs

42

and sufferings. To one of Tom's bent, the combination was irresistible, and he fell at once under Hudson's spell. One of his many engaging points is that, delighted though he always was by his own successes, he never sought to magnify them by belittling the share of others: and he admitted freely that to Hudson was due in great measure his lifelong interest in Irish music.

But the two friends had not to depend only on the airs which Hudson had collected. In 1792, a Protestant patriot named Dr James MacDonnell, seeing the old harp music of Ireland vanishing, had arranged a festival in Belfast to which the last of the harpers were bidden. Only nine could be found. The nine played all they could remember, and a young man named Edward Bunting was given the task of setting down the airs as they were played. Bunting became a violent convert to Irish music, and travelled about the country on his own, collecting more airs and variants. Four years after the festival, he issued his first collection of over sixty airs, none of which had ever appeared in print.

The two friends had a copy of Bunting's volume, and it inspired Moore with his first idea of setting words to the native airs. He approached Bunting, who, with a purist's scorn, would have none of this proposal to graft words to harp music. His refusal has been ascribed to churlishness, but it is only fair to give him credit for his musicianship. He could hardly be expected to see what Moore, technically no musician, saw by instinct. It is to Tom's credit that, where many a man would have borne a grudge for the rebuff, he paid generous tribute, on more than one occasion, to Bunting's work for Irish music, and to the great benefit which he personally had derived from it.

An air which Tom and Hudson often played was *The Little Red Fox*. This, to which Tom was soon to write the words "Let Erin remember", he must have heard from Hudson, for it does not appear in Bunting's volumes till 1840. One day, when they were playing together, Robert Emmet came in. He sat in the

window, and did not seem to be listening. They came to *The
Little Red Fox*. Suddenly Emmet started upright.

"Oh," he cried, "that I were at the head of twenty thousand
men, marching to that air!"

This is interesting for its bearing on the charge, so often made
against Moore, of tampering with the country airs and altering
them to suit his purpose. The charge will have to be considered
later, but here is one instance at least on which Moore may be
acquitted. The air as given by Bunting is a quick tune in three-
four time, completely different, in spirit and character, from
the noble swing of "Let Erin remember". It has been assumed,
therefore, that Moore altered the time: that the quick version is
genuine, and Moore's spurious. But nobody, least of all Emmet,
could have imagined leading an army to the jiggle-joggle of
the air as given by Bunting. Two versions of it must have been
current, as of so many others, and Hudson picked up the more
dignified. There is, of course, the faint chance that Moore saw
the possibilities of the original air, and suggested playing it
slowly: but, as Hudson was his tutor in Irish music, it is very
unlikely.

II

Robert Emmet, thus introduced, takes the centre of the stage.
To him was given the greatest admiration Tom Moore had for
any man. While still an undergraduate, Emmet had attained a
spiritual maturity which set him far above his fellows. His character was almost perfectly poised. Unshakable in courage and
conviction, powerful in intellect, a born leader of men, he was as
gentle in manner and as tenderly considerate as any woman. His
face was serene, till inward passion lit it up, his bearing calm and
easy. His appreciation of character was immediate, his judgment forbearing. Tom worshipped him from the first, and
was rewarded with his affection, but not his confidence. He

knew better than entrust to the weaker vessel what it could not contain.

When Tom entered Trinity, Emmet was already a figure in the university. To such of the undergraduates whose thoughts were not all upon sport and "diversion", he was a portent. The dons regarded him with misgiving, because of his political activities. He was a leading member of the Debating Society, to which undergraduates were admitted as a preliminary to entering the "authorized" Historical Society. Tom joined, but did not speak. He was content to admire the eloquence of others, and particularly Emmet's, upon such subjects as "Whether an Aristocracy or a Democracy is most favourable to the advancement of science and literature?" and "Whether a soldier was bound, on all occasions, to obey the orders of his commanding officer?"

After a few months of this, Emmet and he were admitted to the Historical Society. There is a slight confusion, on the subject of this society, between Moore's two accounts. In the *Memoirs*, he says that it had been "put down by the fellows, but continued in defiance of them to hold its sittings *out*side the walls". Possibly this is a mistake for the Debating Society, which is described early in 1797, as it was in that year that he submitted, for the Literary Medal, his *Ode upon Nothing, with Notes by Trismegistus Rustifustius, D.D., etc., etc.* This brought him his first real notoriety in the university. It was a satire against pedagogues and pedants, and there were solemn complaints of its "licence" and "immorality". Moore himself was chosen to read it out, and did so with great abandon, acting the various parts, and following it up with a spirited defence against the charge of immorality. The whole performance excited roars of laughter and applause: but the charge had touched Tom, and he hastened to make plain that he felt very much the suggestion that he had seriously attacked the laws of morality and good taste, and made amends by having the *Ode* removed from the Society's books.

It was probably Hudson who introduced Tom to Emmet.

The acquaintance rapidly grew to a friendship, which moved Tom's new tutor, one Phipps, to warn him against being seen too much in public with such a firebrand. This, of course, made him all the more anxious to be associated with Emmet in every possible way. But Phipps need not have worried. The limits to the association were set by Emmet himself. He knew Tom's mother, and he knew Tom. Only once in Tom's hearing did he allude to the United Irishmen, and he never proposed that Tom should be enrolled. Tom attributes this to Emmet's realization of the watchful anxiety with which he was regarded at home, and to his reluctance to increase it. Anastasia had no wish that her boy should be caught up in a revolutionary society, which might endanger his prospects, if not his life. She worried continually lest his impulsive nature, or his sense of loyalty to his comrades, should lead him astray. Emmet must have known all this, for Anastasia was never one to keep her anxieties to herself, and his "forbearance" was without doubt partly due to it: but he saw from the first that Tom, burning with romantic enthusiasm, was not of the stuff of which rebels are made. It was both kinder and wiser, on all accounts, to leave him out. So Tom remained, throughout, ignorant of more than the vaguest outline of what was planned.

His own attitude towards the whole situation is a naïf mixture of wistful desire and self-knowledge. He admired the men of action, and longed to be of their company. He was no coward, even if his courage was of the theatrical order. He welcomed, when it came, the chance of standing up and making a brave gesture. But he was built for peaceful ways, and knew his own measure. "Timid to try the mountain's height" had more than one application: and, elsewhere, he says frankly that he was "constantly tied to my mother's apron strings".

III

He made at least a flutter to escape them. In the autumn of 1797, a paper named *The Press* was founded by a number of the United Irishmen, notably Emmet's older brother, Thomas Addis Emmet, and Arthur O'Connor. Every line of this was avidly devoured at 12 Aungier Street, where Tom read it aloud to the family. It was a medium-sized publication of two sheets, appearing every two days, and costing twopence-halfpenny. The first page contained as a rule a political letter signed "Montanus", Robert Emmet's pseudonym; an article; and several advertisements. The middle pages carried general news and more advertisements, and the back page was given up to the "French Republic", with an article or two on the leading figures in the Revolution.

Tom soon became ambitious to see himself in print in these inspiring pages, but dreaded what his mother might say. At last he submitted an imitation of Ossian. His second contribution was a great deal bolder. It was an open "Letter to the Students of Trinity College", and appeared in the sixtieth number. For the light it sheds on its author, it is worth giving in full:

To Montanus.

SIR,

Instigated by a particular perusal of your 8th letter, by a publication which lately appeared in the *Dublin Journal, purporting* to be from "A Loyal Student of Trinity College", I have the satisfaction now to assure you of my hearty concurrence in, and perfect conviction of the truth of the sentiments you have there professed. Sir, you have if I mistake not, divided your subject into three parts, namely, the improbability of any change in the English Administration; the prospect of advantage to Ireland from that change if accomplished; and lastly the probable effects of peace with France, in producing a redress of grievances in

Ireland. The insufficiency of any of these measures, to produce
that desirable object, a removal of the existing abuses in the
executive government of Ireland, you have already demon-
strated. But to consider the points singly. The removal of the
present flagitious and corrupt ministry, is as you assert, a vain,
delusive hope; it is supposing that men, who from their station
and consequent power, have been enabled to practise every
cruelty and injustice against the people, from whom that power
is derived, who have aggrandized themselves and their adherents
with the spoils wrung from the hands of industry, and the unsuspecting credulity of the people, who have sported with the
sufferings, and trampled on the rights of their country, that these
very men, should by *resigning* their power, expose themselves to
the *just* vengeance of the nation they have injured and oppressed.
Sir, I agree with you that they will never do it; nay more, should
they even incline to do it, the interests of the monied men so
closely connected with the present system of corruption, as you
have fully shown, will never suffer them to effect that act of
justice. But, Sir, the improbability, I had nearly said impossibility of this ever happening, induces me to pass on to the second
question, namely, the probable effects of this change of ministry
effected, on the affairs of Ireland; and here will any unprejudiced
mind, will any Irishman say, that an English minister, whose
interest, the history of the country will shew, has ever been, to
limit the commerce of Ireland, discountenance her manufactures,
and humble her spirit of independence; that a minister chosen by
the English people, and whose object we must suppose to be
popularity, will risk the loss of the affections of that people, by
any concessions to a country whose wants and dependence on
them, have ever been the chief source of their wealth and power;
concessions which must, by lessening those wants (I mean in a
commercial sense, which I conceive to be the staple of either
country) materially affect the interests of that people by whom
they are supplied; but of what avail would these concessions be,

THE TRIAL OF ROBERT EMMET

supposing them granted, in redressing the original grievances of this country? "Concessions such as these, are of little moment to the sum of things, unless it be to prove that the worst of men are sensible of the injuries they have done us, and perhaps to demonstrate to us the imminent danger of our situation. The mischief lies too deep, to be cured by any remedy less than some great convulsion, which may either carry back the Constitution to its original principles, or utterly destroy it." I fully agree with you, that the most liberal and enlightened man in Ireland would not be able, if chosen minister, to follow the dictates of his wisdom in redressing the wrongs of Ireland. Now, Sir, to the third and last question, namely the probable effects of peace between England and France, on the affairs of Ireland. And here I must beg leave to say a few words—If we look into the history of this country, since the time of its conquest by Great Britain, she (*sic*) shall find that it has ever been the policy of the English Cabinet to make large promises whenever she wanted our assistance in the prosecution of her wars; but where shall we look for the accomplishment of any of her promises? Were we not at the conclusion of the American War, promised a free trade? Did we obtain it, *in the extent wished for*? No; after a few petty concessions, the popular voice was sunk, their leaders bribed and pensioned, and the question buried in oblivion. I will be told several restrictions were at that time taken off the commerce of Ireland, and that they did obtain a free trade—*in name*. The restrictions taken off, were such as injured Ireland in the extreme, but did not benefit *Great Britain*—such as well became the English ministry to take off. But, Sir, it seems to be a necessary consequence, when a nation becomes so corrupt or enervated to give up her liberties, at the time she has a right to expect, and a power to enforce them, that she should become the dupe of her own folly, and sink in abject slavery beneath those burthens she had not spirit to remove. Such, Sir, would be the consequences of an *unconditional* peace—unconditional with respect to the grievances of

Ireland. Then would we experience redoubled coercion, and merciless extinction of the champions of liberty—for "violence and oppression at home, can only be supported by treachery and submission abroad". When the civil rights of the people are daringly invaded on one side, what have we to expect, but that their political rights should be deserted and betrayed, in the same proportions on the other. Thus, Sir, have I endeavoured to expound what seemed to me the purport of your eighth letter.

As to the address of *thanks* you have received from a *loyal student of Trinity College* on the subject, I should incline to pass it over unregarded, did it not contain many errors, which as I conceive I may rectify I shall beg leave to notice them. You, as the orator of your party, have been accused of inconsistancies (*sic*), which did not exist. First "you do *not* deplore the fate of Ireland on the conclusion of a *safe* and *honourable peace*, but you express your fears that a peace in which her interests were neglected would be *neither safe nor honourable*;" secondly "you do *not* deny that a change of Ministry would meliorate the condition of Ireland;" on the contrary you say "a resort to new men could not make us worse, it might perhaps snatch us from perdition." But you *do* say, that an English Minister however liberal and well meaning would be subject to error in his judgment of the state of this country, from the wrong information he would receive, if an English interest continued to predominate in the Irish government, and thus unknowing the disease, he would be inefficient to apply a remedy. Thirdly, you do *not* (if I conceive you right) assert the insufficiency of *any* reformation in parliament, there is a wide difference between the reformation that parliament is capable of, and the flimsy reform which an English Minister could, consistently with his political existence, make in favour of this Country. But fourthly I know not where to look for the foundation of that assertion that you deny, a redress of the military grievances, or a repeal to military law would be sufficient to restore the happiness of Ireland. Your words I believe are these, supposing a peace to have been effected. "Then the military force that now overspreads the country, and fills it with outrage and devastation will be augmented daily with ferocious swarms and undisciplined human hordes, breathing slaughter and longing after confiscation." On the whole there is not (in my opinion) any grounds for the mighty fears of our Loyal Student. He says he hopes the letter of Mundanus, by disclosing the secrets of his heart will make converts to the cause of Loyalty. I hope this simple explanation of the meaning of Mundanus' letter as it must appear to every *disinterested* Man, will make a convert of him. I wish for no enemies. This is not a time to express a difference of Political opinion. No, we should all have one common cause, the welfare of our country; we should all Unite, rally round her standard, and recover our Heaven-born rights, our principles from the grasp of Tyranick ministers.

A PATRIOTIC FRESHMAN.

At first, only Hudson knew that Tom was the author. When the fateful issue arrived at Aungier Street, Tom composed himself as best he might, and managed to read it aloud without arousing the suspicions of the family. Next day, however, Hudson inadvertently let out the secret. The Moores were thrown into consternation. They voted the letter "very bold", and Mrs Moore earnestly begged Tom to promise that he would never attempt anything of the kind again: and, he says simply, "as any wish of hers was to me a law", he gave her his word.

Another rebuke for the letter came from an unexpected quarter. Emmet, on one of the country walks which he and Tom often took together, began to talk about the letter, and Tom admitted that he had written it. Emmet then said, very gently, that, although the contents had pleased him in one sense, he was sorry that public attention had thus been drawn to Trinity. It might alarm the authorities, and set them enquiring too closely into the work which he and others were quietly carrying on. Talk and letters were not what was wanted, but action. Tom's feelings were not at all hurt by the rebuke.

"I could not help being struck with the manliness of the view which I saw he took of what men ought to do in such times and circumstances, namely not to *talk* or *write* about their intentions, but to *act*."

It only made him admire Emmet more, and long to be one of the men of action.

IV

In the number of *The Press* which contained Moore's letter appeared the following brief item of news: "Lord Moira takes his seat this day." Neither Tom nor his future patron ever noted the coincidence.

V

Not long afterwards came Moore's chief gesture as a man of action. His letter does not seem to have attracted any attention, but the college authorities, aware of what was brewing, resolved upon an "Inquisition" to purge the university of its rebels. A tribunal was set up, under no less a person than the Lord Chancellor Fitzgibbon, a violent Orangeman, and a number of undergraduates were summoned to appear before it. Emmet saw at once that he stood no chance, and he, John Brown, and the brothers Corbet fled before the enquiry began.

Tom was not one of those summoned to attend on the first day, but he was present, and eagerly followed the proceedings. One after another, the undergraduates broke under Fitzgibbon's pitiless questioning, and gave evidence incriminating their comrades. Presently Dacre Hamilton, a close friend of Emmet's, was called to the stand. Hamilton had even less to do with politics than Moore. He was a mathematician, a simple and innocent creature, and his friendship with Emmet was purely personal:

but the fact of it made him suspect. Questioned about Emmet's affairs, he refused to answer, and was punished by dismissal from the university, which meant permanent exclusion from all the learned professions.

No. 12 Aungier Street was a place of gloom that evening. Neither Tom nor his parents could blind themselves to the fact that he was likely to be called next day. Anastasia saw the collapse of all her hopes, but neither she nor her husband—"my dear honest father", as Moore affectionately calls him—hesitated for a second. If Tom were asked questions which would lead to the incrimination of others, he must follow Hamilton's example, let the cost be what it might.

Sure enough, next day he was called, and presently found himself face to face with Fitzgibbon and the fierce anti-Catholic propagandist, Dr Duigenan. He was asked, in the usual form, to swear that he would tell "the truth, the whole truth, and nothing but the truth".

"I have an objection, my lord," he said, in a clear, firm voice, "to taking this oath."

Fitzgibbon scowled. "What's your objection, sir?" he asked sternly.

"I have no fear, my lord, that anything I might say would criminate myself, but it might tend to criminate others; and I must say that I despise that person's character who could be led under any circumstances to criminate his associates."

Fitzgibbon eyed him.

"How old are you, sir?" he enquired.

"Between seventeen and eighteen."

"H'm." He turned, and said something under his breath to Duigenan. Duigenan whispered back. Then he again addressed Tom.

"We cannot allow any person to remain in this university who refuses to take this oath."

It looked like a deadlock: but Tom replied, "I shall then, my lord, take the oath, still reserving to myself the right of refusing to answer any such questions as I have described."

"We do not sit here to argue with you, sir," growled Fitz-gibbon: but he allowed Tom to take the oath, and proceeded to cross-examine him on the United Irish Societies. Here Tom could answer freely every question that was put to him. Thanks to Emmet, he knew nothing at all, and his ignorance was apparent even to Fitzgibbon. The Chancellor turned once more to Duigenan, and they conferred anew. Duigenan was loath to let Moore go, and, prompted by him, Fitzgibbon asked one last question.

"When such are the answers you are able to give, pray what was the cause of your great repugnance to taking the oath?"

"I have already told you, my lord, my chief reasons; in addition to which, it was the first oath I ever took, and it was, I think a very natural hesitation."

One of the fellows, sitting by, here interrupted, "That's the best answer that has been given yet," and Tom was excused. His friends all crowded round him with congratulations: "not so much, I could see," he tells us, "on my acquittal by my judges, as on the manner in which I had acquitted *myself*": and his reception at Aungier Street was rapturous.

It was a theatrical appearance, and his complacency at the end is unpleasing, but it was not bad for a boy of seventeen, under formidable questioning, and with a great deal to lose: especially for a boy tied to his mother's apron strings.

VI

When the rebellion broke, in May 1798, Moore was ill in bed. The plans of the United Irishmen had received a disastrous set-back in March, when Major Sirr, at the head of the Government troops, had raided Oliver Bond's house in Bridge Street and captured many of the leaders, including Edward Hudson.

Hudson was imprisoned for several months in Kilmainham gaol, hearing from day to day of comrades led out to execution, and expecting his own. He survived, however, and was condemned to exile. Before he left, Tom obtained leave to see him. He found that his old friend had beguiled the time by covering the walls of his cell with drawings illustrating the legendary origin of the Irish harp!

Hudson was lucky. Few figures of any importance in the rebellion were left alive. Those who had not fallen at the Curragh or at Vinegar Hill died on the gallows, like the two Sheares, Munroe, and McCracken. Wolfe Tone cheated the hangman by taking his own life, Fitzgerald died of wounds. Emmet survived to lead another rising five years later. It failed: he was tried and condemned to death. In the gaol where he lay awaiting execution, his character impressed all who came in contact with him. The turnkey who attended him, a man hardened by years of prison conditions, fell under his spell. As Emmet was being led to his death, the turnkey, tears streaming down his cheeks, stood in the stone passage to bid him farewell. Emmet's arms were pinioned: he could not shake hands. Leaning forward, he gently kissed the turnkey's cheek. The turnkey fainted.

VII

Moore was on the point of sailing to take up his appointment in Bermuda when Emmet died. He makes no mention of it in his letters, but one of the first poems in the *Irish Melodies*, published five years afterwards, had an application which was immediately recognized in Ireland. Emmet, speaking from the dock, had finished with these words:

"I have but one request to ask at my departure from this world. It is the charity of silence. Let no man write my epitaph. When my country shall have taken her place among the nations of the earth, then, and not till then, let my epitaph be written."

This is Moore's lyric:

> O breathe not his name, let it sleep in the shade,
> Where cold and unhonour'd his relics are laid:
> Sad, silent, and dark, be the tears that we shed,
> As the night-dew that falls on the grass o'er his head.
>
> But the night-dew that falls, though in silence it weeps,
> Shall brighten with verdure the grave where he sleeps;
> And the tear that we shed, though in secret it rolls,
> Shall long keep his memory green in our souls.

It is noteworthy how far superior Emmet's words are to Moore's—was "verdure" an echo from the toast at Napper Tandy's dinner?—and how much more poetry is in them. The difference epitomizes, not unfairly, the contrast between the two natures. Moore did better when he sang of Sarah Curran, Emmet's love.

> She is far from the land where her young hero sleeps,
>   And lovers are round her, sighing:
> But coldly she turns from their gaze, and weeps,
>   For her heart in his grave is lying.
>
> She sings the wild song of her dear native plains,
>   Every note which he lov'd awaking;—
> Ah! little they think who delight in her strains,
>   How the heart of the Minstrel is breaking.
>
> He had liv'd for his love, for his country he died,
>   They were all that to life had entwin'd him;
> Nor soon shall the tears of his country be dried,]
>   Now long will his love stay behind him.
>
> Oh ! make her a grave where the sunbeams rest,
>   When they promise a glorious morrow;
> They'll shine o'er her sleep, like a smile from the West,
>   From her own lov'd island of sorrow.

A popular modern setting has made this one of the best-known of Moore's lyrics, and it is admired by thousands who have no idea of the circumstances that inspired it.

The impression left upon Moore's mind by the rising of 1798

and all connected with it was deep and lasting. He bears witness to it fearlessly in his *Life* of Fitzgerald, written many years afterwards.

... "Though so many years have since gone by, the impression of horror and indignation which the acts of the government of the day left upon my mind is, I confess, at this moment far too fully alive, to allow me the callousness of a historian in speaking of them."

VIII

It is on these years that half the charges made against Moore are based, so we may as well look at them now. Two generations of patriotic Irishmen have had little but scorn for Moore, as poet and patriot. Part of this decline is due to a normal and proper reaction against the exaggerated fame he enjoyed in his lifetime, and for years afterwards: part of it is legitimate: and the rest is due to an unfortunate trait in the Irish character.

The Irishman, particularly the Dubliner, is loath to praise a compatriot. A certain degree of local reputation he will allow, but, the moment it spreads outside, and particularly if it is recognized in England, he sets himself at once to belittle it. Nothing so rouses his spleen as to have English people come over and praise an Irishman. This, perhaps, is natural: but one can hear in Dublin, during a single day, more disparagement and denigration of noted Irishmen than hostile journalists elsewhere could invent in a twelvemonth. The city, in many ways the most stimulating in the world, breeds a sour mood, an *accidie*, blown up of climate, indolence, and drink, which infects the natural generosity of her sons. They recognize it in their hearts, and resent bitterly those who break away from it and achieve success elsewhere. So, in bar and club, the disappointed lawyers, doctors, journalists sit, consoling themselves by jeering at all who have escaped the miasma.

The case against Moore, however, had deeper origins than this natural talent for disparagement. It was galling to see a reputation made abroad, and worse to see how the bourgeoisie and the common people took the *Melodies* to their hearts. From a newer generation, who wanted action, Moore's apparent defeatism, his mourning over past glories, excited anger and contempt: and they found, with savage pleasure, a real charge against the man himself. After the privilege of Emmet's friendship, he went to England and accepted the hospitality of his friend's executioners. After writing his letter in *The Press*, and expressing his hatred of Ireland's oppressors, he spent the rest of his life among them, became the darling of their drawing-rooms, and toadied to their prince. The "impression of horror and indignation" caused by the acts of the English Government cannot have been very deep.

Undoubtedly, there are grounds for the charge. Moore came over to London, won success there, made friends of noblemen, met the Prince, and was delighted with himself about it all. But life is not as simple as it can look on paper. Moore was up against an ancient paradox. Arrived in London, he found a cultured and intelligent society which knew nothing of what had been happening in Ireland, and which, individually and collectively, was incapable of any of the actions done in its name. It is a problem which has baffled stronger natures than Moore's. These people showed him nothing but friendliness, and to friendliness his own nature was readily susceptible. To blame the wrongs of Ireland on any of them would have been academic and childish. They were in no way responsible. If, on the other hand, he came to know them well, and to be accepted among them, then, by tactful representation, conveyed to the right quarter, he might get something done. Thus—if it troubled him —he may have quieted his conscience. And, if his own personal success went to his head, and, for a time, blinded him to his memories, few but the more fanatical logicians among his countrymen will find it in their hearts to judge him harshly. We have no evidence that his love of Ireland cooled, and much evidence that he was outspoken in her behalf. All that Moore could do, he did, and very effective it was. He was no hero, but no coward: and he is hardly to be blamed if the way of least resistance happened to be the way in which he could do his country the greatest service.

The core of the matter is that many Irishmen cannot forgive him for not having died with Emmet. Even in our day, the best way to be sure of a fair name in Ireland is to die for her. Many a famous Irishman has been *felix opportunitate mortis*. Those who live will be disparaged, sooner or later. There are men of whom the genius of their country, or of the art they practise, takes especial care. They are needed. Moore was needed, and the genius of Ireland preserved him for her service.

CHAPTER VI

BREAKING AWAY

Beginnings of social life—B.A.—Tom crosses to England—A
lunatic and a sponger—Lodgings in Portman Square—The
Middle Temple—Introduction to Lord Moira—Plans for
Anacreon—Return home

TOM'S days at Trinity were near their irresponsible close. The
examinations, and the anxieties of politics, were after all only
incidents in a gay and happy round of pleasures. His preference
for feminine society was, if anything, strengthened, and to that
society his singing was the readiest passport. His voice, the fact
that he accompanied himself, and his mercurial and amiable
temperament made him a welcome guest in any society. Chief
among the families he frequented was that of Grierson, the
King's Printer, who, with a house in Harcourt Street and another
at Rathfarnham, entertained beyond his means. Another was
that of Joseph Atkinson, of the Ordnance Board, who, if not as
prodigal, gave dinners and dances, and was no less fond of Tom's
music. Sir George Shee, who was a good musician, was struck at
once by the young singer's quality, and had him to dinner to
meet Lord Clare. Dr Kearney, the Provost of Trinity, liked him
well, and bade him often to his house, where Mrs Kearney and
her daughters made much of him. It was all a pleasant foretaste
of the conquests ahead.

Kearney's goodwill took a more definite form than benevolent
hospitality. For some time now Tom had had the run of Marsh's
library, and had made a real start on his project of translating
Anacreon. When he was nineteen, Anastasia presented him with
a copy of Gail's edition, which gave him great delight, and con-

firmed him in his design. He worked hard, till he had translated twenty of the Odes, then took them to Kearney, with the modest suggestion that he be awarded a classical premium for his labours.

The old Provost scratched his chin. The work was good, he said, very good indeed. At the same time, he doubted whether the Board could be brought to reward the translation of work so "amatory and convivial". However, he urged Tom to continue his work, translate the whole of the Odes, and publish them. He had little doubt they would succeed. "And," he added, with a twinkle, "the young people will like it."

The task was to occupy some years, but it was not by any means the only verse upon which Tom was busy. To this period belong a great many of the *Juvenile Poems*, soon to be published as the work of "Thomas Little". He had plenty to keep him occupied, between his verse, his music, and his insatiable appetite for company.

II

At the end of 1798 Tom graduated as a B.A., and left Trinity. The next thing was to eat his dinners at the Middle Temple, where he and Beresford Burston had been entered some time previously. It was no easy task for the Moores to find the fees, and the money necessary to keep their boy in London; but Anastasia had been saving for a long time, and, when at last he set sail in April of 1799, there were some extra guineas sewn into the waistband of his pantaloons. The good woman also stitched in a scapular, blessed by the priest, to keep her darling from harm. Tom knew all about the guineas, but nothing about the scapular.

From what he himself has told us, it is easy to picture the start of his journey. With all his goods in a vast portmanteau, he set out from Aungier Street. The farewells were done, the handkerchiefs waved, and, as the packet stood out from the South Wall,

Tom looked back at the little smoky city in loneliness and misgiving. Ahead, the Bay was ominously dotted with "white
horses", and an east wind robbed the mountains of colour.
Beyond lay the unknown life of London and the rigours of the
Middle Temple. True, he had a purpose nearer his heart, that of
gaining subscribers to enable him to publish his *Anacreon*, but the
thought of touting for them seemed unattractive enough on the
sloping deck in the cold grey morning. Then the packet began to
get the full force of the wind, and Tom took refuge below.

The passage was long and rough, and they did not reach Holyhead till night. Cold, and barely recovered from sickness, Tom
hurried to book a place in the Chester mail, which left next
morning. All the places were booked, but, by great good fortune, he found a gentleman who did not wish to travel. The
gentleman sold Tom his place, and advised him to answer in his
name when the list of passengers was called over. This Tom did,
only to be rebuked by a fellow-traveller, who pointed out the
danger of an *alias* in such troubled times. Thoroughly frightened,
Tom got little sleep, despite his fatigue, and hurried first thing in
the morning to have his booking changed to his own name.

Arrived at Chester, tired, dirty, and discouraged, he tramped
the streets, still feeling guilty over the substitution. At breakfast
next morning he was accosted by a lunatic, who set the inn in an
uproar, and boasted of having killed a woman and child in
Warrington the night before. The lunatic took a fancy to Tom,
and suggested that they should explore Chester together, but
Tom excused himself.

He soon had enough of Chester. The next coach did not leave
for a couple of days. Unable to bear the prospect, Tom took a
place in the mail, where he fell in with even more doubtful company. A seedy-looking young man, sizing Tom up, attached
himself firmly, and, after speaking of his wealth and prospects,
suggested that they should see the metropolis together. Nothing
would do him but that Tom and he should put up at the same

inn at Charing Cross. His luggage, he said, had been sent on in advance: but, curse it! it had not arrived. His linen was none too clean after the journey: perhaps Mr Moore——?

But Mr Moore remained strangely deaf to hints, and kept the key of his portmanteau firmly in his breeches pocket. The stranger did not appear to resent this lack of response. He became more assiduous than ever, charging the waiter, as they sat at breakfast, to take Mr Moore's coat, and brush it well, before they both set out to see the city. Tom, however, did not want to see the city. He wanted to go straight to his friend Mr Masterson, in Manchester Street, Manchester Square. Very well: the stranger would accompany him. Arm-in-arm they walked to the door, where the stranger, leaving him, charged him to meet him again in a couple of hours.

Masterson greeted Tom, then looked about him.

"What have you done with your luggage?" he asked.

"Left them at the inn."

"Did you give them in charge to the master of the house?"

"No."

"Did you get them booked?"

"No." Tom's heart was sinking still further.

"Have you the key of the room?"

"No."

"Off you go, this minute, and secure them."

And, in a hackney coach, Tom hurried back post-haste to Charing Cross, and was mightily relieved to find his portmanteau safe. He left a message for the stranger, regretting that he could not keep his engagement to meet him, and drove back to Manchester Street with the portmanteau. The journey was safely over.

III

It had been expensive. The actual crossing cost a guinea. From Holyhead to Chester cost £1 10s. 6d., and his decision to take the speedy mail, instead of waiting for the coach, took £3 13s. 6d. from his pocket. Another two guineas added for "contingent expenses" made a formidable total. Mr Masterson, however, was able to console him by saying that this was pretty much the average figure, and recommending him next time to go by Park Gate, which was considerably cheaper. He carried on the good work of economizing by finding his guest a comfortable lodging at the house of a woman who did washing for his wife: and here, at No. 44 George Street, Portman Square, Tom found himself master of a comfortable little room on the second floor, at the modest sum of six shillings a week.

The lodging, like all others, had its drawbacks. Portman Square was full of poor French émigrés, and there were two at No. 44. One, an old curé, occupied the room next to Tom's. The wall was thin, and, as the head of his bed was against one side of the wall and the head of Tom's against the other, Tom received his snores at maximum strength. The second émigré, a bishop, lived downstairs. He had many visitors, but no servant to announce them, and so anticipated a later practice by hanging up in the hall a square board, with "The Bishop's at home" on one side, and "The Bishop's gone out" on the other.

Tom had breakfast snugly by his fire. Lunch he also took at home. It was usually cold, and cost him about a shilling. For dinner, if he had no invitation, he went to one or another of the many cheap French restaurants in the neighbourhood. A specimen menu for dinner consisted of soup, bouilli, rice pudding, and a tankard of porter: total, ninepence-halfpenny.

It was not an extravagant mode of life, and, stimulated by the letters of introduction Tom had brought, there were a good many invitations, mostly from Irish people, to lighten the cost still further. One such friend was Martin Archer Shee, later President of the Royal Academy. His brother-in-law, Nugent, an engraver, was not prosperous enough for dinner, but was good for a chat and a cup of tea. The Mastersons were a tower of strength. Mr Masterson lent him a piano for his own use, and at their house there was always plenty of music. Sally, his old friend, who had acted with him, had become a good pianist, and was also learning the harp. Then there was McMahon, a Dublin apothecary, who had come over to London, and whose wife, when Tom was hard up, offered to lend him money to pay his fees at the Middle Temple. Tom managed without her help, remarking that "such generous offers came too rarely in this world to allow themselves to be forgotten". As a matter of fact, they came his way fairly often. The landlady of his second lodging, in Bury Street, when a tailor was pressing him for settlement of a bill, offered him the use of her savings. The kindness from a poor woman to whom he was practically a stranger moved him to tears. Very gently he declined her offer, "and went and thanked God upon my knees for the many sweet things of this kind He continually throws in my way".

It must be said for Moore, that, though a kind man himself, he never failed to be surprised and grateful for the kindness showered upon him, and never took credit for his own power to charm and please. He enjoyed his success, but never presumed on it, or took it as his right.

IV

In spite of these friends, Tom was often lonely and homesick during his first weeks in London. He persevered with his letters of introduction, but was unlucky in many cases. Most of them brought him polite notes of regret, and invitations to call "in the morning". He went one night to the theatre, but did not enjoy it properly. He hated going alone, and there was no one to bear him company.

His initiation at the Middle Temple accentuated his feeling of strangeness. (Beresford Burston seems to have disappeared.) One of his first duties was to give a small dinner to his brother

6

Templars. Knowing nobody, he had no idea whom to invite. Fortunately, a young man came to his rescue, and offered to collect the statutory number of guests. Tom was greatly relieved. His new friend provided the diners, and Tom footed the bill: but the occasion did not help him socially, for he never saw any of his guests again.

Then, suddenly, his world brightened. A letter of introduction from Joe Atkinson found its mark, and he was bidden to call upon Lord Moira.

The first Earl of Moira was a wealthy and cultured man who divided his time between England and Dublin, where he had a fine house on the south quays. He entertained lavishly, owned a fine collection of pictures, a library which he threw open to all, and was in general a patron of the arts. His manners were of the best, free from snobbery, courteous alike to the humblest and the highest. He "neither displayed his rank nor departed from it." In politics, he was looked upon as a coming man, destined for high honours; and—a great point with Tom—he was well disposed towards the Catholics. For several years, he was to be the young poet's most influential friend and patron, and to procure him entry into the most exclusive society.

Tom's first visit, in the morning, lasted for nearly an hour, and he pleased his lordship so well that he was bidden to dine on the following Saturday. A bare three weeks later, the tide was flowing with a vengeance, and he was writing to his mother that he now need never be alone. Indeed, the difficulty was to be alone. He was being reproached on all sides for his neglect of visiting. Lady Peshall, Mrs Latouche, Mrs Cologan—there was a superabundance of willing hostesses. At the house of the last he met Dr John Wolcot, better known as "Peter Pindar", the satirist; but, while delighted to meet such a celebrity, Tom found him coarse and disappointing, and made no attempt to follow up the acquaintance.

Tom's chief personal friend in London was a young man called

Dr Thomas Hume, of whose character he had the highest
opinion. Foremost in Hume's characteristics was his capacity for
friendship. He was remarkably sensitive to the moods of his
companion; and Tom, for all his expansiveness and high spirits,
had fits of deep despondency. Hume does not figure much on
the purely social side of Moore's life. He was interested in his
work, and chiefly in the completion of *Anacreon*.

Tom was writing busily, in the intervals of his visits and
gaiety: yet, in spite of friends and occupation, his moods of
despondency grew. He was ashamed of them, and bewailed
them in his regular letters to his parents. "Melancholy little
whims", "melancholy complainings", "querulous irritation"—
they all find place in his letters: but, when his parents showed
that they were worried, he was full of contrition and apologies.
The plain fact of the matter was that Tom was homesick. The
relationship between him and his parents was always most affectionate, and he had never been so long away from them. The
time spent at Blackrock with the Burstons did not count. That
was near home: he could see them at a couple of hours' notice.
But now he was three hundred miles from Aungier Street.

"My darling mother, shall we meet in summer? Oh! how I
long for it. Tell me that you wish it,—that you approve of it,—
and I will fly to you. . . ."

But Anastasia, much though she must have wished it, did not
approve, as Tom knew in his heart.

"I think the wearisomeness of this place is making me bilious.
. . . I wish prudence did not keep me away from you, dearest
mother, and I should exchange all my fineries for Irish stew and
salt fish immediately."

Soon, however, he had a reason which could overcome even
prudence. London was getting very hot, and work would be
difficult. Books were not published in summer, and there was
nothing for him to do but prepare for his *début*, which he could
do just as well in Ireland. As for his legal studies, they could be

carried on better in Ireland than in London. The public libraries
in London were not good, and he knew no lawyers well enough
to borrow books of them, whereas in Dublin everything would
be ready to his hand. Moreover, Hume had very kindly offered
to try to have some of his poems published. Though there was
little hope of getting money for an unknown author, yet perhaps
Hume might screw out of the bookseller something towards his
passage.

The publisher was Stockdale, of Piccadilly, and, as Tom had
feared, he did not want to part with any money. If anything, he
would have liked the young poet to contribute to the cost of
publication, and it looks from one of Tom's letters as if his father
had to advance the passage money.

"Oh, father! I hope I may one day or other repay you; but
Heaven knows how! I am now in such a disposition that one
word from you would decide me in staying here. . . . I shall feel
happy, *very* happy in seeing you, but indeed I shall feel disappointed at the idea of not having in some measure lightened
the burthen which is on you. If I can add, however, one moment
of happiness to my poor mother's life by returning, I shall hope
that we cannot regret it."

The last sentence, so pleasantly disingenuous, with its flavour
of masculine conspiracy for the benefit of the weaker sex, suggests that young men of twenty change but little.

The upshot of the negotiations with Stockdale was that he
should publish the translation of *Anacreon* as soon as it was ready.
This was more than enough for Tom, and, by July 2nd, he was
impatiently waiting at Park Gate for the packet. His impatience
led him to call that singularly attractive place "insipid", but, as
the same adjective was applied to his anonymous travelling-
companion, it need not be counted against him.

He reached Dublin on the 4th or 5th, and received a rapturous
welcome from the family. At once he settled down to work, but
sweetened it with a return to the accustomed gay life, going out

to dinner with Joe Atkinson, John Stevenson, and other old friends, singing—he hardly dared face Billy Warren, because he had brought back with him so little that was new—and dancing through the short summer nights.

CHAPTER VII

THE CAREER BEGUN

Anacreon nearly ready—A scholar's criticism—Tom falls ill—
State folk—Début as a singer—The Prince's leave—Meeting
with the Prince—*Anacreon*—Donington Hall—The social round
—"Mr. Thomas Little"—A visit from Carpenter—*The Gipsy
Prince*—Financial worries—The "Little" poems

TOM left Dublin on the 26th October, and by the 27th was in
Chester, after a pleasant and uneventful journey. He could not
secure a place on the mail, and had to wait till the next day. He
had a friend with him, named Hobart, and the pair took advantage of the delay to go with a pretty little travelling acquaintance
to the theatre.

An undated letter to his mother, inserted at this point in the
first volume of the *Memoirs*, suggests that on his way back to
town Tom paid his first visit to Donington Park, the country
home of Lord Moira. The probability is that the letter has been
misplaced. It is true that, writing in 1833, Moore says that, to the
best of his recollection, he first went to Donington on his way
back from this first homecoming, and mentions the incident of
being shown to his bedroom by his host. But, in a letter in the
eighth volume, dated December 31, 1800, he tells his mother,
"Nothing can be more princely than the style of this place, nor
anything more flatteringly polite than my reception here," and
goes on to relate the same incident. He would hardly tell his
mother a second time about a place he must have already described, if he had been there, nor again relate the same incident
about his host.

The beginning of November saw him in London, working

quietly at home. His chief concern now was the publication of
Anacreon. He was working night and day over the manuscript,
retouching and revising. The excellent Hume, in his absence, had
carried on all the negotiations with Stockdale, and seen to the
announcement of the forthcoming publication in the Reviews.
Subscriptions were coming in. Tom had two guineas in hard
cash "from Mr Campbell and Mr Tinker . . . the only guineas I
ever kissed . . . and I have locked them up religiously". He had
great hopes of the Dublin subscription, and urged his parents not
to be too modest about soliciting their friends. In all, he hoped to
clear no less than a hundred guineas. The first proofs "of the
printing of the proposals" were ready early in December, and,
apart from a small delay over the drawings, all was going splen-
didly. These were being executed in Dublin by one Cuming, to
whom the Odes were sent, enclosed in Moore's letters home, and
who was apparently very dilatory over his work. Nugent was
doing the engravings.

Then, again through Hume's good offices, four of the Odes
were submitted for criticism to Dr Lawrence, a friend of Burke.
The scholar's reply was cautious. The Odes
"are, in many parts, very elegant and poetical; and, in some
passages, Mr Moore has added a pretty turn not to be found in
the original. To confess the truth, however, they are in not a few
places, rather more paraphrastical than suits my notion (perhaps
an incorrect notion) of translation."

He went on, at considerable length, to suggest emendations
and improvements, ending with the fear lest Hume and the
author should find him "too long, minute, and impertinent".
The author, however, reported himself in his next letter home
well satisfied.

"Dr Lawrence has read my Anacreon; paid wonderful attention to it: and has written a Greek ode himself, which he allows
me to publish."

All promised well. He was going everywhere in society, and

his letters are full of the great ones he encountered. He was meeting stage folk, being taken to the opera, and there were suggestions that he might compose for it. He was studying music more seriously, and taking lessons in "thorough bass". A glee of his was published by Longmans. Johnstone, of Covent Garden, to whom he had been introduced, sang his songs in company. And now, for the first time, he got a real chance to sing them himself. Hitherto, he had sung only at the houses of friends.

Fortunately, we have an onlooker to supplement his own account of this *début*, a Miss Berry. The occasion was a formidable one. Well-known singers had been performing to a brilliant company, when suddenly the short, chubby figure, looking much younger even than his years, was led to the piano. Tom himself was too much overcome by the occasion to notice anything, but Miss Berry records the "contemptuous titter" which went up at his appearance. Once he began, it was another matter. The fashionable audience was spellbound, and Tom, as he left the piano, was gratified in the midst of all the applause to hear a lady observe, "And he's going to the Bar—what a pity." So great a sensation did Tom make that a noted lawyer, "old Hammersley", sent for him, and advised him not to let his head be turned by the admiration his talents won him, but to persevere in his profession.

As Miss Berry confessed that she did not care for Tom in those days, but found him too well pleased with himself, her testimony is probably to be trusted.

II

All this time, subscriptions for *Anacreon* continued to roll in. Tom now had about fifty. The Marquis of Lansdowne had subscribed, and asked the poet to call. Tom had the Duke of Bedford's name, and Mrs Fitzherbert's. The significance of the latter could not be missed: but, before anything else could happen,

Tom fell victim to sudden illness. He was taken with a severe pain in the side, which his physician, Dr Baillie, tried to get rid of in the good old-fashioned way with a dose of calomel. The dose failed, and an abscess began to form. Woolriche the surgeon was called in, and came for some time twice a day. Tom belittled the whole thing, so as not to alarm his mother, and said nothing about it till he was well again. By the time he wrote to his mother, he was sitting up, weak, but in good spirits, eating well, and d.. .king porter and old port. In a letter a week or so later to his Uncle Richard, whom he always called his "darling Brother", he admits the seriousness of the illness.[1]

"This has been a most delicious day, and I have been basking about the streets in great happiness; everything looked so new and so bright to me—the coaches all made of gold and the women of silver; besides, everyone was so glad to see me, and I saw one poor man who had been as ill as myself, and we met like two newly-raised bodies on the day of resurrection,—so glad to see each other's bones with a little flesh on them again. . . . Well, it is a most sweet thing to feel health returning, and if my side but keeps well, and the sun keeps shining, I have some very, very, happy weeks before me. I am now in the 8th week of my illness, and this is the first day I have *walked* out, though I have been twice with Lady D.[2] in the carriage. I hated coming back to my room and sofa to-day, but as it was the first time, I could not venture to stay out."

This was in March. In May, Tom was perfectly well again, going to parties, and enjoying a holiday to which he felt his illness entitled him. *Anacreon* was in the press: he had nothing more to worry about. He met a number of society people and men of letters, of whom the most important was William Godwin.

By June, he was combining work and parties. One of his pro-

---

[1] He learned, many years afterwards, that it was even more serious than he knew, and that his life had been in danger.
[2] Lady Donegal.

ductions was a Greek Ode, which he proposed, should Dr. Lawrence approve, to prefix to *Anacreon*. If successful, it would be a snub to the fellows of Trinity, of whom only two, the Provost and Tom's own tutor, had subscribed to his *magnum opus*. Their abstention annoyed him very much, but, secure in the general approval, he merely thought the worse of them, dismissing them as "scoundrelly monks" and "a cursed corporation of boobies".

In the meantime, his many meetings with Johnstone and other stage folk were bearing fruit, and he was working at an opera, *The Gipsy Prince*. He was not quite easy in his mind about this project, as the plot was not his own. Anastasia was consulted about it, as about everything else, for he knew how she would hate him to be associated with anything that did not succeed. He was keeping his work at it a secret, he told her, in case it should not be a success. Still, there should be money in it, and that was always a consideration.

Then came the event for which, once he had Mrs Fitzherbert's subscription, he must have been secretly hoping.

My dear Mother,
I have got the Prince's name, and his permission that I should *dedicate* Anacreon to him. Hurra! hurra!

The dedication and the hurras have never been forgiven him in Ireland, and one can understand why. Those who sang his Irish melodies, and worshipped him as the author, knew nothing about such matters, and cared less. To them, he was the fine flower of patriotism. The public does not enquire deeply into the history of those whom it chooses to honour. There were many to be jealous of Moore during his lifetime, but not until the reaction against him began, in comparatively recent times, were his countrymen extreme to mark what he had done amiss. For the defence, Moore himself, with his frankness and naïveté, is the best advocate.

He had already written to his parents about a *déjeuner* at Sir John Coghill's, when he sang with Lord Dudley. All his songs were encored, and, to crown everything, a young girl told him that the Prince had expressed great curiosity about his birth and parentage—which, to his credit, he never made the slightest effort to conceal. At the beginning of July, he sent his mother the first bound copy of the *Odes of Anacreon*, translated into English verse with Notes, by Thomas Moore, Esq., of the Middle Temple. He was wild with excitement, and could not wait for an acknowledgment. "How did you look at it? What did you feel? Oh! I know what you felt, and I know how you looked!"

He planned to come home, but there was much to occupy him, and he was waiting to be introduced to the Prince. Then, on August 3rd, came the memorable day.

August 4, 1800.

I was yesterday introduced to his Royal Highness George, Prince of Wales. He is beyond doubt a man of very fascinating manners. When I was presented to him, he said he was very happy to know a *man of my abilities*; and when I thanked him for the honour he did me in permitting the dedication of Anacreon, he stopped me and said, the honour was *entirely* his, in being *allowed* to put his name to a work of such merit. He then said that he hoped when he returned to town in the winter, we should have many opportunities of *enjoying each other's society*; that he was passionately fond of music, and had long heard of my talents in that way. Is not all this very fine? But, my dearest mother, it has cost me a *new coat*; for the introduction was unfortunately deferred till my former one was grown confoundedly shabby, and I got a coat made up in six hours; however, it cannot be helped; I got it on an economical plan, by giving two guineas and an *old coat*, whereas the usual price of a coat here is near four pounds. By the bye, I am still in my other tailor's debt. To change the topic, I have heard Lord Moira's opinion of my Anacreon (not from himself, for, when I saw him, he very elegantly thanked me for a vast deal of gratification which it had given him); but he had spoken a vast deal of it to a gentleman who told *me*: said there were scarce any of the *best* poets who had been so strictly grammatical in language as I had been,—that the notes discovered a great extent of reading,—and that, in short, it was a very superior work.

Do not let any one read this letter but yourselves; none but a father and a mother can bear such egotising vanity; but I know who I am writing to—that they are interested in what is said of me, and that they are too partial not to tolerate my speaking of myself.

This letter is Tom Moore's epitome, and I could never find it in my heart to be angry with the man who wrote it. "But, my dearest mother, it has cost me a *new coat*": and the economies: "By the bye, I am still in my other tailor's debt"—and then, immediately, something about *Anacreon*: and finally, the very genuine admonition at the end: it is hard to resist him.

He was twenty-two. He was writing to his mother, whose every prayer and every effort had been for his advancement, and who could hardly have dreamed of such success as was now coming his way. If you blame Tom for dedicating his book to the Prince, you must blame Jack and Anastasia too, those friends of the United Irishmen, in whose house the forbidden uniform had been paraded, who had disapproved of plots and armed rebellion, but faced the disappointment of all their hopes in their darling son rather than that he should endanger a comrade. He was doing what they would have him do. He saw no dishonour in it, nor did they. He was following his star. Emmet would not have followed such a star, but Emmet would not have stood aside from politics at his mother's word. To blame a man for not being somebody else is waste of time. Moore was made for the sunny side of life, and very decently and honourably he comported himself thereon. Few men have stood prosperity better. He was the minstrel boy who was never called upon to go to the war, who played his harp in the drawing-room instead of on the battlefield: and we must take him as he was.

III

No detailed account of the *Anacreon* is necessary. Dr Lawrence's comments dispose of it as a translation. As verse, it is skilful, fluent, and superficial, with a certain pleasing freshness and high spirits. Appearing when it did, it deserves more interest than its qualities as verse can claim; but not very much. It was enriched with a great variety of footnotes, which brought on Moore the charge of pedantry—a charge which, in secret, he must have found rather flattering. He had more than once expressed anxiety on this score, remarking that the society of Burston and Hall, at Trinity, had been a valuable antidote. Actually, the motive for the notes is clear. Tom knew very well that he was no scholar, but was anxious to appear one. He knew a good deal, and had the examinee's knack of setting out his knowledge so that it looked like samples instead of the whole stock. From the point of view of scholarship, his was the magpie mind, collecting a great variety of information on no fixed plan, and content to display it. Hence the extraordinary collection of odd authors cited in the notes to *Anacreon*.

IV

Tom went home shortly after meeting the Prince, and stayed in Dublin till December. His singing during this visit made a great impression. London had given him confidence, and practice had improved his voice. He left a day or two after Christmas, probably crossing this time by Liverpool, and reached Manchester on the 29th, having done the last twenty-six miles of his journey in a canal boat, at the modest fare of three shillings. The slow movement was a relief after the rattle of the mail-coach, and, save for the night journey to Derby which lay ahead, he was in good spirits.

Two days later, he arrived at Donington Park, where he was to stay for several days. Despite all his *déjeuners* and *soirées*, this was the most formidable social ordeal he had yet undergone, a long way indeed from the little grocer's shop in Aungier Street. He had hoped to arrive in time for dinner on the previous evening, but the roads were deep in snow, and in places impassable, so that he had to go a long way round, and did not arrive till two o'clock on the 31st. He was received with a kindness and cordiality which prevented him from being overawed by the magnificence of his surroundings. Lord Moira was all courtesy, and Lady Charlotte regretted very much that Moore's visit had not overlapped the Prince's. The Prince, she told her delighted guest, had regretted it too. When bedtime came, Lord Moira himself insisted on seeing Tom to his room, going in front of him down the long gallery, candle in hand, and wishing him good night at the door. Small wonder that Tom could not sleep, but sat down at once to write to his beloved mother and tell her all about it.

His only discomfort during his visit—at least the only discomfort to which he confessed—was caused by his huge portmanteau. It contained most of his possessions, he could not bring himself to unpack it altogether, and as, in his happy-go-lucky way, he had not had the foresight to put all he was likely to want at Donington on top, he had to stoop over the thing and root about in it, causing such confusion that he felt he dared not stay more than a day or two. The task of repacking it was more than he could face. Anyway, much as he appreciated his host's kindness, his library, and his excellent piano, he was anxious to get back to London. Doubtless Anastasia read between the lines, even more easily than we may. Despite his moments of exultation, when, fresh from Lord Moira's encouragement, he could write, "Dearest Mother! there is no fear of my not doing *every-thing*. Keep up your spirits, my little woman, and you'll find I'll make you as rich as a nabob," the visit was an ordeal, and Moore's alternating moods must have given him unhappy moments of loneliness. He stayed till January 4th, on the morning of which breakfast was served an hour earlier than usual to accommodate him, and his host requested that he should come again on his first opportunity.

Then followed months of the utmost brilliance. The poet was fairly launched. The *Morning Post* dubbed him "Anacreon Moore", and the name stuck for years. Invitations poured in, at the rate of three to six a night. He attended all he could, and gleefully reported them all to his mother, adding, characteristically, that he was taking "old Hammersley's" advice, and not neglecting his legal studies. One night, Lady Harrington's servant chased him to two or three places with a ticket for the king's concert, the "Ancient Music", a function so select that only those who had attended the court before were usually invited. "These attentions from such great people are no harm, but they are flattering." Flattering indeed. Lord Moira called at his lodging in person. He was bidden to the Countess of Cork. Monk Lewis expressed "the greatest agonies" of regret at having come in late one night and missed his songs. He and Lady Charlotte Rawdon were given a double encore. At a grand ball, the Prince came up. "How-d'you-do, Moore? I am glad to see you." In short,

"How d'you do, my dearest mother? Did you see my name in the paper among the lists of company at most of the late routs? This is a foolish custom adopted here, of printing the names of the most *distinguished persons* that are at the great parties, and Mr *Moore*, I assure you, is not forgotten."

One of Tom's most attractive qualities is his affection for his mother. His first concern was to share everything with her: his first happiness to know that she was well.

"All I desire is that my dear ones at home may be as contented and easy in mind as I am. Tell me are you all happy and comfortable? I do not hear from you half often enough."

He was a good son: and, as many good sons do not, he was to make as good a husband.

In the intervals of "racketting" he was busy on *The Gipsy Prince*. He read the libretto to Suett and to Jack Bannister the comedian one evening after dinner. Suett in particular was delighted with his part. The piece was not produced, however. It was too late in the season, and Colman the manager, though he liked it, found it on too lavish a scale for his theatre and hoped that Moore would do him something else. One worry which Tom had on his mind, a debt of £70 to Hume, was cleared by the sale of the copyright of *Anacreon*, of which a new edition had been called for. Its success had paved the way for a new volume, *The Poetical Works of the late Thos. Little, Esq.*, published by Carpenter.

When they came out, Moore was at Donington. He had found the gay London life both tiring and expensive, and, early in the spring, had planned to go off to the country for at least a fortnight "incog". Lord Moira came to his rescue, with the offer of Donington Park. He and his family were in town, so "Mr Moore" could be as quiet as he pleased, have the library to himself, and give his inspiration full scope. So, at the end of April, he slipped quietly from town, and disappeared for a month to Donington. He was not used to solitude, and did not care for it, but the time did not lie heavy on his hands. He rose and went to bed early, ate well, went rook shooting, sang every evening, grew rosy cheeked, and had only one care in the world—the difficulty of getting his letters from home.

v

By the time he returned to London, the poems were out, and "Mr Thomas Little" was enjoying a flattering reception.

Everyone was talking of them, and Carpenter was selling a steady twenty copies a day. The publisher was on a good thing, and he knew it. He deferred publishing the new edition of *Anacreon*, taken over from Stockdale, till Christmas, and encouraged the poet to draw on him in advance for his expenses. Then, choosing his time, he called upon Tom one morning at his lodgings. It was twelve o'clock, but Tom, who had been to a ball the night before, was still in bed. Carpenter bade him good morning, and came straight to business.

"Well, Mr Moore, I have been looking over your account with me, and I find the balance against you to be almost sixty pounds."

Tom shot up in bed, all sleepiness banished, and stared at him in consternation.

"What *is* to be done?" he cried.

"Now, now, Mr Moore. Pray, don't distress yourself." And Carpenter explained, in the kindest of tones, that if Mr Moore would make over to him the copyright of "Little's" poems, he would be happy to cancel the whole account.

Tom beamed in joy and gratitude.

"My dear fellow! Most willingly! and thanks for the relief you have given me."

The publisher bowed himself out, well satisfied. Some years later, he admitted that he was still making close on two hundred a year from the volume.

Tom, all unconscious of how he had been swindled, went on enjoying himself mightily, until the gay life proved too expensive, and he planned another retreat to Donington. He went there, probably, about the end of June, and also perhaps to Ireland, since there is a gap of several months in his letters home. At the end of December, Tom was at the Moiras', a member of a distinguished party which included Curran the orator. From there he wrote to Mary Godfrey, Lady Donegal's sister, telling her how much he wanted to get back to London, and received

7

in return a letter, dated December 27th, so salutary and so charming that it must be quoted in full:

"I have this moment received your letter, and *me voici la plume à la main pour y répondre*; not to tell you what we can make of you, for God only knows what you are good for, or whether you are good for anything, but to lament and groan over your restless disposition. Your talents might fit you for everything, and your idleness unfits you for anything. You want to come to town, I know you do, merely to get away from those country-bred, sentimental ladies, the Muses, and I pray that you may have no other ladies in view to supply their place. You really might, if you pleased, study all the morning, and amuse yourself all the evening. I intreat you to make an effort and not to devote every hour and moment of your existence to pleasure. You know my sermons make you laugh—*tant mieux*. I never despair of you when you laugh; if you yawned I should give up the thing as hopeless." . . .

On receiving the letter, she had "resolved to answer it immediately, to encourage you to remain at your post. Nothing ever was more disinterested than this advice, and I never shall cease to admire myself for giving it, for if I followed my own inclinations, which in general don't lead me astray like yours, I would say 'Come up to town by all means, and the oftener we see you the better.' I consult your interest when I say the contrary. But yet if you do come, if the truth must come out, I shall most heartily rejoice to see you, and so shall we all. Say pretty things for me to Lady Charlotte about love and friendship, and writing to each other. I shall give you a *carte blanche* upon the occasion, for I suspect she does not care the least in the world for me—it is all stage trick and fine acting: this is quite *entre nous*. Remember me to Lord Forbes. God bless you, and make a good man of you (I believe it is almost impossible)."

He did not take the advice. Protesting that he was coming up really on business, to get some more of his music published, he travelled with Curran, who kept him in fits of laughter the whole way, and arrived in town on January 3rd, to find that the second edition of *Anacreon* had appeared on New Year's Day. It had as a frontispiece his own portrait, "engraved by Jas. Heath from a Miniature by A. Plimer". It began to sell well, and Stevenson, who had set a glee from it, *Lady Fair*, was encouraged to publish at once. He and Moore were at work on *The Gipsy Prince*, but for some reason Stevenson withdrew, much to Moore's chagrin, and the music was entrusted to Michael Kelly, of whose academic abilities he had a poor opinion. But Kelly could write a catchy tune, and Moore had to admit that he did his work well.

On July 24th,[1] *The Gipsy Prince* was put on at the Haymarket, Colman having apparently overcome the difficulties of which he complained. Despite the title page of the printed copy, which stated that it was "now Performing with Universal Applause at the Theatre Royal, Haymarket", the operetta failed to attract the public, and was withdrawn after a few performances. Moore makes no reference to it, but his next letter was written in September.

The rest of the year was spent between London and Donington, with a visit to Wales in September. When "Anacreon Moore" saw fit to attend the Union Masquerade, a ticket for which cost fifteen guineas, it is small wonder that London proved expensive. For a while he had peace at Donington, amusing himself with Dalby, Lord Forbes' tutor, by looking at Jupiter through a telescope: but presently the house was full, and he was wishing "all the duchesses and marchionesses *chez le diable*". Even so, he wrote, or got material for writing, witness the verses headed "To his Serene Highness the Duke of Mont-

[1] Kelly, in his reminiscences, gives the date as 1801. This is not possible, since Moore refers to the forthcoming production in more than one letter dated 1802.

pensier, on his portrait of the Lady Adelaide Forbes, Donington Park, 1802".

During the summer, his purse seems to have run dry. He lay low for a while, and put in some hard work. Monk Lewis, with whom he was now on terms of close friendship, wrote to ask where the deuce he had got to, and reported that Count Beaujolais (brother to Louis Philippe) had been looking for him everywhere. Finally, a report went round that he was dead.

The financial situation had become really difficult. Tom was in debt to tradesmen, and had had to borrow from his uncle Richard. There seemed, at the beginning of the year, a strong prospect of Lord Moira coming into power, and Tom was doing all he could to obtain a position or a pension through his agency. Moira proved very friendly, and the idea was put forward that Tom should go to Brunswick with Lord Forbes. Nothing came of it. Moira entertained his protégé to dinner at the Cocoa Tree, condoled with him on his disappointment, and gave him to understand that any influence he had—and his prospects looked brighter than ever—would be used in his behalf. To leave nothing untried, Tom had written to Monk Lewis, who told him pretty plainly that no recommendation from him was likely to have the least effect, and could suggest nothing better than "some trifling situation in the India House".

And so the year closed, Tom's only adventure of note being a descent down a Welsh coal-mine. He went down in a bucket, and—his own words—expected to kick it before it brought him up again.

VI

Whatever else might be said of them, the poems of "Thomas Little" could not be accused of pedantry. True, they were not innocent of footnotes, but their general tone was remote from the schools. They were facile, graceful, occasionally witty, conventionally phrased, and musical. While it is hard to speak of them as a whole, since they were written over several years, in the best of them Moore's technique is improving, and he shows real originality. Many are squibs of the slightest kind:

ON A SQUINTING POETESS

To no *one* Muse does she her glance confine,
But has an eye, at once, to *all the Nine*!

or

TO PHILLIS

Phillis, you little rosy rake,
  That heart of yours I long to rifle:
Come, give it me, and do not make
  So much ado about a *trifle*!

But there is a genuine originality, something all Moore's own. The best of the poems are remarkable in two ways. One of them was the boldness of his metrical experiments, in which he anticipated by many years the practice of later poets.

THE GENIUS OF HARMONY

An Irregular Ode

Ad harmoniam canere mundum.—CICERO, *de Nat. Deor.,* . . . lib. III.

There lies a shell beneath the waves,
In many a hollow winding wreath'd,
  Such as of old
Echoed the breath that warbling sea-maids breath'd;
  This magic shell,
From the white bosom of a syren fell,
As once she wander'd by the tide that laves
  Sicilia's sands of gold,
    It bears
Upon its shining side the mystic notes
  Of those entrancing airs,
The genii of the deep were wont to swell,
When heaven's eternal orbs their midnight music roll'd! . . .

Similarly,

THE FALL OF HEBE

A Dithyrambic Ode

'Twas on a day
When the immortals at their banquet lay;
The bowl
Sparkled with starry dew,
The weeping of those myriad urns of light,
Within those orbs, the almighty Power,
At nature's dawning hour,
Stor'd the rich fluid of ethereal soul.
Around,
Soft odorous clouds, that upward wing their flight
From eastern isles
(Where they have bath'd them in the orient ray,
And with rich fragrance all their bosoms fill'd),
In circles flew, and, melting as they flew,
A liquid daybreak o'er the board distill'd.

Another was a note which had been dumb in English poetry
for a long time: since the days of Rochester and Sedley, from
whom Moore, assiduous in Marsh's library, had caught it.

LOVE AND MARRIAGE

Eque brevi verbo ferre perenne malum.—SECUNDUS, eleg. vii.

Still the question I must parry,
Still a wayward truant prove:
Where I love, I must not marry;
Where I marry, cannot love.

Were she fairest of creation,
With the least presuming mind;
Learned without affectation;
Not deceitful, yet refin'd;

Wise enough, but never rigid;
Gay, but not too lightly free;
Chaste as snow, and yet not frigid;
Fond, yet satisfied with me:

Were she all this ten times over,
  All that heav'n to earth allows,
I should be too much her lover
  Ever to become her spouse.

Love will never bear enslaving;
  Summer garments suit him best;
Bliss itself is not worth having,
  If we're by compulsion blest.

If all the verses were as good as the first and fourth, Moore
would have written one of the best poems of its kind in English.
"Mr Little" had no use for the eighteenth century. For once, he
was ahead of his time—a compliment one cannot pay him afterwards, as man or poet. Burns had leaped like a comet into the
sky, and *Lyrical Ballads* had ranged the rebels against the old
school. Moore was not in the van of the new freedom, but he
was going gaily along, doing something new and unfashionable
with such grace and charm that no one realized what it was. The
success of the "Little" poems is easy to understand. They ran
easily, they were musical, they made no demands on the intelligence, they were mildly *risqué*: and they had this freshness, this
limpid note, which sounded happily in ears accustomed to the
measures of Johnson and Crabbe. It is often the lesser men who
do most to change popular taste, handing on the discoveries of
their betters in an easier, more palatable form. Moore's influence
was enormous, as was to be proved by his celebrity in America
and Canada, won on the strength of Anacreon and Little alone.
In the great loosening of the muscles of English poetry which the
first thirty years of the new century brought about, he had his
honourable share.

CHAPTER VIII

TRAVEL AND ADVENTURE

A laureateship declined—A poet abroad—A letter from John
Moore—Farewell to England—The voyage—Arrival in Ber-
muda — Disappointments — A good friend — New York —
Moore's travels—Hudson again—An Indian Chief—Niagara
—Moore's views on America—Home again

THE spring of 1803 found Tom still without the post he was
looking for. Money was tight, but he had no fewer than three
invitations to stay in the country, which would mean a considerable saving. He worked hard, making fair copies of his poems,
and bewailing the labour. By May, his finances were sufficiently
in order for him to send five pounds for Ellen's music lessons,
with an apology for the smallness of the sum.

Then came the offer of a post, specially created for him. Lord
Moira and Joe Atkinson seem to have got together and persuaded the Chief Secretary for Ireland to establish an Irish
Laureateship, on the same lines as the English. Moore consulted
his father, who advised him against the proposal. We cannot be
sure whether he was at first dazzled by it, or whether what he
said to his mother had been in his mind from the start. He told
her that nothing could have made him accept the salary but the
fear that she and his father were in need: but, since they were not
"in instant necessity", he gladly turned the offer down.

"Feeble as my hopes are of advancement under government,
I should be silly to resign them, without absolute necessity, for a
gift which would authorise them to consider me provided for,
and leave me without a chance of any other and further advantage. . . ."

Shrewd enough: but he had consulted a good many people on the subject, and the good sense may have been theirs, rather than his.

He felt a little natural anxiety about the reaction of Lord Moira and Joe Atkinson to his refusal, but Moira reassured him very pleasantly, and he wrote off at once to his mother a full statement of his reasons. Money difficulties were met by Carpenter, who promised to pay him a hundred a year on account of future transactions: and on the strength of this he at once sent Catherine a new piano, "not as good by any means as I could wish for her, but sweet toned, and of course much better than the wretched machine she has at present".

The last fortnight in July and the first week of August he spent at Donington. Then he went up to town on business. It was real business this time. Lord Moira had once again been active on his behalf, and had secured the offer of a Government post in Bermuda, a registrarship in the naval prize-court. Moore wrote in vague terms to prepare his mother for the possibility that he might be sent abroad. Then, as soon as the offer was definitely made, he sought his father's advice. Jack Moore has hitherto been rather a shadowy figure in his son's life, and this, the only letter of his which is extant, is so admirable that he must be given the centre of the stage:

DUBLIN,
Aug. 16, 1803.

MY DEAREST TOM,

I regretted very much not having written to you on the receipt of your letter of the 7th, but I wished to have a fuller account of the situation of this appointment, which we had reason to expect from yourself, and which we have had this day by your letter. Your uncle came here yesterday for the purpose of disclosing the whole secret to your mother, so that we only anticipated what you had done of yourself to-day. There could be no such deception carried on with her, where you, or indeed any one of her family, were concerned, for she seems to know everything respecting them by instinct. It would not be doing her the justice she well deserves to exclude her from such confidence. Her fears are greatly removed and relieved by the various accounts we have of this island, possessing good air and almost every other advantage that can possibly be wished for: there is nothing un-pleasant in it but the distance, and Heaven knows that ought to be reckoned a blessing to be almost any distance from these two countries at present. Poor Kate came to town to-day in conse-quence of my having written to her on this business, for there is no one ought to be more interested in your affairs than her, and my poor child knows it. However, after all that was natural for her to feel on such a separation, she was quite delighted, and said she wished to accompany you. She returned back to Atkinson's; he, A., does not know of this business, nor do I think it right he should until it's all determined; for though he is, I believe, one of the best of men, he blabs a little too much. However you know when and how to let him know of it. Your uncle Joice wrote you yesterday; he is one of the best of creatures; he mentioned his wish to know something certain of the emoluments of this place, which was very natural, but your letter of this day clears up that point. For my particular part I think with you, that there is a singular chance, as well as a special interference of Providence, in your getting so honourable a situation at this very critical time. I am sure no one living can possibly feel more sensibly than your poor mother and me do at losing that comfort we so long enjoyed, of at least hearing from you once every week of your life that you were absent from us; for surely no parents had ever such happiness in a child; and much as we regret the wide separa-tion which this situation of yours will for some time cause between us, we give you our full concurrence, and may the Almighty God spare and prosper you as you deserve. Your own good sense, I hope, will always direct you. It will be most material, and I hope what you will be able to accomplish, that of being called to the bar either here or in London; for it would give you not only sanction and consequence at present, but give you an honourable profession after. I need not suggest those things to you, for I am sure you will not leave any thing undone. I should be glad you would now write to us more frequently, as you may suppose our anxiety about you will be every day increasing, and I hope you will be able to come to see us before your departure. You will hear from me again in a post or two. Your mother joins me in love to you, and I am, my dearest child, your ever affectionate,

JOHN MOORE.

"Surely no parents had ever such happiness in a child." It is a fine tribute, not lightly won, and Moore's detractors must swallow it as best they can.

To one so affectionate as Tom, the idea of a long separation from his dear ones was too painful to be dwelt on. He busied himself with the hundred and one things to be done before his departure. Uncle Richard once more came to the rescue with a gift of money. Tom sold his piano, left a last batch of songs with Stevenson, and, sore at heart but in the highest hopes, set sail from Spithead, on board the frigate *Phaeton*, on September 25th, 1803.

II

The voyage began fairly, with good weather and the promise of a comfortable trip. Off the Hebrides, they met a ship bound for Lisbon, and Tom, in the faint hope of its ultimately reaching her, sent a letter to his mother. Characteristically he had already settled down to the life of the ship. Before starting, he made friends with two fellow-voyagers, a Mr and Mrs Merry, and he now set about making friends with all on board. The officers he liked particularly, and reported of them, at the end of the voyage, that they were the best set of fellows he had ever encountered. There was, as he realized, a prejudice to overcome. He did not realize how great. "I thought you," the first lieutenant told him afterwards, "the damnedest conceited little fellow I ever saw, with your glass cocked up to your eye": and he gave the poet a far from complimentary imitation of his first appearance.

That Moore won them all over we know on better evidence than his own. A midshipman, one Scott, wrote in his *Recollections*, some thirty years later, that they knew nothing of Moore's poetry, but that he was the life and soul of the company, and that "the loss of his fascinating society was frequently and loudly lamented by the officers long after he had quitted us in America". The lessons of Burston and Hall had been well learned, and Tom's natural genius for friendship had been strengthened by an understanding of how to approach people on common ground. His secret was that he enjoyed life and genuinely liked his company. Save for the few people to whom, like Wolcot, he took an aversion, he could get on with anyone: and against his preference for the ladies, and his drawing-room conquests, must be set his success with the officers of the *Phaeton*.

Although he had fits of homesickness, and felt very much the lack of letters from home, Tom found the voyage full of interest. There were flying fish and turtles to be admired, and the ardours of the journey, the rough weather and the violent changes of temperature, taught him one valuable lesson.

"I am much more hardy, dear mother, than I ever imagined; and I begin to think it was your extreme tenderness that made either of us imagine that I was delicate."

The *Phaeton* reached Norfolk, Virginia, early in November. Tom said good-bye to passengers and officers with a sinking heart. He had become attached to them all, and they to him. They were his last link with the world he knew, and he now must go among strangers. So, with mutual expressions of regret, they parted, and Tom went ashore, clasping his letters of introduction, to call upon the British Consul. In a few minutes, his spirits had bounded up again. The first thing he saw, as he entered the consul's drawing-room, was a harpsichord: and Colonel Hamilton and his wife gave him a cordial reception, the consul being much impressed by a letter from Lord Henry Stewart, and even more so by the mention "by accident" of the magic name of Lord Moira. ("I shall, of course," Tom observes, "mention all this when I write to Lord M.")

In the evening, there was music. He was further delighted to see some of his own songs among the music-books, but nearly wept for homesickness when a young lady played some of the pieces which he had heard Billy Warren teach his sister. A local periodical spoke well of "Little" and *Anacreon*. Tom had a net to keep off the mosquitoes, which revenged themselves upon poor Mrs Merry. Better still, he heard good accounts of Bermuda, and expected to set sail in a few days at the latest. He wrote a long letter home, and was happy.

Actually, some two months passed before he left the hospitable Colonel Hamilton, during which he had the mortification of receiving back one of his letters, undelivered, five weeks after he had sent it off. The ship which carried it had been driven back by rough weather. At last, however, a warship put in, and the captain offered to take the distinguished traveller gratis, thereby saving him between twenty and thirty guineas. The *Driver*, under Captain Compton, set sail about January 3rd. Moore, though glad to be gone, felt some regret at leaving his kind host and hostess. Mrs Hamilton cried, and the Colonel gave him letters of introduction to everyone who could conceivably be of service.

The *Driver* ran into some of the worst weather her officers could remember. For three days she dared not put on a stitch of sail, and, at meals, officers and their passenger had to be tied to the table. Moore confirmed his new-found hardiness by refusing to be disconcerted, and eating a vast dinner of steak and onions during the worst gale of the trip. Despite the gales, the voyage took only a week.

Bermuda, to the eye of fancy, was a romantic and delightful spot, and Moore proceeded to take full advantage of it. He wrote to Lady Donegal a verse epistle, full of nymphs and grots, zephyrs and whatnot, in his most lush manner, but confessed in a letter home that, when it came to nymphs, the island was disappointing. From the delightful little white houses appeared, not the appropriate naiads, but a few miserable and ugly negroes. Even so, the verses to Lady Donegal, rubbish though they are, are interesting in that they are about the first instance in Moore of natural description. He seems to have had little eye for nature, indeed little visual sense at all.[1] The beauties of Dublin and Wicklow, the marvel of a summer trip by boat to Dalkey Island, provoked no comment from him. Of his childhood days at Sandymount, with its magic views over the sands at low tide, and of the autumn he spent at Blackrock, he left no visual record. His Journal, which begins in 1818 and continues to his last years, tells us almost everything about people but what they looked like. "A fine handsome man", "a pretty girl", "an ugly woman": he hardly ever gets beyond the vaguest descriptions.[2] Yet personalities interested him more than anything else in life. Nature was never more than a background for the human scene —often as not a backcloth. Niagara moved him, but to a religious ecstasy. He felt the gloom of Glendalough on a dark day, but as atmosphere rather than in visual images. And, in his hymn to the "sweet Vale of Avoca", he expressly tells us that it was not the beauty of the place that so moved him, but "something more exquisite still": adding that

> the best charms of nature improve
> When we see them reflected in looks that we love.

---

[1] The most vivid touch in his account of his life in Bermuda is the description of a dish of green peas smoking every day on the table.

[2] An exception is the picture of Byron at La Mira, on p. 223 (note).

This being so, it is surprising that we get as much from him about Bermuda as we do.

III

The island was disappointing in more particulars than the plainness of its females. Moore's post turned out to be something very different from what had been represented. The emoluments were small. Nothing but a war with Spain could give the prize-court enough to do to make it pay. He resolved therefore to stay only so long as was needed for the writing which he had in hand, and then to sail for home. This decision cheered him enormously. It meant that he was facing Ireland, instead of having his back turned to it, and he settled down to enjoy himself for all he was fit. To one of his fame and talents, this offered no difficulty, and in spite of the plainness of the ladies, there were at least two claimants to be the original of the "Nea" to whom certain of his Bermuda verses were addressed. "The ideal . . ." he wrote in 1841, "was made out of two real ones."

His one sorrow was that no letter had come from home. The only news he had, in a newspaper, told him of the death of an old friend, and made him almost afraid to open another, so that his longing for news from home was mingled with dread. But the moods of despondency were quickly over, and the change had made him feel better in health than ever before. Roses were in bloom, there were green peas for dinner : what more could a man want? So, between miscellaneous verses, songs for Stevenson, and entertainment from the hospitable islanders, the four months passed. The collaboration with Stevenson was becoming valuable. Stevenson's setting as a glee of Moore's *Give me the Harp of Epic Song* had so delighted the Viceroy, Lord Hardwick, that he was rewarded with a knighthood, and the work for Carpenter, which was to adjust Moore's finances, may well have been a collection of songs for his friend.

At the end of April, Moore appointed a deputy to look after his responsibilities, and took a passage in the Boston frigate, under Captain Douglas, for New York. He arrived, bursting with health and spirits, after a nine days' voyage, having made a staunch and faithful friend of the captain. After the voyage, they were not to meet again for five years. When they did, Douglas, who had some money in the bank, put it at Moore's disposal.

"Now, my dear little fellow," he said, "here is a blank check, which you may fill up while I am away, for as much of that as you may want."

If Moore had been careless of other people's money, as he was of his own, he might have taken advantage of many offers of this kind: but he never exploited his gift for making friends, and remained, to the end of his life, in a state of gratified surprise at each fresh evidence of it. Three years later, when Douglas had become an admiral, he offered Moore the Secretaryship in Jamaica, an offer which Moore instantly appreciated at its worth, for he was by that time dead out with the Prince, whom Douglas ran grave risk of offending by this open profession of friendship.

The trip, besides winning him this good friend, gave Moore the chance to see something of America. Of New York he thought very poorly. It had a certain picturesqueness, but he found the town depressing, and the inhabitants stupid, without taste and feeling. From New York he sailed to Norfolk, where he stayed with the Hamiltons, and received from the kind-hearted Mrs Hamilton a pair of ear-rings for Catherine. Thence he travelled by coach to Washington, to stay with the Merrys, and on to Baltimore, in a state of increasing indignation at the discomfort of his journey. His fellow-passengers consisted mostly of "squalling children, stinking negroes, and republicans smoking cigars": and the coaches themselves seemed to him emblematic of the Government, "filled with a motley mixture, all 'hail fellow well met', driving through mud and filth, which *bespatters* them as they raise it, and risking an *upset* at every step. God comfort their capacities!"

It does not come prettily from a Dubliner of the time, who should have been prepared for a little tolerance in the matter of dirt and discomfort. This is the one instance in which Moore shows himself less than generous. His good friend Douglas, in a letter dated June 29th, takes him goodnaturedly but bluntly to task for showing too little consideration for people who were doing their best to please him.

"Now, my good fellow, allow me to advise you not to be *too careless* about the *warm reception you received* at Philadelphia: in my opinion, these new acquaintances ought always to be treated with the greatest *respect* and *attention*. I wish you had come down yesterday, as I do think few of your friends would feel much more gratified by taking you by the hand than myself."

One blushes for Moore, that he of all men should have earned such a rebuke. On no other recorded occasion does his "readiness to please and be pleased" appear to have deserted him. The kindest conclusion we can come to is that the uncomfortable stage-coach upset him, and that a temporary fit of peevishness was to blame. In a letter to his mother, written three days before Douglas's rebuke, he picks on Philadelphia as the one place which received him cordially, and which he was sorry to leave. The inhabitants of "the only place in America which can boast of any literary society" knew who their visitor was, "but their affectionate attentions were far beyond this deference to reputation". He was "quite caressed" and was sorry to leave.

While there, he met again his old friend, the exiled Edward Hudson. Far from finding him "cured of republicanism", as he expected, he found him firmer than ever. The meeting was not a success. It is easy to picture: Moore arriving, expansive, full of humorous and scornful comment on the country and its ways, rattling on for some time before he saw, from his friend's unsmiling face, that his jests were not appreciated. Try to retrieve

8

it as he might, the harm was done. "I feel awkward with Hudson now; he has perhaps had reason to confirm him in his politics, and God knows I see every reason to change mine." It is frank, at any rate: and we may imagine what Hudson, his ancient loyalties strengthened by exile, thought of the fêted and successful traveller.

From Philadelphia, Moore went to Passaick Falls, which he found "sweetly romantic". A week in New York, which he left quickly on a report of yellow fever, a trip up the Hudson to Saratoga, where his request for washing materials gave some offence, a visit to Seenectady (*sic*), and a journey along the Mohawk River, were the next stages in his journey. He visited a camp of Oneida Indians, and was delighted with the old chief, whose gentleness and courtesy he contrasted favourably with the manners of the newer inhabitants. He travelled on to Niagara, in a waggon, evidently feeling a bit better, for while he still complained, he admitted that living was cheap and that "powerful curiosity sweetens all discomforts". Niagara made on him as great an impression as any of his hosts could desire. After the Rapids, which he called a "prelibation" of the grandeur that was to come, he saw the Falls themselves. Then:

"Never shall I forget the impression I felt at the first glimpse of them which we got as the carriage passed over the hill that overlooks them. We were not near enough to be agitated by the terrific effects of the scene; but saw through the trees this mighty flow of waters descending with calm magnificence, and received enough of its grandeur to set imagination on the wing; imagination which, even at Niagara, can outrun reality. I felt as if approaching the very residence of the Deity; the tears started into my eyes; and I remained, for moments after we had lost sight of the scene, in that delicious absorption which pious enthusiasm alone can produce. We arrived at the New Ladder and descended to the bottom. Here all its awful sublimities rushed full upon me. But the former exquisite sensation was gone. I now saw all. The string that had been touched by the first impulse, and which *fancy* would have kept for ever in vibration, now rested at *reality*. Yet, though there was no more to imagine, there was much to feel. My whole heart and soul ascended towards the Divinity, in a swell of devout admiration, which I never before experienced. Oh! bring the atheist here, and he cannot return an atheist! I pity the man who can coldly sit down to write a description of these ineffable wonders; much more do I pity him who can submit them to the admeasurement of gallons and yards. It is impossible by pen or pencil to convey even a faint idea of their magnificence. Painting is lifeless; and the most burning words of poetry have all been lavished upon inferior and ordinary subjects. We must have new combinations of language to describe the Falls of Niagara."

At Niagara, and on his way to Quebec, he received gratify-ing evidence of his fame. A watchmaker at Niagara would take no payment for a job, asking Moore to accept it as the only mark of respect he could pay to one he had heard so much of, but had never expected to meet. The captain of the boat which took him across Lake Ontario would likewise take nothing, and said he would be glad to give free passage to all the poet's friends. Moore responded with delight: "This is the very nectar of life, and I hope, I *trust*, it is not vanity to which the cordial owes its sweetness."

His temper was now quite restored, and the "barbarous folk" forgotten. At Halifax and Windsor he was made very welcome, the Governor of Nova Scotia insisting that he be present at the first examination of the new university. The Governor of Lower Canada begged a ship's captain to defer sailing by one day, so that Mr Moore should dine at his house. Moore, long overdue, had feared that Douglas would be already gone, but the gallant captain was still refitting: and, after a joyous letter home, and a message to Carpenter that he was bringing a fat packet of "poetic travels", he set sail for England early in October.

IV

Moore's travels in the New World show him at his worst, and his previous biographers have skated lightly over them. American life at the time was raw and uncomfortable: Dickens, who followed many years later, had something to say about it in *Martin Chuzzlewit*: and Moore, far from all he knew and liked, bumped about in bad coaches over worse roads, had a good deal to put up with. But in despising simple people for their ignorance of literature he was showing himself more "barren of intellect" than they. He must have received considerable provocation, since he could get on perfectly well with the unlettered, but he was at fault in shutting himself off from experience which might have done him good, and such conduct as Douglas's letter hints at was unpardonable. That it was only a temporary lapse is evident from the number of friends he made, and the general rush to do him honour. He made himself pleasant, particularly to the ladies. He sang his songs, though music in America was but "whistling in the wilderness". He was, except on the occasion noted, his usual friendly and expansive self. But he did not care for the New World, and he was glad to leave it.

It is only fair to add that he afterwards expressed regret for a good many of the comments he had made, particularly those in which he aspersed the principle of democracy.[1]

He carried away with him two favourable impressions, stamped on him by the ladies and by the scenery. The ladies he praised highly. They were kind and charming, and they evoked a suitable number of complimentary and amatory poems. As for the scenery, its natural magnificence really got through to him. His letters are full of wonder and description. In one, he says that one might easily surrender everything else in life, to remain for ever with such loveliness: and so alien a sentiment, facile in reaction though he was, meant a good deal.

[1] For an American reply to Moore's strictures, see Appendix B.

The best thing he brought back was his *Canadian Boat Song*,[1] inspired by his trip on the St Lawrence. He arranged it as a glee for three voices, and it was published by Carpenter in the year after his return.

v

Moore arrived at Plymouth on November 12th, at once wrote joyfully to his mother, and hurried on to town. His first concern was to fix up matters with Carpenter, and pay his debts, particularly that which he owed his beloved uncle. At supper at Lord Harrington's he met both Lord Moira and the Prince. The Prince walked over and laid a hand on his shoulder.

"I am very glad to see you home again, Moore," he cried. "From the reports I heard, I was afraid we had lost you. I assure you, it was a subject of general concern."

All was well. The playboy was safe home again.

[1] Not to be confused with the immeasurably superior poem, containing the verse

"From the lone shieling on the misty island,"

which some persons lacking ear and sense have claimed for him.

PART TWO

HEYDAY

Go where glory waits thee,
And when fame elates thee,
Oh, then remember me!

CHAPTER IX

THE MAN OF ACTION

AT twenty-five, Moore was set in the course he was to follow
till his last years. His character was formed, and the road to success lay open before him. Little was to happen that was not an
intensification of experiences he had already met. Even his marriage, that great blessing and mainstay of his life, grew naturally
from his love for his mother, and eventually took its place. The
only new thing to come was sorrow, and against that he fortified himself with an evasion natural to his temperament. From
this point, we shall learn much of his relations with others, shall
see his faculties deepen, his craft mature, and his wit mellow:
unless we have missed contact, we shall come to feel a strong
affection for him: but we shall learn little that is new about the
essential man. The qualities that won Byron, Scott, Rogers,
Canning, and Sydney Smith were those that had attracted his
first friends. The performance that delighted Creevey and Leigh
Hunt and angered Hazlitt—"Mr Moore converts the wild harp
of Erin into a musical snuff-box"—had been heard already in
the drawing-rooms, and the conquest of those drawing-rooms
opened the way to Holland House and Lady Blessington's. He
was to fall heavily into debt, but he had been in debt already.
His politics had got him out of favour once, and were to do so
again. He had made one attempt to be the man of action, and

his next was to be as inconclusive. He had done a good deal of acting as a child, and was to be an actor for a while in earnest. In a word, the years chronicled in such detail are both prelude and parable to all that followed.

And, though for the next twenty-five years Moore lived through one of the most exciting periods of British history, it was to have as little bearing on his life as had the period just past. The Peninsular War, the Act of Union even, had no effect on him. Of the war with France we get a casual mention or two, but the nearest it touched him was its possible effect on his emoluments at Bermuda. Creature of his age though Moore was, it is almost meaningless to set him against it. To its major concerns he was as irrelevant as a thrush. He lived in a special world, its concerns artistic and sociable rather than social, and nine-tenths of what went on outside found no mention in his pages. He had a finger in many pies: hardly a biography of the time can avoid his name: yet he was detached from it all, and his record limited by the narrow focus of his own interests.

Moore's approach to life was personal, direct, and feminine. He was interested in people rather than in movements, in results rather than in methods. Although he was more than once invited to stand for Parliament, although he had at one time a reputation as a political thinker, and although he was copious and occasionally effective in political satire, he had no natural interest in politics as such, and remained to the end an amateur. "I begin at last ", he wrote to Lady Donegal in 1808, "to find out that *politics* is the only thing indeed in this country . . . so I am writing politics." He had the poet's knack of seeing where a course was leading more clearly than did those engaged upon it, but he looked to politics only as a means of realising certain principles of his own, and turned from any party that did not immediately proceed to give effect to them. So stubborn was his fidelity to principle that no party could rely on him.

For general ideas he had little aptitude. He romanticised them,

made them personal, or turned them into a safety valve, an
outlet for his Irish combativeness. He was exceedingly perceptive, and saw as quickly as any man the way the wind blew or
was likely to blow. He was, when stimulated or provoked, an
acute social critic. Yet, left to himself, he would contentedly
confine his interests to a narrow range, and look at nothing
beyond his short and well-shaped nose.

The record of his life for the next thirty-five years is exceedingly full. Apart from Lord John Russell's eight-volume edition
of his Journal and Letters, there is a mass of outside testimony,
and newspaper references almost beyond counting. Collections
of letters exist which were unknown to Russell. Fresh material
offers on all sides. The problem is not one of discovery, but of
selection. To chronicle this, the prime of Moore's life and
activity, as fully as we have chronicled his early years, would
require as much space as Lord Russell's eight volumes. What
is worse, it would be pointless. Moore, like many men whose
characters lack profundity, remained consistent. He had few sudden turns and surprises. If ever he darted off at an angle, the
flight was brief, and he speedily returned to the even tenor of
his way. There were ups and downs, but, until the last years,
his life was played out in the same comfortable, happy, normal
key, its occasional divagations into the minor only serving to
accentuate the main aspiring harmony: "I thank God for my
cheerful disposition," and "Lean upon God, Bessy. Lean upon
God."

II

The first incident of note after Moore's return from America
was the affair of Jeffrey and the *Edinburgh Review*. The first seven
months of 1805 he spent in hard work. The task for Carpenter
did not go as fast as he had hoped, and in August he was still
talking about the necessity for finishing it, and asking his mother

to forgive him for not coming over till it was done. Early in September, however, it was ready, and Lord Moira, in the stiff phraseology he affected on paper, accepted the exceedingly flowery dedication of *Epistles, Odes and other Poems*. Moore was able to go home, but not for long. He was back at the beginning of November, and, in a letter to his mother, actually mentions an event of the greater world, the death of Nelson.

Early in 1806, politics became very exciting. In other words, there seemed every chance that Lord Moira would "come in". Moore was anxious lest he be forgotten, but a breakfast with the noble earl put all his doubts to rest. Still, nothing happened: and, to tease him further, came another bout of illness, an abscess which had to be opened more than once, and laid him by for a while. Before he was about again, Lord Moira sent him the offer of a small post, to keep him going till he found something better. In a tactful letter, Moore declined it. He explained that his real purpose was to provide for his parents in Dublin, and to "elevate" them "above the struggling exigencies" of their "present situation": and that, therefore, it might be easier for Moira to find some little post for his father. Moira complied at once, and in less than a month John Moore received the gift of a barrack-mastership in Dublin. Tom was to have "one of the Irish commissionerships", as soon as things in England were settled. He did not care to leave London until this was arranged, but Moira assured him that absence would not prejudice his chances, and so he went down to visit Lady Donegal and Mary Godfrey at Worthing.

There, as he breakfasted in bed one morning, was brought up to him the current number of the *Edinburgh Review*. *Odes and Epistles* had appeared, and he was eagerly waiting the *Review*. He hurriedly turned over the pages, and came upon this:

"A singular sweetness and melody of versification—smooth copious and familiar diction—with some brilliancy of fancy and some flow of classical erudition might have raised Mr Moore to

an innocent distinction among the song writers and occasional
poets of his day, but he is indebted we fear for the celebrity he
actually enjoys to accomplishments of a different description;
and may boast, if the boast can please him, of being the most
licentious of modern versifiers, and the most poetical of those
who in our times, have devoted their talents to the propagation
of immorality. We regard his book indeed as a public nuisance
and would willingly tramp it down by one short movement of
contempt and indignation, had we not reason to apprehend, that
it was abetted by patrons who are entitled to a more respectful
remonstrance, and by admirers who may require a more extended exposition of their dangers.

"There is nothing, it will be allowed, more indefensible than
a cold-blooded attempt to corrupt the purity of an innocent
heart; and we can scarcely conceive any being more truly despic-
able than he who, without the apology of an unruly passion or
tumultuous desires, sits down to ransack the impure places of
his memory for inflammatory images and expressions and com-
mits them laboriously to writing, for the purpose of insinuating
pollution into the minds of unknown and unsuspecting readers.

"This is almost a new crime among us. While France has to
blush for so many tomes of 'Poesies Erotiques' we have little to
answer for but the coarse indecencies of Rochester and Dryden;
and these, though sufficiently offensive to delicacy and good
taste can scarcely be regarded as dangerous. There is an antidote
to the poison they contain, in the open and undignified pro-
fligacy with which it is presented. If they are wicked they have
the honesty at least to profess wickedness. The mark of the beast
is set visibly on their foreheads; and though they have the boldness to recommend vice, they want the effrontery to make her
pass for virtue. In their grossest immoralities too they scarcely
even seem to be perfectly in earnest, and appear neither to wish
nor hope to make proselytes.

"They indulge their own vein of gross riot and debauchery;

but they do not seek to corrupt the principles of their readers; and are contented to be regarded as profligate, if they are admired at the same time for wit and originality.

"The immorality of Mr Moore is infinitely more insidious and malignant. It seems to be his aim to impose corruption upon his readers, by concealing it under the mask of refinement; to reconcile them imperceptibly to the most vile and vulgar sensuality by blending its language with that of exalted feeling and tender emotion; and to steal impurity into their hearts, by gently perverting the most simple and generous of their affections.

"In the execution of this unworthy task, he labours with a perseverance both ludicrous and detestable. He may be seen in every page running round the Paltry circle of his deductions with incredible zeal and anxiety, and stimulating this jaded fancy for new images of impurity, with as much melancholy industry as ever outcast of the muses hunted for epithets or metre. . . .

". . . A poet of a luxuriant imagination may give too warm a colouring to the representation of innocent endearments, or be betrayed into indelicacies in delineating the allurements of some fair seducer, while it is obviously his general intention to give attraction to the picture of virtue, and to put the reader on his guard against the assault of temptation.

"Mr Moore has no such apology; he takes care to intimate to us in every page, that the raptures which he celebrates do not spring from the excesses of an innocent love, or the extravagance of a romantic attachment; but are the unhallowed fruits of cheap and vulgar prostitution, the inspiration of casual amours, and the chorus of habitual debauchery. He is at pains to let the world know that he is still fonder of roving than of loving, and that all the Caras and the Fannys, with whom he holds dalliance in these pages, have had each a long series of preceding lovers, as highly favoured as their present poetical paramour, that they meet without any purpose of constancy, and do not think it necessary to grace their connexion with any professions of esteem or permanent attachment. The greater part of the book is filled with serious and elaborate descriptions of the ecstasies of such an intercourse, and with passionate exhortations to snatch the joys, which are thus abundantly poured forth from 'the fertile fount of sense'.

"To us, indeed, the perpetual kissing and twining and panting of these amorous persons is rather ludicrous than seductive; and their eternal sobbing and whining raises no emotion in our bosoms but those of disgust and contempt. Even to younger men, we believe, the book will not be very dangerous; nor is it upon their account that we feel the indignation and alarm which we have already endeavoured to express. The life and conversation of our sex, we are afraid, is seldom so pure as to leave them much to learn from publications of this description; and they commonly know enough of the reality, to be aware of the absurd illusion and exaggerations of such poetical voluptuaries. In them therefore, such a composition can work neither corruption nor deception, and it will in general be despised and thrown aside, as a tissue of sickly and fantastical conceits, equally remote from truth and respectability. It is upon the other sex, that we conceive its effects may be most pernicious; and it is chiefly as an insult to their delicacy, and an attack upon their purity, that we are disposed to resent its publication. . . .

"We have been induced to enter this strong protest, and to express ourselves thus warmly against this and the former publications of this author, both from what we hear of the circulation which they have already obtained, and from our conviction that they are calculated, if not strongly denounced to the public, to produce, at this moment, peculiar and irremediable mischief. The style of composition, as we have already hinted is almost new in this country; it is less offensive than the old fashion of obscenity; and for these reasons, perhaps, it is less likely to excite the suspicion of the modist, or to become the object of precaution to those who watch over the morals of the young and inexperienced. We certainly have known it a permitted study where performances infinitely less pernicious, were rigidly interdicted. . . .

"There is one other consideration which has helped to excite our apprehension on occasion of this particular performance. Many of the pieces are dedicated to persons of the first consideration in the country, both for rank and accomplishments, and the author appears to consider the greater part of them as his intimate friends, and undoubted patrons and admirers. Now, this we will confess is to us a very alarming consideration. By these channels the book will easily pass into circulation in those classes of society, which it is of most importance to keep free of contamination, and from which its reputation and its influence will descend with the greatest effect to the great body of the community. In this reading and opulent country there are no fashions which diffuse themselves so fast as those of literature and immorality. . . .

"On looking back to the volume with a view to estimate its poetical merits impartially, as separated from its sins of morality, we were surprised to find how little praise it could lay claim to; and are more and more convinced that its popularity is owing almost entirely to the seduction of the subjects on which it is employed. . . ."

There was a good deal more, and all of it hostile.

Moore was angered, as well he might have been, but his mercurial spirits bounded up again, and, discussing the review with Lady Donegal and Mary Godfrey, he made light of it. Then something really interesting happened. Moore conceived the idea of challenging Jeffrey to a duel. By what process he thought himself into such an attitude is hard to guess. He says himself that it was not done in anger (as we can well believe), but that his Irish love of a fight, and his vanity, had a good deal to say. This will not do. Moore's instinct was to keep out of rows, and this was a quite unnecessary row, and a dangerous one. When the idea first came into his head, he only played with it. Edinburgh was a long way off, and he could afford neither the time nor the money to go there. In face of this, he must have nursed the thought, and worked himself up, till he saw himself once more as the man of action. Then, chance took a hand. Returning to London, he discovered that Jeffrey was there! What was more, Rogers, coming from dinner at Lord Fincastle's, repeated a significant conversation. Jeffrey had been at the dinner, and his host, happening to mention Moore, described him as possessing "great amenity of manners".

Jeffrey laughed.

"I am afraid," he said, "he would not show much amenity to me."

So Jeffrey acknowledged the blow he had struck, and realized how it must sting a man of spirit! Moore took a deep breath, and wrote to his friend Woolrich, asking him to help him. Woolrich in reply suggested that Moore was acting hastily, in anger, and begged him to think it over. This settled Moore's last doubt. He wrote to Hume, who undertook at once to do what he wanted. A challenge was sent to Jeffrey, in such terms that there could be only one reply. The part of the review to which Moore took particular exception was the accusation that he had set out to corrupt the minds of his readers, and on this point he gave Jeffrey the lie direct.

Jeffrey accepted the challenge, and referred Hume to a friend of his named Horner. The next thing was to get the pistols. Hume, though he had been in a duel, possessed none. Moore was prejudiced against them, having nearly blown off his thumb while fooling about with someone else's. A friend named William Spencer undertook to provide them, and Moore bought in Bond Street enough powder and shot for twenty duels. On the evening before the day arranged, Spencer produced a pair of pistols, with the assurance that they were too good for the

9

occasion. Moore then sat down and wrote noble letters of farewell to Lady Donegal and Mary Godfrey, to be delivered if
Jeffrey killed him. It was decided that he had better not sleep at
home, and, as Hume's lodging had few amenities, Moore took
the sheets from his bed and went along in a hackney coach
to spend the night at his friend's.

He slept well, for the later part of the night at least, and Hume
had to rouse him. The *rendezvous* was at Chalk Farm, and
thither they drove off, to find Jeffrey and several of his friends
already waiting.

The place chosen was well screened with trees, and Hume
and Horner agreed that it was highly suitable. However, Horner
was anxious. He had seen some men hanging suspiciously about,
and did not wish the proceedings to begin till he was satisfied
that they were gone. He hunted about, but could not see them,
and at last he and Hume retired behind the trees to load the
pistols, leaving the two principals together.

There was a short silence. Then Jeffrey spoke.

"What a beautiful morning it is!"

"Yes," assented Moore, with a smile. "A morning made for
better purposes."

Jeffrey sighed. The meeting was none of his seeking. Then,
as their seconds delayed, neither being expert at the business, he
and Moore began to walk slowly up and down together. At one
turn, they came in sight of the seconds, busy at their task. Moore
at once told his opponent a story of Billy Egan, the barrister,
who, engaged in a similar business, was also walking up and
down while the loading was going on. His antagonist, thinking
he was trying to steal some advantage, called to him angrily to
stay where he was.

"Don't make yourself unaisy, my dear fellow," replied Egan.
"Sure, isn't it bad enough to take the dose, without being by
at the mixing up?"

Moore seems to have been confident, or, at any rate, to have felt little fear. He thought the story *à propos*, as indeed it was, and his main concern was not to fall short of the occasion. Jeffrey smiled wanly, and the seconds, their task at last complete, marched importantly out, set the combatants at their posts, and gave each his pistol. Then they stepped back, and Moore and Jeffrey stood, pistols raised in the air, awaiting the signal.

It never came. Police officers suddenly emerged from the thicket at Jeffrey's back. The nearest knocked Jeffrey's pistol out of his hand with his staff, and the other rushed over and disarmed Moore. Horner's suspicious characters had not gone far after all. So the affair ended in anticlimax, and the duellists were driven off, each in his own conveyance, to Bow Street. On the way Hume confided that Horner had known nothing whatever about firearms, and that in the end he had had to load both pistols himself.

While waiting to be bailed out, the parties conversed in the most amiable manner. The conversation soon became literary, and Jeffrey poured forth all the riches of his vocabulary and of his fancy, as if he had been sitting in his own armchair instead of on a bench in a police station. Moore responded at once, and the two beamed at each other in new-found amity. Jeffrey had taken a fancy to his challenger the moment he set eyes on him. From this time on, they were firm friends.

Spencer, to whom Moore had sent word of his plight, now turned up with Rogers,[1] and the pair were bound over to keep the peace, and released. In the excitement of getting away, they forgot to reclaim the pistols. When Moore remembered, Hume had gone off to join his wife in the country, so he went back to Bow Street alone.

This time he met with a very different reception. The chief officer refused to give them up, saying, with an unpleasant leer, that it appeared to the magistrate there had been foul play in-

[1] Samuel Rogers, the poet.

tended: for Moore's pistol had a bullet in it, but Jeffrey's had none.

Moore was at first incredulous, then stared aghast. Hume—his second—had on his own confession attended to the loading of both pistols! Once let that get about, and his character was gone for ever. He rushed round to Horner, and by great good luck found him at home. To his relief, Horner pooh-poohed the suggestion.

"Don't mind what these fellows say," he cried. "I myself saw your friend put the bullet into Jeffrey's pistol, and shall go with you instantly to the officer and set the matter right."

So back to Bow Street they went again, where Horner's testimony removed the magistrate's suspicions, and both the pistols and the incriminating bullet were returned. But the mischief had been done. A report of the affair had got about, and a mischievous journalist, by substituting the word "pellet" for "bullet" added a last touch of absurdity to the story. It appeared in all the papers, without Hume's testimony, and Moore found himself exposed to ridicule and contempt. He wrote at once to his friends, explaining the facts of the case; Horner drew up a statement, which the magistrate certified; and arrangements were made to have it published in the papers which had carried the first report.

Nothing was wanted but Hume's signature, and this, to Moore's amazement, he declined to give. The rush of ridicule and publicity had been too much for him. He took fright, said that he "did not know who Mr Horner was", and refused to have anything more to do with the matter. Moore was furious. There was nothing he could do but write to the papers himself, and his letter, coming from the interested party, naturally carried no weight. Many years passed before he forgave Hume.

Another friendship was severed, when he found out how the police had happened so pat upon the duel. Spencer had told Lord

Fincastle about it over the dinner-table, and Lord Fincastle had communicated with Bow Street. In his first mortification, Moore told Lady Donegal he would rather have lost a limb than borne the ridicule: but in a day or so he felt much better. Lord Moira praised his conduct, Horner said at Holland House that he had borne himself with a "mixture of feeling and forti-tude", and, finally, Rogers arranged a meeting between him and Jeffrey, at which the latter apologized handsomely for the "intemperance" of the review, acknowledged that, in his own opinion and that of his friends, it contained "too much that was exceptionable" ("too much" is a pleasant touch), and rounded the matter off with a signed tribute to "the fairness and spirit" which Moore had shown.

So the little poet came off well again, without loss of liberty or blood, as at the inquisition at Trinity. The ridicule was soon forgotten, and he had gained a friend, besides several flattering tributes to his honour and manhood.

As to the main object of Jeffrey's attack, the supposed licen-tiousness of the *Odes and Epistles*, it is hard to-day to see what all the fuss was about. Moore was frequently attacked on the same ground, and his reputation for literary immorality was sufficient both to make critics complain that the young Byron was following in his footsteps, and to lead Byron to call him "the melodious advocate of lust". The mistake was to take Moore seriously. His friend Joe Atkinson defended him by saying that he was "an infant sporting on the bosom of Venus": a phrase with which, in all its implications, we may be content.

III

All this was about the end of August 1806. The earlier part of the year had been spent in work, and in wondering whether Lord Moira would come in—a speculation which was to occupy Moore, off and on, for many months. He was, as usual, hard up, but Carpenter offered a welcome piece of pot-boiling. Arthur Murphy, the incredibly florid translator of Tacitus, was busy on a translation of Sallust, and Moore was offered £40 to contribute a Life to it. He did so, and the money enabled him to hurry over to Dublin.

"Well," enquires Mary Godfrey, on October 2nd, "how are you after your seasickness, and how do you feel yourself in Dublin, after your brilliant career here among the learned and the dissipated? If it were not for the extreme joy which I know you feel at being with your family again, I should grieve for the change; but you have contrived, God knows how! amidst the pleasures of the world, to preserve all your home, fireside affections true and genuine as you brought them out with you; and this is a trait in your character that I think beyond all praise. . . ."

No "contrivance" was necessary. Moore had that genuine simplicity that never outgrows the loves of childhood. With the notable exception of Byron, Mary Godfrey is the best and most individual of all Moore's correspondents. She laughed at him, rated him, and praised him, all justly. A sentence after the last quoted above, she is deriding him; then she goes on to tell him that he has got universal credit for his conduct in the affair with Jeffrey.

"In short, I am quite agreeably surprised to find the turn it has all taken in your favour. You don't know how happy we feel at it, for I am sure you don't know to this good day how much we care for you. But never take a pistol in your hand again while you live."

Moore actually did not answer till late in February of the next year. He had the grace to admit that he was ashamed of himself, but pleaded that he had been busy, studying three and a half hours a day in Marsh's library, and going his usual round of parties, etc.

"I have written nothing since I came here, except *one song*, which is everybody says the *best* I have ever composed, and I rather prefer it myself to most of them. When am I to sing it to you? Oh! *when, when?* I am an unfortunate rascal, that's certain."

This was the nearest he came to mentioning a suggestion that was to determine his fame for ever. William Power, a music seller of Dublin, impressed doubtless by Moore's renown as a singer, and (very likely) by the success of the song aforesaid, proposed to him that he should write words to a number of Irish airs, and that Sir John Stevenson should help in the arranging.

About a week after his letter Moore left Dublin for Donington, where he remained till June. He wrote off almost at once to his mother, to ask Power for Bunting's *Irish Airs*, which, characteristically, he had forgotten to bring, and for Miss Owenson's,[1] which the Atkinsons had. The fact that he had "forgotten" the Bunting book, and that the manifesto for the project, in the form of a letter from him to Stevenson, was dated April 1807, suggests very strongly that the proposal had been made while he was in Dublin.

An extract from the manifesto, which Power issued to draw attention to the series, shows that Moore fully realized the difficulties ahead of him:

"The task which you propose to me, of adapting words to these airs, is by no means easy. The Poet, who would follow the various sentiments which they express, must feel and understand that rapid fluctuation of spirits, that unaccountable mixture of gloom and levity, which composes the character of my countrymen, and has deeply tinged their Music. Even in their liveliest strains we find some melancholy note intrude—some minor Third or flat Seventh—which throws its shade as it passes, and makes even mirth interesting. If Burns had been an Irishman (and I would willingly give up all our claims upon Ossian for

[1] Miss Owenson, afterwards Lady Morgan, the novelist, had a reputation in Dublin as a singer.

him), his heart would have been proud of such music, and his genius would have made it immortal.

"Another difficulty (which is, however, purely mechanical) arises from the irregular structure of many of those airs, and the lawless kind of metre which it will in consequence be necessary to adapt to them. In these instances, the Poet must write, not to the eye, but to the ear; and must be content to have his verses of that description which Cicero mentions, '*Quos si cantu spoliaveris, nuda remanebit oratio.*' That beautiful Air, 'The Twisting of the Rope', which has all the romantic character of the Swiss *Ranz des Vaches*, is one of those wild and sentimental rakes which it will not be very easy to tie down in sober wedlock with Poetry. However, notwithstanding all these difficulties, and the very moderate portion of talent which I can bring to surmount them, the design appears to me so truly National that I shall feel much pleasure in giving it all the assistance in my power."

He remained at Donington, working steadily, until the end of May, when a house-party descended upon him, and he was obliged to stop for a while and join in the fun. He was not only working at the *Melodies*. Indeed, he seems to have postponed them, for he wrote in April that his mother need not send him Miss Owenson's Airs after all: they would keep till he came to Dublin. He had begun the satiric poems which were to appear in the year following as *Corruption and Intolerance*.

After the house-party, he visited Lady Donegal at Tonbridge, and crossed to Dublin some time in August. The first two numbers of the *Melodies* appeared in April 1808, and it is pleasant to realize that many of them must have been written in Ireland.

The only other event of 1807 was a letter from Stockholm, electing Moore to be a Knight (3rd Class) of the Order of St Joachim. As the sum of £52 10s. was demanded for "fees of honour", it is hardly surprising that he did not accept the distinction.

CHAPTER X

THE "IRISH MELODIES"

The *Irish Melodies*—Written to be sung—Moore's verse technique—Consideration for the singer—Criticisms of the *Melodies*
—Sir Charles Stanford—Moore's apologia—Moore on Bunting
—Moore's own singing of the *Melodies*—Light verse—Fame
and effect of the *Melodies*

THE first number of the *Irish Melodies* appeared in 1808, the tenth
and last in 1834. The best of them were written by 1815, the last
four numbers showing a decline in quality, but for practical
purposes they may be taken as a whole. They are the pinnacle of
Moore's work, his title to immortality: and nine-tenths of the
criticism of them that has appeared has been on a wrong basis.

The essential point about the *Melodies* is that Moore intended
them to reach his audience *through the mouth of a singer.* Words
and music are indivisible. The lyric for each Melody is a lyric,
not a poem: that is to say, it is the words of a song. Moore was
writing for the voice, primarily for his own voice. He tested each
one out himself, again and again, and his first care was to find
words which (*a*) fitted the air, and (*b*) were singable. "I shall
finish the number . . . this month," he writes to Power in 1812.
"I am sorry to find that there is no air in it at all likely to suit my
own singing, which does not tell well for the number." [1] To
print by themselves the words of any of the *Melodies*, and judge
them as a poem, is to put them to a test for which they were not
meant. Moore never envisaged the printing of the words without the music, and only gave his consent, very reluctantly, when

[1] This was not conceit. A clause in Moore's agreement enjoined that he
should visit town at regular intervals and make a vogue for his latest songs by
singing them publicly.

he found that a pirated edition, full of errors, was already on the market.

That some of the words stand very well by themselves—as poems—is beside the point. They can never so achieve a fraction of their full effect. "'*O si sic omnia!*'" exclaimed Tennyson, in his praise of *Oft in the Stilly Night*, but he too was making the mistake of judging it in the library instead of in the music-room.

This is no academic point, but the core of the whole matter. The *Melodies*—as poems—have often been attacked for their blandness, their limpidity, their lack of thought. But the poet whose words are to be heard from a singer has above all things to be clear and immediate in expression. If his sense is not instantly apparent, if his metaphors are not reinforced and rammed home with easy parallels, they are gone, and the singer, from the audience's point of view, is singing gibberish. Any practised lyric writer will bear this out. The sentences must be short, the syntax crystal clear, and the meaning such as can be taken in without effort and at one hearing by a number of people at once.

Let us see what Moore could do within these limitations. This first example is taken, not from the *Irish Melodies*, but from the *National Melodies*. Still, it is a typical example of Moore's workmanship.

OFT IN THE STILLY NIGHT

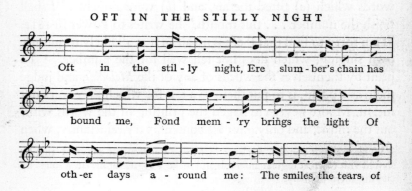

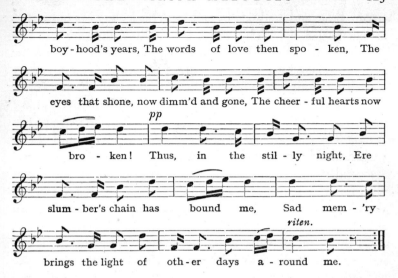

boy - hood's years, The words   of love then spo - ken, The

eyes   that shone, now dimm'd and gone, The cheer - ful hearts now

pp

bro - ken! Thus,   in   the   stil - ly   night, Ere

slum - ber's chain has   bound   me,   Sad   mem - 'ry

riten.

brings the light of   oth - er   days   a - round   me.

When I remember all
    The friends, so link'd together,
I have seen around me fall,
    Like leaves in wintry weather;
        I feel like one,
        Who treads alone
Some banquet-hall deserted,
    Whose lights are fled,
    Whose garlands dead,
        And all but he departed!
Thus, in the stilly night,
    'Ere slumber's chain has bound me,
Sad Memory brings the light
    Of other days around me.

The mood is not profound, but it is epitomized perfectly. Graceful, melancholy, and flowing, the song is a model of its kind.

II

Naturally, it was by a poetic technique that Moore secured his effects, but this was, in the *Melodies*, subordinated always to the end in view, and used side by side with his feeling for music and his personal skill with his voice. Of the limitations his task imposed on him as a poet he was well aware. "I am better able", he said, "to vouch for the sound than for the sense." Happily, they were limitations which did his poetic ability little, if any, harm. He was too flowery, and all the better for pruning.[1] Even so, the floweriness would burgeon out unsuitably. The first verse of *Has Sorrow Thy Young Days Shaded*, written for the tenor Braham, was admirably spare, and the poet complaisantly offered to send a second verse "applicable to any purpose" the singer might wish for. We may safely assume that it was the last verse, and that the nonsense about "our Lagenian mine" was put in as an afterthought. Singers invariably leave it out.

Of sheer surface verse technique Moore had plenty. It is unfashionable nowadays, and there are poets who deny its existence altogether: but Moore, as anyone who studies him carefully will discover, knew a thing or two about sound and rhythm and the craft of verse in general. In the *Melodies*, he was concerned with sound and rhythm only. His arrangement of vowel sounds is primarily a singer's, but some of the verses are very good to speak. The management of the o's (and r's) in

> Though lost to Mononia, and cold in the grave,
> He returns to Kincora no more . . .

and the short e's in

> Ere the emerald gem of the western world
> Was set in the crown of a stranger . . .

shows a skill, a sheer knowledge of the business, that earns the respect of anyone who has realized that such problems

---

[1] "You are quite right," he wrote to Leigh Hunt, "about the conceits that disfigure my poetry; but you (and others) are quite as wrong in supposing that I *hunt* after them—my greatest difficulty is to *hunt them* away. . . . In short, St Anthony's temptations are nothing to what an Irish fancy has to undergo from all its own brood of Will o'the Wisps and hobgoblins."

exist. It must be admitted that his concentration on sound led Moore to write many things that look loose and silly in verse alone.

> There is not in this wide world a valley so sweet
> As that vale in whose bosom the bright waters meet . . .

Why "vale"? It is inexcusable. And "bright" is a pointless adjective. But complete the words with the air from which they should never be parted:

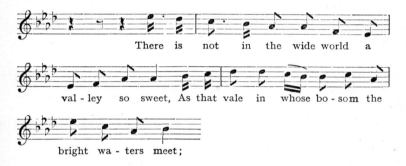

The broad sound of "vale" is precisely needed at its point in the phrase, and the sharp lift gives "bright" a sparkle which at once makes it significant and exact. Once more it is made obvious that we cannot, without injustice and stultification, consider the words apart from the air.

The kind of skill, both verbal and rhythmical, which Moore used can soon be illustrated. Few quotations will be necessary. Take the first stanza of *I saw from the beach*.

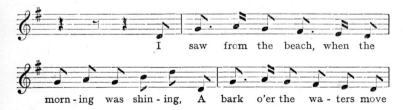

glo - rious - ly on; I came when the sun o'er that beach was de - clin - ing, The bark was still there, but the wa - ters were gone.

These are some of the most purely vocal lines ever set down. The voice cannot help singing them. Moore always flatters one's voice. The professional instantly notices a new ease, a vocal line and words that bring out the best in him without his having to do anything about it—often indeed, despite Moore's own instructions for singing the *Melodies*, the less he does the better. The amateur decides, with gratified surprise, that he is a better singer than he thought.

As music, the phrases alone are not too easy to sing, but Moore has transformed them. First of all, his lines have an astonishing forward flow, an impulse running right through from the first word to the last. The placing of the consonants at the accented parts is beyond praise. "Shining", at the end of the first line— Moore was very fond of a breath-attack to brighten the last important vowel in a phrase, when the lungs might be getting empty: "gloriously", with the slight delay of the double consonant, the pictorial vigour of the word, opening into the ring and brightness of the rising "on": the supreme aptness of "declining", which so naturally, and again so pictorially, comprehends that awkward little run of notes: when a singer finds this sort of thing, he thanks God, and gets on with his singing.

No one has ever so considered the voice. For instance, in one of his silliest lyrics, *Believe me if all those endearing young charms,* there is something to help the voice up to every high note in the first stanza. Certainly, without the abundant contemporary testimony, one can tell just what sort of Irish voice Moore had, from the very way in which he places his vowels. The succession of e's in that first line

> Believe me, if all those endearing young charms,

and the caution with which he leads to the open a of charms, with a y to clear the way, almost enables one to hear his voice take the phrase. Moore, as singer or lyrist, was never afraid of an open vowel, but he almost always made the approach easy. When he took no particular pains to do so—as happened seldom —it was probably in one of the airs which did not suit his own voice. It is noteworthy, in this connection, how many of his songs suit men better than women, and tenors or light baritones rather than basses. The only *Melody* that has attained universal popularity with women is *The Last Rose of Summer*, and that is as much due to the perspicacious Flotow (who included it bodily in *Marta*) as to its native virtues. It does, however, perfectly suit the soprano voice.

There is little to be gained by cataloguing the felicities of Moore's writing for the voice in these *Melodies*. A quarter of an hour at the piano will be more convincing than pages of exposition. William Power's suggestion found the one man able to effect a magic synthesis. Moore brought to his task a musical ear, a voice, a high metrical skill, and a mysterious quality of which he himself knew nothing—the power to articulate, in his mannered, feminine way, the soul of a country.

Here, to conclude quotations, are two more of the *Melodies*, the former little known outside Ireland.

Si - lent, O Moyle, be the roar of thy wa - ter;

Break not, ye breez - es, your chain of re-pose, While,

mur - mur - ing mourn - ful - ly, Lit's lone - ly daugh-ter

Tells to the night - star her tale of woes.

When shall the swan, her death - note sing - ing,

Sleep, with wings in dark - ness furl'd?

When will heav'n, its sweet bell ring - ing,

Call my spi - rit from this storm - y world?

Sadly, oh Moyle, to thy winter-wave weeping,
Fate bids me languish long ages away;
Yet still in her darkness doth Erin lie sleeping,
Still doth the pure light its dawning delay.
When will that day-star, mildly springing,
Warm our isle with peace and love?
When will heaven, its sweet bell ringing,
Call my spirit to the fields above?

The legend it embodies has told against this song's popularity, but the air is a fine one, and Moore has caught its tone and colour with astounding sensitiveness.

The second is his masterpiece.

Of harp that once through Tara's halls
  The soul of music shed,
Now hangs as mute on Tara's walls,
  As if that soul were fled.—
So sleeps the pride of former days,
  So glory's thrill is o'er,
And hearts, that once beat high for praise,
  Now feel that pulse no more.

D. Maclise, R.A.   E. E. Becker

AN ETCHING BY DANIEL MACLISE, R.A.
From Moore's Irish Melodies

At the mid hour of night, when stars are weep-ing, I fly To the lone vale we lov'd, when life shone warm in thine eye; And I think oft, if spi-rits can steal from the re-gions of air To re--vi-sit past scenes of de-light, Thou wilt come to me there, And tell me our love is re-mem-ber'd, e'en in the sky.

Then I sing the wild song 'twas once such pleasure to hear!
When our voices commingling breath'd, like one, on the ear;
And, as Echo far off through the vale my sad orison rolls,
I think, oh my love! 'tis thy voice from the Kingdom of Souls,
Faintly answering still the notes that once were so dear.

In the mouth of a sensitive singer, this is one of the loveliest songs in the language.

III

The popularity of the *Melodies* of course invited many attacks, of which the chief has been that Moore altered the national airs to suit his purpose, and destroyed their character. This attack was strongly developed by Sir Charles Stanford, who pointed out that many of the airs in Moore's version differed markedly from the versions given by Bunting, and accused Moore of emasculating them for the drawing-room. As an example, he took the air known as *The Little Red Fox*, and compared it to Moore's *Let Erin remember the Days of Old*. Bunting's version is a quick dance tune. Moore's, which Stanford admits has gained enormously in dignity, is a march at half the time.

The first answer to this is that folk tunes exist all over the country in different shapes, and no single one can be pitched on as the correct version. For example, *The Little Red Fox* reached Moore and Bunting quite independently. Bunting did not get his till 1839, and the volume on which Stanford relied was published in 1840. Moore knew the air in his undergraduate days, probably from Hudson, and played it to Emmet: and in any case he received another version, the slow one, in 1806, and published it without alteration. The same applies to all the airs. Bunting is not evidence one way or the other. To prove his case, Stanford would need to show that Moore had access to no other version of any disputed air than that given by Bunting: a sheer impossibility.

As to altering the airs—of course Moore altered some of them. He had to. Many of Bunting's airs, as we have seen, were taken down from harpers. No great knowledge of music is needed to realize that, to transform an air plucked from the strings of a harp to one able to be sung *legato* by the human voice, certain modifications are unavoidable. The surprising thing is, not the number of airs Moore changed, but the number he somehow contrived to leave as they were.

Even where the airs were songs already, with Irish words, Moore was in little better case. He had been credited, in such a piece as *At the Mid Hour of Night*, with catching something of the characteristic rhythms of Gaelic poetry. If he did, it was solely through his sensitiveness to the curve and movement of the air, for he knew nothing of Gaelic, and was unable to read a word of it. The air taught him all he knew.

Undoubtedly, therefore, Moore made changes where he felt

they were needed: and modern musical opinion supports him.
Bunting made changes too, with less excuse, since he was not
adapting for a particular purpose. And, since Moore had a col-
laborator, more changes appeared in the final versions than he
intended. Stevenson made the piano arrangements, and his
academic sense was often offended by the scale and accidentals
of the native airs. He regularized them accordingly, despite
Moore's protests, adding florid passages and harmonies of an
ecclesiastical type, so that Moore, in his own performance, very
often did not use the published version at all.

"It has always been", he writes, "a subject of some mortification to me that my songs, as they are set, give such a very im-
perfect notion of the manner in which I wish them to be performed, and that more of that peculiarity of character which I
believe they possess as I sing them myself, is lost in the process
they must undergo for publication; but the truth is, that, not
being sufficiently practised in the rules of composition to rely
upon the accuracy of my own harmonic arrangements, I am
obliged to submit my rude sketches to the eye of a professor
before they can encounter the criticism of the musical world, and
as it too frequently happens that they are indebted for their
originality to the violation of some established law, the hand
that corrects their errors is almost sure to destroy their character,
and the few little flowers they boast are pulled away with the
weeds. In singing them myself, however, I pay no such deference
to criticism, but usually give both air and harmony according to
my own first conception of them, with all their original faults,
but at the same time, all their original freshness. I know I shall be
told, by the learned musician, that whatever infringes the rules of
composition must be disagreeable to the ear, and that according
to the pure ethics of the art, nothing can possibly be pleasant that
is wrong; but I am sorry to say that I am lawless enough to
disagree with him. . . ."

Many years later, in 1840, when Bunting's second collection

(that referred to by Stanford) had appeared, Moore commented upon it in his Journal, giving a different emphasis to the question of changes.

"Received from the Cramers a copy of Bunting's newly published collection of Irish airs, which they have often written to me about, as likely (they hoped) to furnish materials for a continuation of the Melodies. Tried them over with some anxiety; as had they contained a sufficient number of beautiful airs to make another volume, I should have felt myself bound to do the best I could with them, though still tremblingly apprehensive lest a failure should be the result. Was rather relieved, I confess, on finding that, with the exception of a few airs, which I have already made use of, the whole volume is a mere mass of trash. Considering the thorn I have been in poor Bunting's side, by supplanting him in the one great object of his life (the connection of his name with the fame of Irish music), the temper in which he now speaks of my success (for some years since he was rather termagant on the subject), is not a little creditable to his good nature and good sense. Speaking of the use which I made of the first volume of airs published by him, he says, 'They were soon adopted as vehicles for the most beautiful popular songs that have perhaps ever been composed by any lyric poet.' He complains strongly, however, of the alterations made in the original airs, and laments that 'the work of the poet was accounted of so paramount an interest that the proper order of song-writing was, in many instances, inverted, and instead of the words being adapted to the tune, the tune was too often adapted to the words, —a solecism which could never have happened had the reputation of the writer not been so great as at once to carry the tunes he designed to make use of altogether out of their old sphere, among the simple and tradition-loving people of the country with whom, in truth, many of the new melodies, to this day, are hardly suspected to be themselves'. He lays the blame of all these alterations upon Stevenson; but poor Sir John was entirely innocent of them, as the whole task of selecting the airs, and in some instances shaping them thus, in particular passages, to the general sentiment which the melody appeared to me to express, was undertaken solely by myself. Had I not ventured on these very allowable liberties, many of the songs now most known and popular would have been still sleeping, with all their authentic dross about them, in Mr. Bunting's first volume. The same charge is brought by him respecting those airs which I took from the second volume of his collection. 'The beauty of Mr Moore's words', he says, 'in a great degree atones for the violence done by the musical arranger to many of the airs which he has adopted'."

There is no subject more full of disputation than folk music, and the argument that has raged over Moore and the various versions of the airs he used is elaborate and fierce: but the consensus of modern opinion is that he altered remarkably little, and then only when it was necessary; and that his alterations seldom did harm.

Even if they had—even if his version of an air was unlike, and weaker than, the original—it would be beside the point, provided that the resulting song was a good one. For any transcription from one medium to another, whether it be of a Bach chorale for orchestra by Stokowski, or Casals' arrangement of the allegretto from the Mozart clarinet quintet as a 'cello solo, the final and only test is whether it comes off. If it does, we may disregard the purist. There are a good many purists—or pedants —in Ireland, and not a few of them have fixed upon the music of the people as their province. The best answer to them is Moore's achievement, musical, poetic, social, and historic. What he did was marvellously well worth doing, and marvellously well he did it.

IV

Moore's performance of his own lyrics, and of every kind of song, was dramatic rather than musical. His speaking voice was a trifle husky, but the minute he began to sing it was clear, soft, and sympathetic. Of contemporary testimony on his singing we have a great deal. He moved even men to tears, and frequently won what is more impressive than applause—the tribute of silence.

On the quality of his singing the evidence is unanimous. Lockhart, Scott's biographer, said that Moore's was "the most exquisite warbling" he ever heard. Leigh Hunt compared his voice to a flute. Willis, in a famous passage which we shall meet in its place, described the effect of his singing. Creevey recorded his delight in it. Sydney Smith [1] declared characteristically in a letter,

"By the Beard of the prelate of Canterbury, by the Cassock of the prelate of York, by the breakfasts of Rogers, by Luttrell's [2] love of side dishes, I swear I had rather hear you sing than any person, male or female. For what is your singing but beautiful poetry floating in fine music and guided by exquisite feeling?"

Singing was the breath of life to Moore. He even "warbled a little" the day before he died. His enunciation was perfect: every word was clear: and the sheer quality of his voice, small though it was in volume, compelled instant attention in the most crowded salon. "It is a kind of admirable recitative, in which every shade of thought is syllabled." Evidently he was a typical Irish singer of the best sort.

Moore's own directions for singers of the *Melodies* are explicit enough:

"There is but one instruction I should venture to give any person desirous of doing justice to the character of these ballads, and that is, to attend as little as possible to the rhythm, or time in singing them. The time, indeed, should always be made to wait upon the feeling, but particularly in this style of musical recitation, where the words ought to be as nearly *spoken* as is consistent with the swell and sweetness of intonation, and where a strict and mechanical observance of time completely destroys all those pauses, lingerings, and abruptnesses, which the expression of passion and tenderness requires. The truth of this remark needs

[1] The famous clergyman and wit.
[2] Another member of the Holland House circle, a wit and diner-out.

but little enforcement to those who have ever heard a song of feeling and delicacy passed along in the unrelenting trammels of an orchestra.''

It is noteworthy in passing that Irish singers as a race are weak in rhythm and time, but Moore's instructions are musically rather shocking. At the same time, for various reasons, they are not as bad as they sound. The test of the born singer is his treatment of rhythm, and an artist can take liberties that would be fatal in anyone else, because, all the time aware of the structure beneath what he is singing, he pays back what he steals. Count McCormack, incomparably the greatest modern interpreter of the *Melodies*, has always struck an inspired mean between Moore's directions and the strictness of the metronome. Some of his early renderings of Irish ballads show exactly the emotional and dramatic freedom which Moore postulated, but, a better musician than Moore, he has understood how much the sheer natural curve of the air, and its rhythm, contribute to the effect of the song. His singing of *The Meeting of the Waters* and *Has Sorrow Thy Young Days Shaded* is unsurpassable, and one can only wish that Moore could hear it from Elysium, to shed tears (as assuredly he would) at his own creation.

The second reason why Moore's directions are not as unmusical as they sound is that, to the modern ear, dramatic singing connotes opera. Moore's performance of his own *Melodies* was dramatic, but in no sense operatic. The difference goes back to a fundamental principle which applies to all folk singing. The natural, untrained voice tends to go thin on a high note, losing in volume what it gains in brightness. The curve of a folk song recognizes this, and takes advantage of it, touching in its high notes lightly. The operatically-trained voice, on the other hand, likes to emphasize its high notes, and has learned to make them the most powerful of all: and a style of composition has arisen to exploit such voices and give them the opportunities which they desire. This is one reason why the trained singer as a rule makes such a mess of folk songs. Moore, as is obvious from the phrasing of his songs, did not favour the operatic method. He allowed his voice to run up naturally into his head, without strain. The operatic method, applied to the *Melodies*, produces horrible effects. Take, as an example, *The Minstrel Boy*. The accepted way of singing it on the concert platform to-day is something like this (second stanza):

molt. accel.   *sost.*

pp The minstrel fell (*cresc.*) but the foeman's (*ff*) ch-a-AIN
        Could not brrring his pro-ou-oud soul under.

molto rit.   *sost.*

ppp The harp he loved never spoke aga-ai-ain
        molto accel.

ff For—he—TORRRE its cho-o-ords asunder.   *etc., etc.*

Besides being vulgar, this utterly destroys the quality of the tune. The lyric does not present a vivid action of half an hour since, but a sorrow of long ago. It should be sung softly and slowly, as it was in the film of Mr O'Flaherty's *The Informer*, when it becomes infinitely more moving, and the beauty of the air is revealed. A sensitive singer, with the faintest of accents, can make a word like "tore" far more effective than can a legion of operatic vociferators.

v

One other quality of Moore's is brought out by the *Melodies*, and that is his excellence as a writer of light verse. Not all the airs on which he sought to "bestow the gift of articulation" were melancholy, and to the gayer of them he worthily responded. The metrical variety to which the airs compelled him was here shown at its happiest.

The time I've lost in wooing,
In watching and pursuing
    The light that lies
    In woman's eyes
Has been my heart's undoing.
Though Wisdom oft has sought me,
I scorn'd the lore she brought me.
    My only books
    Were woman's looks,
And folly's all they've taught me.

In its kind, there is nothing better in the language. The pupil of Prior, Rochester, and Sedley could more than hold his own. These lighter lyrics, while best in company with the airs to which they were written, can stand very happily by themselves.

> Then awake!—the heavens look bright, my dear,
> 'Tis never too late for delight, my dear,
>   And the best of all ways
>   To lengthen our days
> Is to steal a few hours from the night, my dear.

VI

The *Melodies*, besides making Moore's name,[1] came as near as anything else to making his fortune. For the first two numbers, he received from Carpenter £50 a song. In August of the year they appeared, he added a postscript to a letter to his mother: "I quite threw away the *Melodies*: they will make that little smooth fellow's fortune." In 1811, after the appearance of the fourth number, the brothers Power offered him £500 a year for the monopoly of his musical work, on condition that he visited town regularly in order to sing his songs in the drawing-rooms and give them the necessary vogue. Moore drew—or rather, over-drew—his £500 for nearly twenty years.

VII

"Moore has done more for the revival of our national spirit than all the political writers whom Ireland has seen for a century."

These words, written by an anonymous journalist in 1810, were both fact and prophecy. He understood, evidently, the real significance of the *Melodies*, but he could not have foretold their fame and influence, any more than could Moore himself. To the

[1] Among the many favourable reviews was one by his old friend John Wilson Croker, in the *Quarterly*.

end of his life, it is improbable that Moore had any real idea of what he had done. He had expressed, as best he knew how, a genuine underlying emotion, his love for Ireland, but he was conscious of the details more than of the spirit beneath. The beauty of the air, the chances it offered him, the scope it gave his voice, came first. The rest belonged to his genius, that passive, feminine gift which enabled this unlikeliest of good-natured, high-principled, feckless creatures to become the mouthpiece of his country. Written for the English drawing-rooms, the *Melodies* took a long time to reach the people of Ireland. That they should be known in Dublin was understandable, and Moore was recognized there before 1820. His fame spread further, and during his lifetime, as the episode of Bannow shows. Still, there is no proof that the people who so rapturously made him welcome knew his songs. These must have made their way slowly. Their intervals and notation were utterly unlike those favoured by the country singers, some of whom still make a wry face at ordinary European singing. The words were in English, and, even though they were soon translated into Irish, it was generally Irish of such a kind that the people would have had as good a chance of understanding the English.

That something was known of the *Melodies*, and that their efficacy was recognized, the following letter proves:

23 CHURCH STREET,
CORK.
14 *Oct.* '41.

SIR,

I have seen a letter addressed by you to Mr. Windele of this city and as the Translator of your inimitable Melodies into the Language of my country I rejoice exceedingly that you feel so much interested in the object which I have in view and thank you, sincerely, for your very kind sentiments in my favor.

Here it is generally believed that your Melodies have done

more to remove the prejudices which existed in England than all that had been done for that purpose previously or subsequently to their publication—that they made known the wrongs of the "Emerald Isle" in the salons of the great coronetted in the land of the Saxon and the Norman is no less true than that "their masters paused at the songs of their captives and wept" and thus smoothed the way for Catholic Emancipation—a greater Revolution than was ever caused by the sword of the warrior or the wiles of the statesman was thus achieved by the Magic of Song.

Strongly impressed with the opinion that this triumph of justice and of right was mainly attributable to your genius I was long anxious, on account of the well told tale of Ireland's wrongs which almost each Melody, independently of its poetic merit, contained, to make known the sentiments—if not the beauties of your immortal Muse—thro' the medium of a translation in which they can be better understood by our People millions of whom still continue to speak the venerable language of ancient Ireland.

My intention is to publish, in a cheap way that the work may become as well known in the cottage as its original is in the residences of the great and noble and that the Melodies as the airs should become Irish. In this object I shall be assisted by many patriotic individuals—the honor, as a subscriber, of your name would do me infinite service—and when I tell you Sir, that my intention is to dedicate to you my humble labour I trust you will concede to me the high privilege of your name as a subscriber and permission to prefix it—to the "Irish Melodies" in Irish.

With much deference,
I have the honor to be,
Sir,
Your obt Hble Servant,
Eugene O'Cavanagh

Thomas Moore Esqr
etc. etc.

Even when we allow the eloquent Mr O'Cavanagh a good measure of flattery, his letter is interesting as evidence.

In the end, the spirit of the *Melodies* overcame all difficulties, and after 1860 they spread everywhere, and retained their hold for more than fifty years, during which Moore was the musical voice of Ireland.

It was not only the plangency of the songs, their nostalgic melancholy, their insistence on the Gael's lost heritage, that so took hold on the Irish people. Looking back to a golden age has long been the characteristic, and the curse, of the Gael. It was the linking up of this nostalgia with the impassioned memory of Emmet, which Moore did more than anyone to keep alive: the proclamation that what had happened within living memory was descended from, and part of, the heroic past: the irresistible suggestion, combining with O'Connell's remorseless cry of "Organize! Organize!", that this lost heritage was a matter for action as well as dream, and might be regained: this was the new spirit, and the *Melodies* became its talisman. The United Irishmen had failed, but Moore, whom they wisely left out of their councils, carried on the torch of their inspiration and "set the heather blazing". His songs were symbols of what was to come, and in singing them men worshipped the beauty of their country and drank a toast to her future. The songs were easy and exciting to sing; they were Irish; they were Ireland. The green-covered book with the harp on the cover was for two generations a part of the furniture of every Irish home, and its contents part of the furniture of every Irish heart: and "Melody Moore" took his place for ever among the architects of the new Ireland.

CHAPTER XI

MARRIAGE AND FAMILY LIFE

Theatricals at Kilkenny—Moore as actor—Miss E. Dyke—
Moore married—Character of Bessy—An episode—The ex-
penses of London—The Moores move to Kegworth—Lord
Moira disappoints—Birth of Barbara and Anastasia—Mayfield
Cottage—Birth and death of Olivia—Barbara's fall—John
Moore dies—Anastasia's illness and death—Tom and Russell

THE wave of enthusiasm for amateur theatricals, which had en-
gulfed among others the excellent Samuel Whyte, spread far
beyond Dublin, and by 1802 had reached Kilkenny. There one
Mr Richard Power, bitten by the craze, assembled a company,
and met with such success that his annual festival grew from a
week to a fortnight, and, in 1809, to three weeks.[1]

How Moore fell in with Mr Power and his troupe is not certain. Probably it was through Joe Atkinson, who, in 1808, the
year of Moore's first appearance at Kilkenny, wrote the prologue
to the festival: for another friend, Isaac Corry, joined the company at the same time. The *Leinster Journal* proclaimed the advent
of "Anacreon Moore", and was soon recording that, on his *début*
as David in Sheridan's *The Rivals*, he "kept the audience in a
roar". He had two more parts in this festival, playing Mungo in
a piece called *The Padlock*, and singing the part of Spado, a comic
brigand, in O'Keefe's *A Castle in Andalusia*. In the latter he had a
line, "True anger raises me; I always appear six foot in a passion," to which the house responded with delight.[2]

---

[1] Creevey says that the receipts for the three weeks were £1,200, of which
£700 paid the expenses, and the rest went to charity.

[2] Moore seems never to have resented his lack of inches. Elizabeth Rennie
tells us: "I remember the very first words he ever addressed to me, when

His experience at the festival excited fresh dreams of writing for the stage, but, busy for the time being, he did nothing about it. The following October saw him again at Kilkenny. He was by now a favourite member of the company, and wisely did nothing to jeopardize his position, keeping to comic parts, and leaving Shakespeare alone. He wrote and spoke the prologue to this three weeks' session—appropriately, for it was one of the most important occasions of his life. The company was not very strong in ladies, and it was the practice to invite two or three professional actresses to strengthen it. In 1808 one of these was a Miss H. Dyke. The invitation to her was repeated in 1809, and she brought with her her sister, Miss E. Dyke, aged only fourteen, a girl of striking beauty. We have no record of the performance of either sister, since the *Leinster Journal*, so prodigal in its praise of Moore, has nothing to say about them; but in the play *Peeping Tom*, Miss E. Dyke played Lady Godiva, opposite Moore in the name part. Moore evidently enjoyed himself, writing a letter to Rogers which drew the injunction, "Don't let the Graces supplant the Muses."

There was no danger of that; but one Grace had supplanted the others. In July 1810 he wrote to Lady Donegal:

"So much for the main subject of my epistle; and now, having made such a bad hand of what I have *not* done, I wish I could give you even a tolerable account of what I *have* done; but, I don't know how it is, both my mind and heart appear to have lain for some time completely *fallow*, and even the usual crop of *wild oats* have not been forthcoming. What is the reason of this? I believe there is in every man's life (at least in every man who has lived as if he knew how to live) one blank interval, which takes place at that period when the gay desires of youth are just gone off, and he has not yet made up his mind as to the feelings

brought across the room to be introduced, at a large evening party assembled at a friend's house, at Maida Hill, were 'Well are you not dreadfully disappointed?—Am I not even less than you expected?'"

or pursuits that succeed them—when the last blossom has fallen away, and yet the fruit continues to look harsh and unpromising —a kind of *interregnum* which takes place upon the demise of *love*, before ambition and worldliness have seated themselves on the vacant throne."

What the astute lady made of this we unfortunately do not know. At any rate, in the following October Moore and Miss E. Dyke once more graced the boards at Kilkenny, for the last time. Moore took only a small part, to the disappointment of the *Leinster Journal*, but he appeared in an interlude, when, to his own piano accompaniment, he gave a *Melologue upon National Music*, which he had originally written to be spoken at a benefit night in Dublin. By the end of the festival his mind was made up, if indeed he had not made it up before. He crossed to London to see what work he could get and what provision he could make: he came back to Dublin: he crossed to London again, and secured a lodging to his liking: and on the 25th of March, 1811, he led Elizabeth Dyke, then aged sixteen, to the altar at St Martin's Church, and married her. She was a Protestant. She had not a penny, and Moore was twice her age.

It was a love match. All the omens were against it, and it turned out ideally. Moore was so conscious of its folly, on paper, that he did not at first dare to tell his parents. When he did, it was some time before his father could bring himself to write, an abstention which greatly worried the sensitive and affectionate Tom. But, in himself, he had no uneasiness. His instincts were sound, as are those of many a mother's darling when it comes to picking a mate, and his Bessy gave him nothing but joy and happiness to the day of his death. His friends, after an interval of stupefaction, approved at once. Rogers took to her at sight, and christened her Psyche: and the severe old bachelor, jealous for his friend's happiness, was hard to please. Lady Loudoun and Lady Charlotte Rawdon were among the first to call. Lord

Moira treated her with a dignified, half-embarrassed consideration. Miss Godfrey, shrewdest of friends, wrote:

"It gave us both great satisfaction to hear so pleasant an
account of your domestic life, as that which your last letter to
Bab contained. Be very sure, my dear Moore, that if you have
got an amiable, sensible wife, extremely attached to you, as I am
certain you have, it is only in the long run of life that you can
know the full value of the treasure you possess. If you did but
see, as I see with bitter regret in a very near connection of my
own, the miserable effects of marrying a vain fool devoted to
fashion, you would bless your stars night and day for your good
fortune; and, to say the truth, you were as likely a gentleman to
get into a scrape in that way as any I know. You were always
the slave of beauty, say what you please to the contrary: it
covered a multitude of sins in your eyes, and I never can cease
wondering at your good luck after all said and done. Money is
all that you want, and it is very provoking to think how much
that detestable trash has to do with our happiness here below."

And soon she and Lady Donegal were sending their "love,
downright honest love to Bessy".

Bessy was worth it. Simple, sensible, affectionate, a careful
manager, generous to a fault, she was the perfect wife and
mother, without any of the dullness such perfection often
brings. She enjoyed, in mingled awe and bliss, the splendours
of Donington Hall: but, loving things, as her husband said, "by
association", she preferred Rogers' friendly house to all Lord
Moira's magnificence. She stayed down in the country, economizing and burying her beauty out of sight, while Tom went up
to town to sing his songs at Holland House and at Lady Blessington's. She trusted him, and her trust was not abused. In return,
she had his complete devotion, and, to the end of their time
together, they were like lovers. No poet ever had a happier
married life—except for one great sorrow. "Why do people
sigh for children?" poor Bessy was to write, in one of her rare

SAMUEL ROGERS
From an engraving

moments of bitterness. "They know not what sorrow will come with them." Of their five children none survived even the father, and the elder son cost them much sorrow before he went the way of little Barbara and the rest. But, in all that concerned their two selves, they were ideally happy. Their home life was as warmhearted and affectionate as that at Aungier Street in the years gone by, and all who came near felt its glow and were welcome. Bessy was popular wherever she went. In Dublin and in Paris she was the toast of the town, for her simplicity no less than for her beauty. All this gave Moore the greatest delight. He was proud of her, and nothing pleased him more than that his friends should appreciate her at her true worth.

The early years especially were full of joy. Moore, the playboy always—"He seemed," wrote Gerald Griffin, many years later, ". . . young as fifteen at heart"—was just the man for his sixteen-year-old bride. Once, going out to dine and finding themselves early, they fell to dancing in a green lane till the half-hour was ended. Another time, when young Tom had just been born, and Moore was reading *The Vicar of Wakefield* to the convalescent Bessy, a young Irishman called at the cottage. The visitor said that

". . . his wife had been delivered of twins on the road, and was lying without any comforts for them at a house in Sandy Lane: never could he have found Bessy in a tenderer mood for such a story. She had a large jug of caudle made instantly, which she gave him, with two little caps and two shifts out of the stock she keeps for the poor, a pound of sugar, some tea, and two shillings; one of which was *my* gift, because he was an Irishman.

"17th.   Our Irish friend did not bring back the pitcher as he promised. Suspicions began to arise; walked to Phipp's; called at the cottage, where the fellow said his wife and twins were lying; found 'twas all a cheat. Sad hardeners of the heart these tricks are."

But the heart was not hardened. That sigh, in which there

II

was no resentment, only a mild sorrow that such tricks [1] could be, expressed permanently the goodness of Moore's nature and the happiness of his life at home. He and Bessy would do the same next day. No amount of "cheats" could sour them or darken their faith in human nature, their belief that all men were as well disposed as they. Moore went on reading *The Vicar of Wakefield* to Bessy that night, and his next entry is:

"18th. Walked my dear Bessy for the first time into the garden; the day delightful. She went round to all her flower beds to examine their state, for she has every little leaf in the garden by heart. Took a ramble afterwards by myself through the Valley of Chitoway, and the fields. Exactly such a day as that described so beautifully by the sacred poet Herbert:

> Sweet day, so cool, so calm, so bright,
>   The bridal of the earth and sky;
> Sweet dews shall weep thy fall to-night,
>   For thou must die.

Wrote some more of my flash epistle; and, in the evening, finished the 'Vicar of Wakefield' to Bessy; we both cried over it. Returned thanks to God most heartily for the recovery of my darling girl, and slept soundly."

In the early years, Moore ran everything, and took charge when Bessy was ill or depressed. Later, it was she who imperceptibly took command, and he came to lean upon her and defer to her judgment—as well he might, for she possessed abundant common sense, and set his welfare above everything.

Nearly twenty years afterwards, when they were once more at Kilkenny, Moore wrote: "In looking along the walk by the river, under the Castle, my sweet Bess and I recollected the time when we used, in our love-making days, to stroll for hours there together. We did not love half so really then as we do now."

In a changing world, such a love match as that of Tom Moore

---

[1] Compare Moore's reception of the legacy hoax, p. 280.

and his Bessy is an inspiration, and there are few women, at any rate, who do not envy it.

II

Now that he was a married man, Moore had to see to getting his living in earnest. The pair lived for a while in Bury Street, very happily, but London was too expensive. All Moore's friends wanted to see Bessy, and that meant entertaining. He and she were bidden to all manner of balls and assemblies, and that meant money for clothes. They stood it for close on a year, then decided to cut down expenses by moving into the country. Where should they go? To be near a library was essential to a literary man, and the Moores decided on a cottage at Kegworth, near Donington Park. This had the additional advantage of being near Lord Moira, whose hopes of high government office continued to rise and fall. For a time it seemed that Lord Moira would get Ireland, and Moore was delighted, both on his own account and because his patron favoured the Catholics; but it became clear that the Prince and the Government did not share his enthusiasm, and Moira ceased to be considered for the post.

The Prince became Regent in 1811, and proceeded at once to disappoint his Whig friends by omitting to turn the Tories out of office. From that moment, Moore would have none of him, and, conscious perhaps that he had shown a little too much pleasure when he first made the Prince's acquaintance, he redressed the balance by spirited abuse. He had, in the past, committed himself rather heavily. There were, for instance, some lines on the Prince's visit to Ireland which, in his new mood, he must have found embarrassing.

> He loves the green Isle and his love is rewarded
> In hearts that have suffered too much to forget . . .

At any rate, the Prince had learned to dissemble his love. It did not extend towards the Catholics. So Moore crossed him off one side of the ledger, and entered him on the other. There were soon as many items on the new page as on the old.

Meantime, his hopes rose and fell with Lord Moira's. Sick of the alternation, Moore longed to cut himself off from patronage. "It has been a sort of *Will o' the Wisp* to me all my life," he wrote, "and the only thing I regret is, that it was not extinguished sooner, for it has led me a sad dance." But he dared not yet. Money was tight: his prospects, despite the Powers' offer, were anything but secure: and the project started at Kilkenny had come to nothing. An opera, *The Blue Stocking*, had been put on at the English Opera House, without success. The papers received it politely, except for *The Times*, but the public was not impressed. Mary Godfrey wrote to console Moore, telling him that, as he had written to please the public, the public was to be blamed for not responding; but this was poor consolation, and Moore wisely made no further attempts upon the theatre.

Actually, Moore, despite his letter to Mary Godfrey about his idleness, had done a good deal since the first appearance of the *Melodies. Corruption and Intolerance* had been followed by a further satire, *The Sceptic*, which fell flat. The third number of the *Melodies* appeared in 1810, the fourth in 1811. He now envisaged a long narrative poem, with an Oriental setting, and, once at Kegworth, worked at it steadily.

Then came two setbacks, one close after the other. Moore, trying to emancipate himself from mental dependence on Lord Moira, was at last beginning to view his patron with a critical eye. In a letter in June 1812, to Miss Godfrey, he permits himself some sharp criticisms, and winds up with a tribute to the noble lord's heart at the expense of his head. Another few months, and he was to find fault with the heart also. In October came the news that Lord Moira was to have India. Moore was given reason to suppose that he was to accompany him as his secretary, and, while at first he hardly dared to hope, he heard others

saying openly that his appointment had been decided. Lord
Moira himself, on the last occasion they met, had been non-
committal, promising, as always, to keep Moore's interests in
the front of his mind. Naturally, Moore was thoroughly un-
settled by all this, and his letters express a painful agitation at
having heard nothing from his patron since the appointment.
Then came a letter, with not a word in it about India. At last
the great man came to Donington. Moore went to see him, but
got a glimpse of him only, shooting in the fields. Moira called
out to him, "You see a schoolboy taking his holiday," and
Moore, repeating the incident to his mother, said: "I am quite
sure Lord Moira means to do nothing for me."

He was right. Moira avoided meeting him for some time, and
at last confessed that he had nothing to give. His Indian patronage on this side was exhausted. If, however, when he got out
there, he found anything suitable, etc. etc. Meantime, he would
leave word with the Ministers at home that they should do
everything in their power for Mr Moore. Moore's reply was
polite but spirited.

"From your hands, my lord, I shall always be most willing to
accept anything, and perhaps it may yet be in your power to
serve me. But I beg you will not take the trouble of applying
for me to the patronage of Ministers, as I would rather struggle
on as I am than take anything that would have the effect of
tying up my tongue under such a system as the present."

Lord Moira received this courteously: he could do little else.
But Moore was indignant, and felt he had a grievance. "He has
certainly not done his duty by me," he wrote to Lady Donegal.
"His *manner*, since his appointment, has been even worse than
his deficiencies of *matter*, but (except to such friends as you) I
shall never complain of him. He served my father when my
father much wanted it, and he and his sister took my dear Bessy
by the hand cordially and seasonably; for all this I give him
complete absolution. . . ."

To Power he was even franker.

"Between ourselves, my dear friend, I have not so much merit in these refusals as I appear to have, for I could see very plainly, through Lord Moira's manner, that there was very little chance of his making any proper exertion for me whatever, and, putting conscience out of the question, policy itself suggested to me that I might as well have the merit of declining what it was quite improbable would ever have been done for me. After this, what do you think of his lordship? I cannot trust myself with speaking of the way he has treated me. Gratitude for the past ties up my tongue."

His dream of hope was over, and he was the better for its loss. So, with Rogers' approbation—"You have acted, my dear Moore, quite nobly and like yourself"—the episode was closed, and Moore learned, also from Rogers, to view his former patron's conduct more leniently. From henceforward, he decided to rely altogether on his own efforts, and Bessy's wise economy helped to make them sufficient.

The second setback, some months later, was the discovery that Byron also was engaged upon a poetic tale of the East. The appearance of *The Giaour* was a sad blow. Following on Rogers' tepid praise of as much of *Lalla Rookh* as he had seen, when the two went for a trip to Dovedale in the summer of 1812, it so discouraged Moore that he almost abandoned it.

"So you insist," he wrote to Mary Godfrey, "upon my taking my poem to Town with me? I will, if I can, you may be sure; but I confess I feel rather downhearted about it. Never was anything more unlucky for me than Byron's invasion of this region, which when I entered it, was as yet untrodden, and whose chief charm consisted in the gloss and novelty of its features; but it will now be overrun with clumsy adventurers, and when I make my appearance, instead of being a leader as I looked to be, I must dwindle into an humble follower—a Byronian. This is disheartening, and I sometimes doubt whether I shall publish it at all; though at the same time, if I may trust my own judgment, I think I never wrote so well before."

However, luckily for himself, he recovered his spirits and continued with the poem.

III

The Moores' first child, Barbara, was born early in 1812. She gave them a little anxiety at first, but soon throve, and was a great joy to them both. In a letter to his mother, before the year's end, he told of the next step in her progress.

"Our little Barbara is growing very amusing. She (what they call) *started* yesterday in walking; that is, got up off the ground by herself, and walked alone to a great distance, without any one near her. Bessy's heart was almost flying out of her mouth all the while with fright, but I held her away, and would not let her assist the young adventurer."

A second daughter, Anastasia Mary, was born at Kegworth in March of the following year. "About six o'clock this morning," Moore tells Mrs Dalby, "my Bessy produced a little girl about the size of a twopenny wax doll." The tiny child took a long time to thrive, and was not helped by being neglected and ill-treated by a nurse. Then the family moved to Mayfield, near Ashbourne, in Derbyshire, and there both the baby and Bessy, whose health had not been too good, recovered strength and flourished. The cottage was "a nutshell of a place", and Bessy fell in love with it at once. The rent was £20 a year, the taxes another three. It was on a terrace above a field, and the first expense was £10 for a paling to keep little Barbara from falling over the edge. She was a funny, pug-nosed little thing. They called her Baboo sometimes, probably in reference to her monkey-like appearance: but she was full of endearing tricks, she rolled happily in the hay outside the door, and her looks began to improve. The neighbours were all kind and welcom-

ing, and Bessy had a great success among them, crowning it
with a triumphant appearance at the local ball.

Ashbourne was a lucky home for the Moores. Tom did some
of his best work there, and the family flourished in the good
country air. The four years were marred by one sorrow. Their
third child, also a girl, called after Byron, though to begin with
she seemed "as strong as a young lioness", lived a short while
only. Bessy, whom the birth had brought very low, sank into
a pitiful state of depression, and Moore took her over to Dublin
to try the effects of sea-bathing. She was received with open
arms by the Moore parents, who had never yet seen her, and
their welcome, plus the rush of Dublin people to offer her
hospitality and do her honour, quite restored her. Then, by
great ill-luck, crossing at the end of September, they struck
rough weather, and by the time the packet reached Holyhead
she was very ill again. It was impossible to move for some days,
but the journey was completed at last, and the sight of her own
cottage, which she had come to love, did something to revive
her. She next developed a cough, and poor Tom was at his
wits' end: but she recovered slowly.

Moore was grieved by this death, but more for Bessy's sake
than for the child's. His attitude towards death was not unusual
in one of his temperament. At the beginning of 1810, he had
lost his beloved Uncle Richard. A letter to Lady Donegal gives
his reaction to the loss.

"You will perceive by my seal that death has been a visitor
in my family; and indeed it is the first time that I have had to
lament the loss of any one very dear to me. My poor uncle, who
went to Madeira, with but faint hopes of recovery from a
decline, died there in four days after his arrival. I am so hourly
prepared for these inroads on our social happiness, that the death
of even the healthiest friend about me could scarcely, I think,
take my heart by surprise; and the effect which such calamities
are likely to have upon me will be seen more in the whole tenor

of my life afterwards, than in any violent or deep-felt grief of
the moment: every succeeding loss will insensibly sink the level
of my spirits, and give a darker and darker tinge to all my future
hopes and feelings. This perhaps is the natural process which
many a heart goes through that has to survive its dearest con-
nections, though I rather think it is not the commonest way of
feeling those events, but that, in general, the impression which
they make is as *short* as it is keen and violent; and surely it is
better to have one moment *darkly blotted*, with the chance of the
next moment's washing it all out, than to possess that kind of
sensibility which puts one's whole life into mourning."

However philosophical his point of view, he shrank from the
actual circumstances of death. Always easily moved to tears, he
feared the shock of something really painful, which he would
have to face in fact rather than in imagination. Life took its
revenge, for, by his life's end, Moore had had to face more
sorrow than most.

In 1817, when *Lalla Rookh* had just appeared, and Moore, at
the pinnacle of his success, had gone off with Rogers to Paris,
he received news that Barbara, the apple of his eye, had fallen
and hurt herself badly. The child lingered for a month, then
died. Moore says little about her death. He had not yet begun
to keep his Journal, and his letters allude to what had happened
without describing it. Moreover, Bessy was prostrate with grief,
and Moore, having to look after her and make arrangements for
a change of house, had too much on his hands to be able to
uxuriate in sorrow. But the scene must have harrowed him,
for when, in December 1825, he heard that old John Moore
was dying, and prepared to cross to Ireland, Bessy prayed that
he would not get there before his father died, and entreated him
not to look upon him afterwards. She knew the effect it would
have upon him.

On his way over, as he lay feeling deadly ill, he overheard a
conversation in the cabin.

"Isn't Mr Moore among the passengers?" a man asked the under-steward.

"I don't know, indeed, sir."

"His father is——" Moore did not catch the word.

"Is he, sir?" said the steward.

This, Moore thought, could only mean one thing: and though he was just on the point of being sick, the shock checked him, and he lay for a long time with his sickness entirely forgotten. As it happened, when he reached Dublin, John Moore was still alive, but past recognizing anyone, and Moore gladly yielded to his sister's suggestion that he should not visit the deathbed. He preferred to remember his father as he saw him last. The subsequent celebration of mass in the bedroom beside the coffin was as much as he could stand: and he loathed the funeral. "Altogether the scene shocked and afflicted me beyond anything: the vulgar apparatus of the ceremony seems such a profanation!"

IV

This experience confirmed him in his shrinking, and the next bereavement found him sensitive to the point of heartlessness. Little Anastasia—"Stasia"—his pet since her sister's death, fell ill. Moore and Bessy were anxious from the first, but the illness fluctuated, giving them occasional grounds for hope. Moore had a premonition of disaster.

"A melancholy week, but lucky for me that I am *obliged* to work, as it, in some degree, distracts my thoughts. The dreadful moment is that interval at night when I have done working and am preparing for bed. It is then everything most dreadful crowds upon me, and the loss not only of this dear child, but of all that I love in the world, seems impending over me."

Anastasia, a gentle, affectionate child, bore her long ordeal bravely and with cheerfulness. One night she asked her father to play some waltzes to her, and hummed them as he played.

Then he had to go to London for a couple of days. There he received a letter from Bessy to say that the child was so much exhausted after her last drive that she could take no more, and that the Doctor warned them the end might be sudden. Moore went back, arriving at five in the morning. He dared not go in at the hall door, but tapped at the back kitchen window, to know what he was to find. Anastasia was no worse, but was upstairs in the room she was never to leave alive.

The end must be told in Moore's own words.

"The next fortnight furnishes but a melancholy detail of the last hours of our darling child, the only consolation of which was that she passed them without suffering, and even in calm and cheerful enjoyment. She had no idea of her danger, nor did Bessy, nor I, nor any of those about her, ever show the least sign of alarm or sorrow in her presence. There are some pious persons who would think this wrong, and who would have disturbed and embittered the last moments of this innocent child with religious exhortations and *preparations* (as they would call it) for another world, as if the whole of her short and stainless life was not a far better preparation than any that their officiousness could afford her. We passed every evening together (she, and I, and her mamma) in some amusement or other, and as it had been seldom in my power to spare so much of my company in this way, it was a treat to her which she enjoyed most thoroughly. 'What nice evenings we have!' she would say to her mamma continually. Sometimes we used to look over together a child's book in which there were pictures from history, and talk of the events and persons they alluded to; at another time, Caroline Fielding's sketch-book and the engravings of Pinelli were an amusement to her; but, in general, what gave her pleasure was either playing a game or two at draughts with me herself, or looking on while her mamma and I played draughts or cribbage, and betting with me as to which should win. However difficult it was to go on cheerfully in such circumstances,

I am convinced that the effort did both Bessy and me much
service, by accustoming us to control our feelings, and, in a certain degree, *hardening* us for the worst. I have already mentioned
her having attempted to sing through a quadrille one evening,
a little before my departure for town, and at the same time she
gave an imitation of a foreigner whom she had heard counter-
feiting the tones of different musical instruments with his voice
at Devizes. A few nights after my return (on the 27th I think)
she said to her mamma, when she was putting her to bed (having been all the evening in most cheerful spirits), 'Shall I try
and sing?' 'Do, love,' said her mamma, and she immediately
sung the line 'When in death I shall calmly recline,' without,
however, (as Bessy is persuaded) having the least idea of applying it to her own situation. In the meantime, the poor child
grew weaker every day, and the swelling in the legs increased.
She continued, however, to eat very well and to sleep comfortably, and sat up every day, employing herself a great part of the
time (for, notwithstanding her years, she was still perfectly a
child) in dressing and undressing a little doll in which she took
great delight.

"March 1st to 12th. Towards the end of this week she began
to have *accesses* of extra weakness in the mornings, so much so
as to make me think, each time, that her last moment was come;
but she revived from them after taking some refreshment, and
the strong cheerful tone of her voice on recovering from what
had appeared to be death seemed wonderful, and even startling.
On Thursday evening (5th) I looked over with her Pinelli's
prints, and she was much amused with and made remarks on
most of the subjects. When she used to close her eyes from
weakness, she would say, 'I can't talk, but do you and mamma
go on talking, for I like to hear you.' On Friday, she was again
alarmingly weak in the morning, and her sweet face still more
sadly altered. That evening she played a game of draughts with
me; but her exhaustion was so great on getting to bed, that

Bessy (who for the last month had slept, or rather lain down on a sofa in her room) sat up the greater part of the night. The dear child, indeed, had often said, 'It is odd, mamma, I never wake in the night, but there I see you and Hannah with your eyes fixed on me, and looking so cheerful and nice.' Poor child, she little knew what those cheerful looks cost. On Saturday morning she was so weak that we thought it better not to move her from her bed, and she dozed away most of the day, occasionally teased by her cough, but without any other suffering. That evening she expressed a wish that mamma and I should play a game at cribbage together, and she would listen to us; but she remained in a drowsy state the whole of the time. As she did not appear to me much weaker than last night, I entreated Bessy to take a little sleep that she might be better able to go through what was yet before her; but though she did not say so, I saw that she would sit up. Next morning (Sunday, 8th) I rose early, and on approaching the room, heard the dear child's voice as strong, I thought, as usual; but, on entering, I saw death plainly in her face. When I asked her how she had slept, she said, 'Pretty well,' in her usual courteous manner; but her voice had a sort of hollow and distant softness not to be described. When I took her hand on leaving her, she said (I thought significantly) 'Good-bye, papa.' I will not attempt to tell what I felt at all this. I went occasionally to listen at the door of the room, but did not go in, as Bessy, knowing what an effect (through my whole future life) such a scene would have upon me, implored me not to be present at it. Thus passed the first of the morning. About eleven o'clock (as Bessy told me afterwards) the poor child, with an appearance rather of wandering in her mind, said, somewhat wildly, 'I shall die, I shall die'; and to which her mamma answered, 'We pray to God continually for you, my dear Anastasia, and I am sure God must love you, for you have been always a good girl.' 'Have I?' she said; 'I thought I was a very naughty girl; but I am glad to hear *you* say that I have been good; for others would perhaps say it out of compliment, but you know me, and must therefore think so, or you would not say it.' 'But everybody thinks the same, my love. All your young friends love you. Lady Lansdowne thinks you a very good girl.' 'Does she, mummy?' said the dear child; and then added, 'Do you think I shall go to Lady Lansdowne's party this year?' I don't know what poor Bessie answered to this. In about three-quarters of an hour or less she called for me, and I came and took her hand for a few seconds, during which Bessy leaned down her head between the poor dying child and me, that I might not see her countenance. As I left the room, too, agonized as her own mind was, my sweet, thoughtful Bessy ran anxiously after me, and giving me a smelling-bottle, exclaimed, 'For God's sake don't *you* get ill.' In about a quarter of an hour afterwards she came to me, and I saw that all was over. I could no longer restrain myself, the feelings I had been so long suppressing found vent, and a fit of loud violent sobbing seized me, in which I felt as if my chest was coming asunder. The last words of my dear child were 'Papa, papa.' Her mother had said, 'My dear, I think I could place you more comfortably; shall I?' to which she answered, 'Yes,' and Bessy placing her hand under her back, gently raised her. That moment was her last. She exclaimed suddenly, 'I am dying, I am dying, Papa! papa!' and expired.

"On the 12th our darling child was conveyed to Bromham churchyard, poor Bessy having gone the night before to see where she was to be laid. Almost all those offices towards the dead which are usually left to others to perform, the mother on this occasion would perform herself, and the last thing she did before the coffin was closed on Wednesday night, was to pull some snowdrops herself and place them within it. She had already, indeed, laid on her dead darling's bosom a bunch of cowslips, which she had smelled to (and with *such* eagerness) the day before her death, and it was singular enough, and seemed to give Bessy pleasure, that though lying there three days they were scarcely at all faded. I had ordered a chaise on the morning of the funeral to take us out of the way of this most dreadful ceremony, (well remembering how it harrowed up all our feelings in following my poor father to the grave) and a most melancholy drive we had of it for two long hours, each bearing up for the sake of the other, but all the worse, in reality, for the effort.

"And such is the end of so many years of fondness and hope; and nothing is now left us but the dream (which may God in his mercy realize) that we shall see our pure child again in a world more worthy of her."

It is a poignant story, but Moore never seems to realize that he had failed his child in leaving her last cries unanswered. Nor does he see the implied reproach in Bessy's words, written some time afterwards:

"Every day only adds to the loneliness of the future, and the happy face of that sweet child is for ever before me, as she used to sit at the other side of the table. But I will try and only think of her as I trust she is—happy and often looking down on those she so tenderly loved. How she thought of and loved *you*! Her dear eyes were always full of light if you but went upstairs and she thought there was a chance of your coming into the parlour."

Preoccupied with his own sensibilities, he forgot his child's: and our sympathy with him is less than it might be. Yet his grief was deep and genuine. He did not touch the piano for months afterwards, and he ends the year's volume with words which cannot be mistaken.

"Here ends the year 1830, and here most gladly do I take leave of this melancholy book, which I have never opened without a fear of lighting upon those pages of it that record the event to me the most saddening of my whole life; the only event that I can look back upon as a real irreparable misfortune; the loss of my sweet Anastasia."

V

Moore's first son, Tom,[1] was born on October 24th, 1818. On the 19th, Moore had been to a ball. He reached home between two and three in the morning, and found Bessy, despite her condition, getting up from bed "to blow the fire for some hot drink" for him. On the night of the 23rd, he went to bed early. At half-past eleven, Bessy called him, and he sent for the midwife, who arrived between one and two;

". . . and at a quarter before four my darling Bessy was safely delivered of a son (and heir *in partibus*), to my unspeakable delight, for never had I felt half such anxiety about her. I walked about the parlour by myself, like one distracted; sometimes stopping to pray, sometimes opening the door to listen; and never was gratitude more fervent than that with which I knelt down to thank God for the dear girl's safety, when all was over—(the maid, by the by, very near catching me on my knees). Went to bed at six o'clock.

"24th. Rose at half-past nine. Bessy and the little hero surprisingly well. Wrote to Lord Lansdowne, Rogers, etc.: Lord Lansdowne's answer most friendly and flattering. I wish he had offered to be godfather; had not courage to ask him. Walked to Devizes for money: drew on Wilkie for 40*l*.: the little prodigal is no sooner born than money is wanted for him. Returned to dinner at five.

"25th (Sunday). Resumed my Sheridan task, from which I have been diverted and disturbed all the last week. At Bessy's request read prayers by her bedside, and joined heartily with her in thanksgiving for her safe delivery."

Bessy was not too well at first, and a nurse had to be found for the baby. "Poor little thing," wrote Moore in his Journal, "with a mother that can give him no milk, and a father that

---

[1] Full names, Thomas Lansdowne Parr.

can give him no money, what business has he in the world?" As things turned out, he had very little business in it.

Russell,[1] the second boy, was five years younger. On this occasion, a physician was to have been in attendance, but, to Bessy's great delight, he did not arrive till half an hour after all was over. She had "a horror of his being even in the house on these occasions". Russell was described by his father as "a little fright, as all such things are". He turned out quiet and gentle, and promised well.

To deal with the two boys now would make the Moores' life seem all sorrow, which it emphatically was not. Their story belongs rather to Tom's last years, and we may look next upon the brighter side of his fortunes.

[1] John Russell.

CHAPTER XII

HEYDAY: SUCCESS AND FRIENDSHIP

Moore and his friends—A visit to Scott—*Lalla Rookh*—The
Moores move to Sloperton—Bad news from Bermuda—Moore
as exile—Travels in Italy—Byron—Paris—A farewell dinner

ON the third morning of Moore's visit to Abbotsford Scott
laid a hand affectionately on his breast.

"Now, my dear Moore," he exclaimed, "we are friends for
life."

The incident was typical of both men. Moore had a genius
for making friends. Few men of his time could boast as many,
and none had fewer enemies. Moore's friends were of all kinds.
He made them naturally, by his eagerness to give and receive
pleasure, by his frankness, his fundamental modesty, his kindness of heart, his great gifts as a talker, and his enjoyment of the
talk of others. The most unlikely and diverse collection of individuals agreed in their affection for him. Emmet spent many
hours walking with him in the country round Dublin, and had
always a gentle and considerate regard for his welfare. Shelley
showed himself pathetically anxious for his good opinion, asking Byron to do his best to mitigate Moore's disapproval of his
atheism, and pledging himself to write to Moore and put his
own case in a better light. Jeffrey took to him at sight, Sydney Smith was a constant companion, Wordsworth expressed
pleasure in his company, Leigh Hunt sang his praises, Byron
wrote a famous eulogy:

"Moore has a peculiarity of talent, or rather talents—poetry,
music, voice—all his own; and an expression in each, which
never was, nor will be, possessed by another. . . . There is

nothing Moore may not do, if he will but seriously set about it. In society he is gentlemanly, gentle, and, altogether, more pleasing than any individual with whom I am acquainted. For his honour, principle, and independence, his conduct to . . . speaks 'trumpet-tongued'. He has but one fault—and that one I daily regret—he is not *here*."

Another friend who, knowing all his weaknesses, admired and loved him, was Samuel Rogers. Intimate though they were, Moore had to mind his p's and q's. "Though in his society one walks upon roses," he confided to Lady Donegal, "it is with constant apprehension of the thorns that are among them." Rogers was a leader of the literary society of the time, a figure to merit deference as well as affection. He was never one to hide his opinions, and there was a touch of the avuncular in his affection for Moore, which was so generously expanded to include Bessy. He ridiculed Moore's love of a lord, and general passion for high society: but Moore, knowing his man, was never offended, and repaid him with an affection as sincere as his own.

Moore's friendship, as we have seen, was by no means confined to writers and artists. He could please sailormen and artisans as well as those who had the measure of his powers. Nor were the ladies behindhand in appreciation. Moore had any number of women friends, from the clear-eyed Mary Godfrey and old Miss Berry, who thought him too jaunty as a young man and liked him better when his locks were grizzled, to the lively Miss Owenson, whom he captivated early with his kindness, and the landlady who offered him the use of her savings. One of his best friends was Mary Shelley,[1] who laboured always to keep up his self-respect and combat his sense of his own short-comings.

"I like him much," she wrote, in the early stages of their friendship. "There is something warm and genuine in his feel-

---

[1] Between 1827 and 1840 he wrote her over eighty letters, in addition to those which have already been published.

ings and manner which is very attractive, and redeems him from
the sin of worldliness with which he has been charged."

Shelley had paid his respects to Moore in *Adonais*:

> . . . from her wilds Ierne sent
> The sweetest lyrist of her saddest wrong. . . . .

but Moore was never easy about Shelley's opinion of him.

"January 18, 19. Received a letter one of these days from Mrs
Shelley, who is about to publish an edition of Shelley's works,
asking me whether I had a copy of his Queen,—that originally
printed for private circulation; as she could not procure one,
and took for granted that I must have been one of those persons
to whom he presented copies. In answering that I was unluckily
not one of them, I added, in a laughing way, that I had never
been much in repute with certain great guns of Parnassus, such
as Wordsworth, Southey, her own Shelley, etc. Received from
her, in consequence, a very kind and flattering reply, in which
she says, 'I cannot help writing one word to say how mistaken
you are. Shelley was too true a poet not to feel your unrivalled
merits, especially in the department of poetry peculiarly your
own,—songs and short poems instinct with the intense principle
of life and love. Such, your unspeakably beautiful poems to Nea;
such, how many others! One of the first things I remember with
Shelley was his repeating to me one of your gems with enthusiasm. In short, be assured that as genius is the best judge of
genius, those poems of yours which you yourself would value
most, were admired by none so much as Shelley. You know
me far too well not to know I speak the exact truth.' "

Dr Parr, when he died, bequeathed Moore a ring, with a
tribute to "his original genius . . . his exquisite sensibility . . .
his independent spirit and his incorruptible integrity." Elizabeth
Rennie, his friend for many years, wrote of him

"His warm and sunshiny nature soon made itself felt by those
approaching him—you caught the all-pervading glow and radi-
ance. He seemed so keenly and vividly to enjoy existence—

making so light of its cares and burdens—on the other hand, so heightening and intensifying the pleasures, that his society exercised over you a species of happy spell, which you grieved to be divorced from and berest of."

Literary history cannot show us a man better loved by his friends, and it is only natural to suppose that he did something to deserve them.

II

The visit to Scott was very happy for host and guest, and the few pages in the Journal that describe it give one as good a picture of Moore and of his private and public popularity as can be found. The incidents tell us how he was regarded: his comments tell us about the man.

"Went up to a room in the sexton's house, which was filled with casts, done by himself, from the ornaments, heads, etc. of the Abbey. Scott, seeing a large niche empty, said, 'Johnny, I'll give you the Virgin and Child to put there.' Seldom have I seen a happier face than Johnny exhibited at this news; it was all over smiles. As we went downstairs, Scott said to him, 'Johnny, if there's another anti-Popish rising, you'll have your house pulled about your ears.' When we got into the carriage, I said, 'You have made that man very happy.' 'Good (said Sir Walter), then there are two of us pleased, for I did not know what to do with the Virgin and Child. Mamma (Lady Scott) will be particularly glad to get rid of it.' A less natural man would have left me under the impression that he had done really a very generous thing. Sir W. bought one of the books giving a description of the Abbey (written every word of it by the sexton), and presented it to me. Went from thence to the cottage of the Lockharts, which is very retired and pretty; and then proceeded to pay a visit to the Fergusons just near. Could not help thinking, during this quiet homely visit, how astonished some of those foreigners would be, to whom the name of Sir Walter Scott is encircled with so much romance, to see the plain, quiet, neighbourly manner with which he took his seat among these old maids and the familiar ease with which they treated him in return; no country squire, with but half an idea in his head, could have fallen into the gossip of a humdrum country visit more unassumingly. This is charming."

Moore picked up, at Scott's dinner-table, a happy story of an encounter between Adam Smith and Dr Johnson "as given by Smith himself".

"Johnson began by attacking Hume. 'I saw,' (said Smith) 'this was meant at me, so I merely put him right as to a matter of fact.' 'Well, what did he say?' 'He said it was a lie.' 'And what did you say to that?' 'I told him he was a son of a b——h.' Good, this, between two sages."

One more anecdote, from the same dinner-party.

"Talking of ghosts, Sir Adam Ferguson said that Scott and he had seen one, at least, while they were once drinking together; a very hideous fellow appeared suddenly between them whom neither of them knew anything about, but whom both saw. Scott did not deny it, but said they were both 'fou', and not very capable of judging whether it was a ghost or not."

A few days later, there was an instance of Moore's popularity with the public. The party went to Edinburgh to the theatre.

"We went into the front boxes, and the moment we appeared, the whole pit rose, turned towards us, and applauded vehemently. Scott said, 'It is you, it is you; you must rise and make your acknowledgment.' I hesitated for some time, but on hearing them shout out 'Moore, Moore,' I rose and bowed my best for two or three minutes. This scene was repeated after the two next acts, and the Irish Melodies were played each time by the orchestra. Soon after my first reception, Jeffrey and two of the ladies arrived, and sat in the front before us, Scott and I being in the second row. He seemed highly pleased the way I was received, and said several times, 'This is quite right. I am glad my countrymen have returned the compliment for me.' . . . Home very tired with my glory, and had to pack for the morning."

It was by no means his only scene of the kind in a theatre. Dublin furnished several, and at the last he assured the crowd that there was no honour he valued so much as that of being considered the poet of Ireland.

III

The point in his literary history at which we last left Moore was when *Lalla Rookh* was but half finished. He soon recovered from his despondency about it, and small wonder. His reputation had suddenly taken a great leap forward, and put him in a position to negotiate royally for its publication. The year 1814 was perhaps Moore's luckiest, as regards his work. Jeffrey asked him formally, with Rogers as intermediary, to become a contributor to the *Edinburgh Review*. Byron dedicated to him his poem *The Corsair*, calling him "the poet of all circles and idol of his own". The contract for *Lalla Rookh* was signed with Longmans in December, and Moore, after refusing Murray's offer of two thousand guineas, was promised three thousand for a poem of stipulated length (the length of Scott's *Rokeby*) of which the publisher had not read a line. Longmans never regretted the bargain, for the poem sold steadily for more than thirty years after its publication. Moore finished it in 1816, but war had made things bad for the book trade, and he agreed to its postponement till more favourable times. The postponement was troublesome, for he was hard up. His father had lost his post as barrack-master, and Moore had to make good the loss. A few months before the appearance of *Lalla Rookh*, he was asking Power for "a few pounds (five or six)" as he was down to his last shilling. Then, in May, the poem was published, and the sky cleared at once. Moore's disposal of his windfall was characteristic. One-third of it he took to clear his debts, and set him on his feet. The remainder he left with Longmans, on their promise to pay his father £100 a year as interest upon it.

The success of the poem was immediate, and Moore was flooded with offers. He had, however, a firm dislike—how strange it sounds to-day!—of miscellaneous journalism and spoke with scorn of "Albumizing, Annualizing, and Periodical-izing", as he called it. Even when in need of money, he refused liberal offers to edit and to contribute to various annuals. An offer of £100 for as many lines of verse, which he could have knocked off in a couple of days, was turned down, as was one of £1,000 a year from Longmans to edit an annual. Not till 1832, when he was in serious need, did he accept an offer (from Marryat) of £500 for contributions to a magazine.

This dislike did not prevent him from enjoying his success to the full. On the strength of the forthcoming publication, the family had moved house to Hornsey. They found the move more than justified financially, and, his mind easy, Moore went off with Rogers to Paris for a holiday, only to be recalled by the news of Barbara's fall.

IV

Of *Lalla Rookh* itself the less said the better. It was a deliberate, set achievement, for which Moore had no qualifications except his technique in verse. He had no knowledge of the East, and little interest in it: and could, on his own confession, work up no enthusiasm until he had detected a parallel between the struggle of the Ghebers against "their haughty Moslem masters" and the Irish resistance to England. Much has been made of that parallel, and there have been many arguments over it, which I do not pro-pose to examine, for the sufficient reason that *Lalla Rookh* is a dull, florid, long poem, uninspired, and without any quality except skilful versification. Moore's writer friends received it coolly, voicing their opinions with more or less frankness, and Moore himself was well aware of its inferiority to the *Melodies*.

He knew, even before he began, that he was going beyond his range, and resolved to "try to make up for his deficiencies in *dash* and vigour by versatility and polish". Once he had hit on his Ghebers, however, with their supposed resemblance to the Irish, he proclaimed that "the spirit that had spoken in the melodies of Ireland soon found itself at home in the East": upon which Mr Stephen Gwynn wittily comments that it found itself about as much at home as is the ordinary European in oriental costume at a fancy dress ball. Had Moore lived to-day, *Lalla Rookh* would have been a novel. Compared with the other second- and third- and fourth-rate work of the period, it is well enough. There was a certain novelty about it, and any wide contemporary success means that the work which enjoys it has something of value for its time. Still, even though the present decade is as unfavourable as could be imagined for judging work in the *Lalla Rookh* idiom, we can be confident that it is a work of no importance: a view in which the best of Moore's contemporaries agreed.

v

In 1817, after a visit to Lady Donegal's town house, under-taken principally in order to cheer Bessy up after her loss, the Moores moved to a cottage at Sloperton, near Devizes, which was to be their home for many years. The cottage was a couple of miles from Bowood, Lord Lansdowne's country seat, and it was at his suggestion that they came to the neighbourhood. Sloperton was an attractive, sheltered spot, in gentle, wooded country, and the village of Bromham was close by. The cottage looked out on a lawn and a quiet garden: everything, cottage, and country round, was after Moore's own heart. The cottage was offered to them for £40 a year, furnished. (By 1829 he was paying only £10 in rent.) Moore was enraptured with it all. Bessy, however, took some time to settle down. She loved the country, but there was nobody she knew. Bowood was splendid for Tom, who was

accustomed to grand folk, but she, despite their kindness, felt at a
loss there. Still, she found plenty to do in the house and in the
village. So charming and naturally friendly a girl could not be
strange for long, and, though she had lost something of her
looks, she was still uncommonly attractive.

Then came a heavy blow. Affairs in Bermuda had long been
unsatisfactory, from Moore's point of view. As early as 1809,
his deputy had proved incompetent, and he had asked Croker,[1]
then Secretary of the Admiralty, to find someone to buy the
deputyship from him. The next deputy would not send in his
accounts, and Moore could not get any information as to his
share of the profits during the American War. Then, on All
Fools' Day, 1818, he received a summons to Doctors' Com-
mons. His deputy had absconded with the proceeds of the sale
of a ship and cargo, which had been left in his hands pending
an appeal to the court at home. "I suppose," Moore wrote
disconsolately to Lady Donegal, "the sum is considerable." It
was: six thousand pounds. Moore had no security for his deputy, and was liable for the whole amount. He expected to
be thrown into prison, but the case was deferred, and did not
come up for hearing till July the 10th of the next year. Meantime, a great deal had happened. Moore's comic series, *The
Fudge Family in Paris*, the fruit of his visit there with Rogers,
had appeared and scored an immediate success, and he was
working hard upon a *Life of Sheridan*, which Murray had
proposed to him on the strength of his stinging verses upon
Sheridan's death. The price for the *Life* was to be a thousand
guineas, so that all promised well, provided only that the Bermuda case were decided in his favour. The defaulting deputy,
whose name does not appear to have been preserved, was the
nephew of a rich merchant named Sheddon. Moore looked to
Sheddon for some redress, but did not seem likely to get it.

[1] J. W. Croker; not to be confused with Thomas Crofton Croker, friend
of James Power the publisher.

Bermuda had become unfortunate in every respect, for Moore presently received the following letter, which must refer to the individual appointed to succeed Mr Sheddon's nephew.

GOVT. HOUSE,

BERMUDAS,

SIR,   18 *January* 1819.

It is with much regret that I have to state to you that I have felt myself called upon to remove Mr John W. Goodrich from the situation of Deputy Registrar of the Vice Admiralty Court of these Islands, in consequence of his gross misconduct and dereliction of duty in delivering the Register of a vessel, seized by the officers of His Majesty's Customs and condemned by the Court to the Master of the vessel in order to prejudice her sale, and to aid the Master in evading the penalties, to which his breach of the British Laws and want of faith in risking the property of British merchants entrusted to him upon freight, so justly subjected him——

And I beg leave to add that at the recommendation of the judge of the Court I have nominated Mr Samuel G. Spencer to succeed Mr John W. Goodrich, and directed the necessary securities to be taken from him for the due performance of the trusts reposed in him; and I have to request that you will be good enough to confirm the appointment, by transmitting your deputation to him accordingly——

I have the honor to be

Sir,

Your most obedient

Humble servant

JAS. COCKBURN

Govr and Comd^r in Chief

And Vice Adm^l

Thomas Moore Esqre,
    Registrar of the Vice Admiralty Court
       of Bermudas.

It is to be hoped that Mr Spencer proved more satisfactory than his predecessors. At any rate, we hear no more about him.

, Then, at long last, the case came up for hearing. It went against Moore, and he learned that, if he did not satisfy the claim against him within two months, he must go to prison. Immediately his friends rallied round, and gave him practical proof of their friendship. Lord Lansdowne offered to advance the whole £6,000. Rogers offered £500, as the first subscription of a fund which Leigh Hunt proposed to raise. Lord John Russell, who had no money available, offered Moore all profits that should be forthcoming from his *Life of Lord Russell*, and his brother, Lord Tavistock, wrote to say that, though he was very poor, he had always admired Moore's independence of mind so much that he "would willingly sacrifice something for him". Jeffrey's letter was characteristic.

JORDAN'S, ST JAMES'S STREET,
Tuesday, May 30, 1818.

MY DEAR MOORE,

What I inclose has been justly owing you, I am ashamed to say, ever since you were so kind as to send me that account of M. de J—— I do not know how long ago; but I did not know your address, and I neglect everything. Will you let me hope for a contribution from you some day soon?

I cannot from my heart resist adding another word. I have heard of your misfortunes, and of the noble way you bear them. Is it very impertinent to say I have 500*l*. entirely at your service, which you may repay when you please; and as much more, which I can advance upon any reasonable security of repayment in seven years?

Perhaps it is very unpardonable in me to say this; but upon my honour I would not make you the offer, if I did not feel that I would accept it without scruple from you.

At all events, pray don't be angry at me, and don't send me a

letter beginning Sir. I shall ask your pardon with the truest submission if I have offended you; but I trust I have not, at all events;
and however this end, no living soul shall ever know of my pre-
sumption but yourself. Believe me, with great respect and
esteem, very faithfully yours, F. JEFFREY.

Moore proceeded to give proof that the tributes to his independence were not misplaced. Grateful as he was for the offers,
and happy though they made him, he gently refused them all,
and determined to rely on his pen and such monies as the Longmans would advance him on the strength of his future work.
There was a debate as to whether he should choose Edinburgh or
Paris for sanctuary. On Lord John Russell's advice, he chose
Paris, and after a fond farewell to Bessy—"Up at six and saw my
darling girl off in the coach. God send I may meet her again in
health and happiness: a nobler hearted creature never breathed!"
—he set off in company with his mentor, just before the pre-
scribed period was over.

While he was away, he had arranged with his publishers to
look after Bessy; and at the beginning of October she wrote her
first letter to the firm. It is worth giving, for we see so little of
her.

GENTLEMEN,

As Mr Moore told me you were good enough to say you
would supply me with money during his absence I beg you will
have the kindness to send me £20 or £30 as soon as convenient
—I have just heard from Mr Moore, he is quite well, and seems
to enjoy his journey very much; and bids me say that he shall be
obliged to you to send for a Box of Papers which he left in Duke
Street to be entrusted to your care till his return.

Yours truly
B. MOORE.

SLOPERTON COTTAGE
Monday.

This was followed a few days later by another, utterly characteristic in its consideration for her husband, and her desire to shield him from anxiety.

SLOPERTON COTTAGE

Oct 7th. 1819.

I have met with a sad accident which I did not mean to inform you of, but fearing that you may hear of it from some other quarter and mention it to Mr Moore, I think it best to tell you that last Saturday I had a fall from my horse and very much bruised my Face, and broke my Nose. The swelling and inflammation are greatly subsided, and Dr Headly does not think it will be much disfigurement therefore I beg you will not even hint it to Mr Moore or to any of my friends in Edingburgh. I received the £30 this morning for which accept my thanks. Will you be good enough to send the Wedding-Cake to Mr Power directly as he is sending me a parcel and that can come with it. The friend who has written this for me will let you know how I am going

Yours truly

BESSY MOORE

Four years later, poor Bessy was to have another accident, and again to damage her nose. Tom was away this time also, and she made a second gallant attempt to hide what had happened, but he came home before the damage had "subsided".

VI

There was something in Moore's make-up which condemned him never to be at his best abroad. The three years that he was out of England, though they began with a much-needed holiday, did him more harm than any other period of his life, and accentuated all the superficial side of his nature. He recovered from their effects as soon as he came home again, but his sojourn in Paris and his travels in Italy came nearer turning his head than any success at home, and we find him for the first time self-conscious and affected, the poet in exile. He *was* in exile: he was homesick, even after Bessy and the family had joined him: and the only alleviation was gay parties in Paris, where he was made much of, and to which he surrendered himself as to a drug. The lapse was neither serious nor lasting, and Moore never lost his charm, as his popularity in Paris shows: but a new note creeps into the Journal, and the writer assumes the opinions and observations proper to Thomas Moore the poet on his travels about Europe.

The holiday began with a hectic few days in Paris. Theatres, the opera, picture shows, fêtes, performing canaries, invitations to dine: "Received a letter to-day from a Sir John Wycherly, of whom I know nothing, apologizing for his taking such a liberty with 'the finest poet of the age', but saying that he has his friend Sir Sidney Smith to dinner, and begging me 'like the bards of old, to waive ceremony and join the party' ": he was delighted with it all, but just as glad to set off for Switzerland and Italy. A glimpse of Mont Blanc at sunset transfixed him with wonder. The panorama of the Alps from the Simplon Pass so moved him that he "alternately shuddered and shed tears".

He did not by any means approve of everything he saw. The gardens of Count Borromeo he found "in wretched taste". For several days, he saw only one pretty Italian girl. The dancers in the opera at Como were "very awkward". The actors at Padua were "all disagreeable".

Lord John Russell kept him company as far as Milan, then went off on his own, and Moore reached Padua alone. From Padua he went to La Mira, Byron's country house, and the two men met for the first time in five years. Byron made much of him, offered him the use of his *palazzo* in Venice, and came to see him there.[1] Before he left, Byron gave him the first part of his Memoirs to take away and read.

Even in Italy, Moore found himself well known, and one of

[1] See Chapter XV.

his companions presented him with an Italian translation of *Lalla Rookh*. He had the usual difficulties of travellers in a strange country, and did not escape being swindled. There was the "cursed *fabbro*", who mended his carriage:

"He came into the room, after I had breakfasted, with a piece of rotten wood in his hand, which at first I almost fancied a bit of the door of Tasso's prison,[1] but which proved to be a fragment taken out of one of my wheels. Four Napoleons was what he asked, and after spending all my Italian in squabbling with him, I was obliged to give three and a half."

Moore went on *viâ* Bologne to Florence, where he was badly bitten by mosquitoes, and fetched up in Rome. Here he saw the sights and was much entertained. The Princess Borghese he thought "a fine creature in her way". She let him kiss her hands, and feel her "matchless" foot. Francis Chantrey, the sculptor, was his constant companion, and Jackson, the painter. (The last person of that name with whom he had hobnobbed was Gentleman Jackson, the boxer, to whom he had gone for materials for *Tom Crib's Memorial to Congress*.) He had a fine time, sat to Bartolini for his portrait, and did not arrive back in Paris till December the 11th. There, he learned that there was no prospect as yet of returning home. The Bermuda situation remained unchanged, and there was nothing to do but arrange for Bessy and the family to come over as soon as possible. They could not come at once, for little Tom was ill, but they came in three weeks' time, during which Moore, homesick and restless, busied himself by seeing everyone he could.

The proposed journey necessitated another letter to Longman.

SLOPERTON COTTAGE

DEAR SIR,   *Dec.* 23rd 1819

This day's Post has brought me your kind letter enclosing £50 for which I am much obliged but must beg you to send me £20

---

[1] He had been looking at Tasso's manuscripts and prison the day before.

more, as I should be very unwilling to leave Sloperton without paying *all* my little Bills—I shall be in Town on tuesday morning when I hope in person to thank you for your very kind attention.

Yours truly
BESSY MOORE.

On Bessy's arrival with the children, Moore gave up gadding about and settled down to work in earnest. Soon they moved to a cottage in the Champs Elysées, where he worked at a sequel to his *Fudge Family* and at a satire which he subsequently thought better of and withdrew. It contained, among other things, an attack on his *bête noire*, Castlereagh. But the poet could not escape from his own popularity, and the invitations still poured in. A respite came when a Monsieur and Madame Villamil offered the loan of a lodge in the gardens of their country house, and Moore began to work on a new project. This, however, needed research, and research once more spelled Paris.

In October, they were back again in the Champs Elysées, and the social life swamped everything. The Moores had to do something to return all the hospitality that was poured upon them, and soon the old game was renewed: Tom ruffled it in the capital, dining and singing, and Bessy stayed in the country, looking after the children, and trying to keep the household books down. Moore, though he began for the first time to feel the strain, and to realize that he was not as young as he had been, enjoyed a great deal of it. He was unhappy in the long absence from home and from his parents, to whom he wrote regularly as often as twice a week, and the dinners and parties and theatres were a distraction at which he gladly grasped.

A visit from Wordsworth did little to cheer him up. The senior poet was taking himself very seriously, complaining of Byron's "plagiarisms" from him, and "holding forth". Moore found him "rather dull", and added that Wordsworth did not understand the give and take of conversation.

As the months went on, his restlessness and his disinclination
to work increased. He pined for England, writing to his publishers that it was impossible for him to continue with *Sheridan*
so far away from all the necessary sources, and drawing on them
for more money until he could come across.

Then Byron came forward with an act of typical generosity.
He knew, of course, of Moore's financial difficulties, and sent
him the remainder of his Memoirs, telling him he might sell them
for what they would fetch. They were not, of course, to be
published till after Byron's death, but he made an absolute gift of
them to Moore, saying that he "should be very glad" if Moore
could "make anything of them *now* in the way of reversion".
Moore demurred, but finally acted on his friend's suggestion,
and Murray agreed to advance him two thousand guineas for the
right of ultimate publication.

Armed with this sum, Moore wished to come over to England secretly and see if he could fix up anything about the
Bermuda business. He crossed with Lord John Russell under the
name of "Mr Dyke". Both were searched at the Customs, and
the official took from Moore a locket containing his children's
hair, and a mother-of-pearl pocket-book which his mother had
given him. As soon as he discovered Lord John's identity, however, the official's manner changed at once, and Moore got his
property back.

Longman, when Moore told him what he intended about
Bermuda, advised him to leave matters as they were, and
"appeared labouring with some mystery". Moore at last got out
of him that Lord Lansdowne had left a thousand pounds at his
disposal, with instructions to try to get the amount of the debt
reduced to that sum. Moore was deeply touched. "How one
such action brightens the whole human race in our eyes!"
Nevertheless, he could not accept the offer. He stole off on a
quick visit to Dublin to see his parents, but dared not stay there
long, for fear word should reach the English authorities, and he

should be arrested. When he returned, however, he found to his delight that the main claim, in respect of which he had been attached, had been compromised on payment of £1,000, and that he was a free man once more. With Longman, he went round to interview Sheddon, to see

"whether he really meant to advance anything towards the sum I am to pay; his conduct all along shabby and shuffling, and now, when brought to the point, his agony at the prospect of being made to bleed, quite ludicrous. Upon my rising from my seat and saying, with a sort of contemptuous air, 'Since Mr Sheddon does not seem inclined to give anything but advice, Mr Longman, I think we may take our leave,' he, with much stammering, proposed to give £200; and, upon Longman saying that really this was not worth while talking about, he was, at last, with much pain and groaning, delivered of £300, having had a very difficult time of it indeed."

To mark his appreciation of Lord Lansdowne's kindness, Moore paid the remainder of the £1,000 out of the money he had offered, and at once repaid him with a draft on Murray against the advance for Byron's manuscript.

He then went back to Paris, to work on a new long poem, *The Loves of the Angels*, returning to England in November.

Before he left, his friends in Paris determined to give him a splendid farewell dinner. The following circular was sent out:

PARIS, *November 2, 1822.*

At a meeting of the personal Friends of Mr Thomas Moore, held this day, it was
Resolved,

That in testimony of the respect and regard with which they consider that Gentleman, and to commemorate in a suitable manner the pleasure which his long residence in this city has afforded to a large circle of his acquaintance, he be invited to partake of a farewell Dinner, previous to his departure from among them.

That in making choice of a social Meeting to celebrate an event that carries with it the deprivation of much of the enjoyment of Mr Moore's Friends during their sojourn abroad, they are desirous of evincing how truly they participate in the satisfaction which is common to all his admirers, on the circumstances of his return to England.

G. WEBSTER, Chairman.

As occasionally happens when Irish people plan such demonstrations, the organization was not what it might have been. The invitations were sent out late and unmethodically, and many people who would have liked to be present received them too late or not at all. Others were unable to come because of the death of Lord Mount Cashell. Lord Trimleston was in the chair. The Reverend Archibald Douglas, to whom the answers to the invitations were sent, kept them all sewn up with red thread, with his statement of accounts for the dinner and the script of his speech proposing Bessy's health. The dinner was held at Robert's on the 11th: here are the main items in the account.

Hire of 26 Decanters for the Bordeau	13
30 Bot^s of Champaigne	150
Roberts Bill	1356
Bard's case of Wine	500
Madeira—dozen	72
Doz^n of Sauterns	60
Music	800

Who "Bard" was is not clear: let us hope it was meant for "the Bard", Tom himself. Bessy was hailed as "a feminine Bayard—*sans peur et sans reproche*".

So the Paris days ended, in high glory, and the family returned to Sloperton. It had been let during their absence, but was fortunately vacant once more.

CHAPTER XIII

HEYDAY (continued)

Moore's extraordinary fame—A visitor to Sloperton—Holland
House—Moore's "fan-mail"—Contemporary descriptions of
Moore—A tour of Ireland

THE story has often been told that Moore and Byron were one
afternoon by the river at Hampton Court, discussing the nature
of fame. As they talked, a boatload of holiday-makers rowed
by, lustily singing one of Moore's *Melodies*.

"There," exclaimed Byron dramatically, laying a hand upon
Moore's shoulder, "*that* is fame."

Moore's popularity in his peak years was certainly astonishing.
He was fêted wherever he went, and everybody, even the
poorest people, knew his name. He was parodied in *Fraser's
Magazine*, the truculent editor, Maginn, attacking him repeatedly. *Lalla Rookh* went into seven editions in a year. *The
Loves of the Angels* brought in a thousand pounds in its first few
months. Coleridge, commenting on the lack of popular appreciation of Wordsworth, remarked acidly that if one of his poems
were put out under the name of Byron, Moore, or Campbell,
it would meet with instant acclaim. It was everywhere regarded
as a privilege to meet the Irish poet. Any memento of him was
treasured as if it had belonged to Royalty. Scott's servant begged
a lock of his hair. A girl who shook hands with him at a dance
covered her hand with her shawl so that no lesser touch should
profane it for the rest of the evening. Mrs Cooper, at Mayfield,
kept a collection of pens with which he wrote *Lalla Rookh*, and
a torn fragment of one of his gloves. Eliza Branigan, his neighbour at Sloperton, preserved, among other relics, "A Piece of the

Scarf and Hat-Band worn by Thomas Moore Esq: at the funeral of Lord Byron, Monday, July 12th,[1] 1824".

Sometimes this popularity had its inconvenient side. On one occasion, when Moore was returning from Dublin in the "Packet", a number of young ladies discovered that he was on board, came to his cabin, and insisted on being kissed all round. Moore, who was already feeling queasy, came out, responded gallantly, then retreated in haste. An older lady, hearing what had happened, knocked at the door and demanded to be kissed as well. Moore managed to comply, and got back just in time.

Gerald Griffin, visiting Sloperton about Moore's candidature for Limerick, begins his account with "Oh, my dear L——, I saw the poet!" That, at least, was how his countrymen regarded him. Griffin's account, taken from a letter which he wrote to a lady residing at Taunton, is worth quoting, both for its liveliness of observation, and because it shows that Moore, caught unawares though he was, did not allow his reputation to make him insensitive to the feelings of others.

"After our first sight and speech of the Irish melodist I opened my writing case to give L—— an account of our day's work then I put it off, I believe until morning . . . and here I come before you with my news, my golden bit of news flat stale and unprofitable. Oh dear L——, I saw the poet! and I spoke to him, and he spoke to me, and it was not to bid me get out of his way, as the King of France did to a man who boasted that his majesty had spoken to him; but it was to shake hands with me and ask me 'How I did, Mr Griffin?' and to speak of 'my fame'. My fame! Tom Moore to talk of fame! Ah, the rogue, he was humbugging, L—— I'm afraid. He knew the soft side of an author's heart, and perhaps had pity on my long melancholy looking figure, and said to himself, 'I will make this poor fellow feel pleasant if I can,' for which, with all his roguery who could help

[1] Miss Branigan, it will be noted, was not quite accurate in her date.

liking him, and being grateful to him?—I should tell you first
how we arrived at the inn at Devizes late in the evening——
Well we asked the waiter—'How far is it to Sloperton Cottage
from Devizes?' 'Sloperton, sir, that's Mr Moore's place, sir; he's
a poet sir. We do all Mr Moore's work.' What ought I to have
done L——? To have flung my arms about his neck for knowing
so much about Moore or to have knocked him down for knowing so little. Well, we learned all we wanted to know, and after
making our arrangements for the following day, went to bed
and slept soundly, and in the morning it was that we hired the
grand cabriolet and set off to Sloperton; drizzling rain, but a
delightful country; such a gentle shower as that which he looked
at Innisfallen—his farewell look, and we drove away until we
came to a cottage, a cottage of gentility with two gateways and
pretty grounds about it, and we alighted and knocked at the
hall door, and there was dead silence and we whispered one
another; and my nerves thrilled as the wind rustled in the creep-
ing shrubs that graced the retreat of Moore. Oh L——, there's
no use in talking but I must be fine—— But the door opened
and a young woman appeared. 'Is Mr Moore at home?' 'I'll see
sir, what name shall I say sir?' Well not to be too particular, we
were shown upstairs, where we found the nightingale in his
cage, in honester language and more to the purpose, we found
an hero in his study, a table before him covered with books and
papers, a drawer half opened and stuffed with letters, a piano also
opened at a little distance and the thief himself, a little man, but
full of spirit, with eyes, hands, feet and frame forever in motion,
looking as if it would be a feat to him to sit for three minutes
quiet in his chair. I am no great observer of proportions, but he
seemed to me to be a neat-made little fellow, tidily buttoned up,
young as fifteen at heart, though with hair that reminded me of
the 'Alps in the sunset'; not handsome perhaps, but something
in the whole cut of him that pleased me: finished as an actor but
without an actor's affectation; easy as a gentleman, but without

some gentleman's formality; in a word we found him a hospitable, warm hearted Irishman, as pleasant as could be himself, and
disposed to make others so. And is this enough? and need I tell
you that the day was spent delightfully, chiefly in listening to his
innumerable jests, and admirable and beautiful similes—beautiful and original as those he throws into his songs, and anecdotes
that would make the Danes laugh—and how we did all we
could, I believe to get him to stand for Limerick; and how we
called again, the day after, and walked with him about his little
garden; and how he told us that he always wrote walking, and
how we came in again and took luncheon and how he walked
with us through the fields and wished us 'good-bye', and left us
to do as well as we could without him."

II

Of all the great houses where Moore was a welcome guest, the
chief was Holland House. This was the most famous salon of the
age. Everyone of note was invited there, and all were glad to go.
The host and hostess were in violent contrast. Lord Holland, who
was six years Moore's senior, was a figure of no particular distinction until he ran away with a wealthy woman who was
already married, and made her Lady Holland as soon as the law
allowed. Quiet, easy-going, and tolerant, he was driven into
public life by his wife, who was by no means content to sit still
and enjoy her title. Holland was an ineffective speaker, and a
martyr to gout, but, subject to those handicaps, he did all that
an enlightened and humane Whig could to champion the
underdog wherever he found him. In the England of the early
eighteen-hundreds, he did not have to look far.

What suited his temperament best was to play the host in his
own house, where he made all welcome with unfailing tact and
charm: qualities which were often needed to offset his wife's lack
of them. "Lack" is too weak a word. There was nothing merely

negative or privative about Lady Holland. Imperious and violent, liable at any moment to plunge from one extreme of emotion to the other, she bullied and cajoled and flattered and insulted her guests till they did not know whether they were on their head or their heels. They submitted, for they all liked her. She had ready sympathies, she commanded affection, and, insupportable though she could be at times, she treated all alike.

A second pacifying influence was that of Miss Fox, Lord Hollands' sister, known to all the intimates of the family as "Aunty". To her lot it fell regularly to soothe the feelings ruffled or outraged by Lady Holland. "True to her angelic mission," says Princess Liechtenstein, who was an habituée of Holland House in her youth, "she brought gladness and shed peace; her understanding was a safe guide for the perplexed." She was "a woman in the best sense of the word".

Moore seldom seems to have come in for the rough side of Lady Holland's tongue. It is true that his pleasure in being an intimate of the house would persuade him to put up with a good deal, but he writes always kindly of her. Once at least, however, she caught him up short. He was dilating at dinner on his proposed life of Sheridan, when she turned upon him.

"This will be a dull book of yours, this *Sheridan*, I fear," she observed.

Moore tried to defend his work, but with poor success. Still, he was an undoubted favourite, and had somehow found the way to handle her ladyship. Probably he took a leaf from Sidney Smith's book, and showed her his independent side. Smith paid no attention to her tantrums, answered her back when she was in a rage, and even laughed at her—all with impunity. Moore could not have gone this far: it was not in his temperament: but the frequency with which he was invited, and Lady Holland's constant care and kindness for him, show that, in his own way, he succeeded.

Only once does he give signs of discomposure and resentment. There lived at Holland House, in continual attendance upon Lord and Lady Holland, a physician by the name of John Allen. It was part of his duty to be the butt of Lady Holland's rages, and she ordered him about in the most outrageous manner. One evening, when she and Allen and a number of others, including Smith, Moore, and Macaulay, were at Rogers's house, Lady Holland flew into a violent passion. Smith, enjoying himself hugely, jeered at her, to the open delight of the company. To their amazement, the physician flared up in her defence. When both had left, the rest began to discuss this portent, Rogers opining that Allen's outburst did him great credit. Moore would not have it. Allen, he said, was a mere slave. His rage was not on Lady Holland's behalf, but on his own. He could not bear the contrast between his servility and their independence. The barb of her tongue had evidently struck home, for Moore was never bitter unless provoked.

Provoked or not, he loved Holland House, where he could meet everybody, talk and listen at his ease, and where he was always welcome. Once, as he came in, he met a distinguished and disgruntled guest putting on his coat in the hall. Lady Holland had sent him away to make room for others. Moore was never so treated. He dined there some hundreds of times, and this, with Rogers's house, was his happiest haunt in London.

The company was astonishingly varied. John Wishaw, writing in November 1815, says

"It is time to say something of my late visit to Holland House, which was a curious moving scene of all nations and languages. Our parties consisted of Bessboroughs and Lord Erskine (*without his star*) [insignia of Thistle], Spaniards of various parties (all of them banished or proscribed), a very intelligent deputy from Buenos Ayres, Rogers and the Romillys just arrived from the Continent, and latterly the great sculptor Canova, and his brother, an Italian Abbate and *savant*. I must not omit Miss Fox and Miss Vernon, who were very generally of our parties and great additions to them. By far the most interesting in the group was Canova. . . ."

"Holland House," wrote Princess Leichtenstein, "was among houses what England is among nations—a common ground, where all opinions could freely breathe . . . from 1799 till 1840 there was hardly in England a distinguished man in politics, science, or literature who had not been a guest at Holland House . . ."

Moore did not appear there till after his return from Bermuda, but he continued to be a guest after 1840. Of his compatriots, Sheridan had been a guest before him, as had Grattan, who "looked upon office as slavery" and "was so full of true courtesy that he made a point even of returning the bow of a child"; Lord Moira, "whose fluent speaking Curran called 'airing his vocabulary' "; and Curran himself, "the embodiment of Irish wit and humour". Others from a long list furnished by Lady Holland to Sir James Mackintosh are Charles James Fox ("of course"), Wishaw, "whose sense made his opinion valuable to have and also difficult to obtain", Macaulay, Sir Philip Francis, Blanco White, George Ellis, "Monk" Lewis, Lord Jeffrey, Thurlow, Eldon, Brougham, Lyndhurst, Sir Humphrey Davy, the Duke of Richmond, Washington Irving, Talleyrand, the Duke of Clarence, the Duc d'Orléans, the Duc de Montpensier, Prince Jules de Polignac, Prince Bariatinsky, the Duchess of Devonshire, Madame de Staël, Metternich, Bannister, and Kemble. Rogers and Sydney Smith were almost counted as belonging to the family.

In such company did Moore find himself at home.

III

Moore's popularity—and accessibility—brought him an enormous "fan-mail". Bad poems ("poets and authors are the pest of my life"), invitations from strangers, declarations of love, begging letters, requests for lectures—all the miscellaneous by-products of success deluged him, as they deluge the successful to-day. Many of these letters he kept, annotating them sometimes in his own hand.

They read amusingly, sometimes pathetically. A lady, alleging that she was an old friend of his, quotes some lines from his "Go where glory waits thee", and ends with the cryptic invitation, "Who can this be? you will say. Come and see." We are not told whether the invitation was accepted.

Another lady's experience was obviously unfortunate.

Dear Mr Moore,

It was me you saw at the Opera last night. I was dying to speak to you. I made so many faces to entice you to come that I was quite mortified. I shall never forgive you for throwing me over unless you promise to come and lunch with me at Wimbledon some day next week——

At present I cannot exactly name the day, but I will let you know——

Yours truly,

I. S. L.

Whatever the rights of it were, Moore kept her letter, as he did the next.

Respected friend

Thomas Moore:

How seldom do persons in a "mediocre" station address those whose names are engraved on the brow of Fame, and yet, in me behold one who attempts it, and to one with whom I am acquainted merely through the medium of his writings.

Nothing would induce me to write to thee with my present intent, if it were not for a slight link that exists between us; thou art a countryman of mine, a native of my own sweet Erin, and this it is that emboldens me to ask a favor of thee, which I trust to thy kindness to grant me. I pray thee keep in mind that I am a member of the Society of Friends, and my style appears, I doubt not, somewhat singular to a person accustomed to the manners of the world, but I am *sincere*, and thy name traced in thy own hand would indeed be a treasure to me, if thou wouldst be so very kind as to send it to me. I almost fear thus to trespass on thy goodnature, but I do hope thou wilt pardon me; I trust implicitly to thy goodness.

I remain thy sincere and admiring friend

I. H.

There is a pleasant touch about the following, which all who have examined old letters with bewilderment will recognize.

I have this day my dear Mr Moore received your Letter. I communicated it to the King.

Inserting a note if possible in the 2nd Edition will be the best, if not, in the 3rd. a Letter in the Times it is not thought necessary to do.

Many thanks for your exactitude

Yrs sinc^y
CHABOT.

On this Moore has written, "Query—the particulars connected with this?"

A great many correspondents wrote in verse. One Henrietta Batten, of Williamstown Cottage, unbosomed herself at some length, ending with the appeal:

From the exile of Erin the melodies roll,
Oh there dearest Romeo give sense to each sound,
And in measures as rich as the soil of thy soul
Let the friend we so loved and so valued be found.

A further epistle from the same lady, very warm and proper, averred

Yes I will guard with exemplary care
The glowing wreath which Romeo bids me wear . . .

She evidently had a useful brogue, but her use of "Romeo" may not be quite as romantic as it sounds. Left to ourselves, we should imagine it to be the lady's ardent fancy. Another letter, recently unearthed, suggests that she had no monopoly in it. Addressed to Mrs Moore, it comes from a Captain F. Romeo, of 92 Abbey Street, Dublin, and is dated July 31st 1819.

"MADAM—

A tribute of respect to the acknowledged and highly admired talents of your illustrious Son, as well as a Similarity of the Letters constituting his and my Name, inspired me some italian verses on his account . . ."

Evidently the Captain's letter got around, and Moore derived his nickname from the anagram.

Oddly enough, the name had been used before, and by Moore himself. When, as a boy, he had exchanged verses with old Miss Hannah Byrne, she had been "Zelia" and he had been "Romeo" —"the anagram", he notes, "of Moore".

The begging letters were often in verse too.

> I pray great Moore you'll lend an ear
> The sufferings of Macraith to hear . . .

As "great Moore" kept the verses, we may presume that he helped the sufferer.

Among the gifts sent him by his admirers was a portrait of himself in wax, which came from a namesake who lived in Tottenham. He was asked his opinion on numberless bad verses, and replied as a rule kindly but truthfully, as when he advised a Dublin grocer's apprentice to stick to the trade that brought him his bread and butter. He received translations of his work into various languages. One, beginning

> Ella e lungi dal suolo ove dorme il suo prode . . .

sent him by one L. Marriott, of Down Street, is endorsed by Moore, "Translation of my song 'She is far from the Land' sent to me with only the signature."

And so the story goes on, uncovering bygone lives and anxieties, and showing how little things have changed.

IV

What Moore lacks in visual description—as Mr Priestley has said, he starves our visual sense—we are happily able to remedy from the eyes of others. There were amongst his contemporaries several who had very sharp eyes indeed, and, owing to his prominence, their eyes were often turned on him. Here are two portraits, one general, the other particular. The first comes from the pen of Leigh Hunt:

"I thought Thomas Moore, when I first knew him, as delightful a person as one could imagine. He could not help being an interesting one: and his sort of talent has this advantage in it, that being of a description intelligible to all, the possessor is equally sure of present and future fame. I never received a visit from him but I felt as if I had been talking with Prior or Sir Charles Sedley. His acquaintance with Lord Byron began by talking of a duel. With me it commenced in as gallant a way, though of a different sort. I had cut up an Opera of his (The Blue Stocking), as unworthy of so great a wit. He came to see me, saying I was very much in the right, and an intercourse took place, which I might have enjoyed to this day, had he valued his real fame as much as I did.

"Mr Moore was lively, polite, bustling, full of amenities and acquiescences, into which he contrived to throw a sort of roughening of cordiality, like the crust of old port. It seemed a happiness to him to say 'yes'. There was just enough of the Irishman in him to flavour his speech and manner. He was a little particular, perhaps, in his orthoepy, but not more so than became a poet; and he appeared to me the last man in the world to cut his country, even for the sake of high life. As to his person, all the world knows that he is as little of stature, as he is great in wit. It is said that an illustrious personage, in a fit of playfulness, once threatened to put him into a wine-cooler; a proposition which Mr Moore took to be more royal than polite. A Spanish gentleman, whom I met on the Continent, and who knew him well, said, in his energetic English, which he spoke none the worse for a wrong vowel or so: 'Now there's Mooerr, Thomas Mooerr: I look upon Mooerr as an active little man.' This is true. He reminds us of those active little great men who abound so remarkably in Clarendon's history. Like them, he would have made an excellent practical partisan, and it would have done him good. Horseback, and a little Irish fighting, would have seen fair play with his good living, and kept his look as juvenile as his spirit. His forehead is long and full of character, with 'bumps' of wit, large and radiant, enough to transport a phrenologist. His eyes are dark and fine, as you would wish to see under a set of vine-leaves: his mouth generous and good-humoured, with dimples; his nose sensual, prominent, and at the same time the reverse of aquiline. There is a very peculiar character in it, as if it were looking forward, and scenting a feast or an orchard. The face, upon the whole, is Irish, not unruffled with care and passion: but festivity is the predominant expression. When Mr Moore was a child, he is said to have been eminently handsome, a Cupid for a picture; and notwithstanding the tricks which both joy and sorrow have played with his face, you can fancy as much. It was a recollection perhaps, to this effect, that induced his friend, Mr Atkinson, to say one afternoon, in defending him from the charge of libertinism, 'Sir, they may talk of Moore as they please; but I tell you what,—I always consider him' (and this argument he thought conclusive), 'I always consider my friend Thomas Moore as an infant sporting on the bosom of Venus.' There was no contesting this; and, in truth, the hearers were very little disposed to contest it, Mr Atkinson having hit upon a defence which was more logical in spirit than chrono-logical in image. When conscience comes, a man's impulses must

SLOPERTON COTTAGE
From a sketch in the National Gallery, Dublin

take thought; but, till then, poetry is only the eloquent and irresistible development of the individual's nature; and Mr Moore's wildest verses were a great deal more innocent than could enter into the imaginations of the old libertines who thought they had a right to use them. I must not, in this portrait, leave out his music. He plays and sings with great taste on the pianoforte, and is known as a graceful composer. His voice, which is a little hoarse in speaking (at least, I used to think so) softens into a breath like that of the flute, when singing. In speaking, he is emphatic in rolling the letter R, perhaps out of a despair of being able to get rid of the national peculiarity."

The other account, by Willis, describes his appearance at dinner at Lady Blessington's.

" 'Mr Moore,' cried the footman, at the bottom of the staircase; 'Mr Moore,' cried the footman at the top: and with his glass at his eye, stumbling over an ottoman between his near-sightedness and the darkness of the room, enters the poet. Half a glance tells you he is at home on the carpet. Sliding his little feet up to Lady Blessington, he made his compliments with a gaiety and an ease combined with a kind of worshipping deference that was worthy of a prime minister at the court of love. With the gentlemen, all of whom he knew, he had a frank, merry manner of a confident favourite, and he was greeted like one. He went from one to the other, straining back his head to look up at them (for, singularly enough, every gentleman in the room was six feet high and upwards), and to every one he said something which, from any one else, would have seemed peculiarly felicitous, but which fell from his lips as if his breath was not more spontaneous.

"Nothing but a short-hand report could retain the delicacy and elegance of Moore's language, and memory itself cannot embody again the kind of frost-work of imagery which was formed and melted on his lips. His voice is soft or firm as the subject requires, but, perhaps, the word gentlemanly describes

14

it better than any other. It is upon a natural key, but, if I may so phrase it, is fused with a high-bred affectation, expressing deference and courtesy, at the same time that its pauses are constructed peculiarly to catch the ear. It would be difficult not to attend to him while he is talking, though the subject were but the shape of a wine-glass. Moore's head is distinctly before me while I write, but I shall find it difficult to describe. His hair, which curled once all over it in long tendrils, unlike anybody else's in the world, and which, probably, suggested his soubriquet of 'Bacchus', is diminished now to a few curls sprinkled with grey, and scattered in a single ring above his ears. His forehead is wrinkled, with the exception of a most prominent development of the organ of gaiety, which, singularly enough, shines with the lustre and smooth polish of a pearl, and is surrounded by a semicircle of lines drawn close about it, like intrenchments against Time. His eyes still sparkle like a champagne bubble, though the invader has drawn his pencillings about the corners: and there is a kind of wintry red, of the tinge of an October leaf, that seems enamelled on his cheek, the eloquent record of the claret his wit has brightened. His mouth is the most characteristic feature of all. The lips are delicately cut, slight and changeable as an aspen; but there is a set-up look about the lower lip— a determination of the muscle to a particular expression, and you fancy that you can almost see wit astride upon it. It is written legibly with the imprint of habitual success. It is arch, confident, and half diffident, as if he was disguising his pleasure at applause, while another bright gleam of fancy was breaking on him. The slightly-tossed nose confirms the fun of expression, and altogether it is a face that sparkles, beams, radiates.[1]

"We went up to coffee and Moore brightened again over his Chasse-café, and went glittering on with criticisms on Grisi, the delicious songstress now ravishing the world, whom he placed above all but Pasta, and whom he thought, with the exception

[1] For Moore's own comments on his appearance, see Appendix D.

that her legs were too short, an incomparable creature. This
introduced music very naturally, and with a great deal of difficulty he was taken to the piano. My letter is getting long, and
I have no time to describe his singing. It is well known, however, that its effect is only equalled by the beauty of his own
words; and, for one, I could have taken him into my heart with
delight. He makes no attempt at music. It is a kind of admirable
recitative, in which every shade of thought is syllabled and dwelt
upon, and the sentiment of the song goes through your blood,
warming you to the very eyelids, and starting your tears, if you
have a soul or sense in you. I have heard of a woman's fainting
at a song of Moore's; and if the burden of it answered by chance
to a secret in the bosom of the listener, I should think from its
comparative effect upon so old a stager as myself, that the heart
would break with it. We all sat around the piano, and after two
or three songs of Lady Blessington's choice, he rambled over the
keys awhile, and sang 'When first I met thee', with a pathos that
beggars description. When the last word had faltered out, he rose
and took Lady Blessington's hand, said good night, and was
gone before a word was uttered. For a full minute after he had
closed the door, no one spoke. I could have wished for myself to
drop silently asleep where I sat, with the tears in my eyes and the
softness upon my heart——

" 'Here's a health to thee, Tom Moore!' "

V

Once he returned from Paris, Moore resumed his *Life of
Sheridan*. It progressed slowly, and he remained, working away
at it more or less steadily, and producing a good deal besides,
until in the summer of 1823 he went over with Lord Lansdowne
to Ireland, to make a tour of the country.

Before they started, Moore went home.

"Off in the coach at six; a very pretty person of the party.

Arrived at Calne a little after five, and expected to find our new carriage (as Bessy promised) in waiting for me. Set off to walk home; met our man William on the way, who told me that the carriage could not come on account of something that was the matter with the harness. Sent him on to Calne, and walked home, which I found rather fatiguing after my sleepless night. Met by Bessy at the door, looking very ill, and her face and nose much disfigured; upon inquiry the secret came out, that on Sunday evening (the evening before last), she and Mrs Phipps and Tom drove out in the little carriage (which Bessy herself had driven two or three times before), and in going down by Sandridge Lodge the pony, from being bitten, they think, by a forest-fly, set off galloping and kicking, without any possibility of being reined in, threw them all into a ditch, ran off with the carriage to Bromham, and knocked both it and himself almost to pieces. Much shocked and mortified, though grateful to God that it had not been worse. Bessy, in protecting little Tom in her arms, came with her unlucky nose to the ground, which is much swollen, though (as Dr Headly says, who has seen it) not broken. The rest of the party escaped with some bruises. What a strange coincidence with my dream! It was a great effort for me to compass the expense of this little luxury; and such is the end of it."

The crossing was rough, as usual when Moore had to travel, and, although assiduously sucking peppermint lozenges, he felt very sick. He disembarked at Howth, and started for Dublin in a chaise, but it broke down, and he and his friend Casey finished the journey in a jaunting car. Then they dined together at Casey's house.

"Never shall forget the welcomeness of his good mutton broth, to which was added some very old port, and an excellent bottle of claret. Went afterwards in a hackney-coach to Abbey Street. Found my dearest father and mother watching for me at the window; my mother not looking so well as when I last saw her, but my father (though, of course, enfeebled by his great age) in excellent health and spirits. Sweet little Nell, too, quite well . . ."

Then came a pleasant incident.

"My mother expressing a strong wish to see Lord Lansdowne, without the fuss of a visit from him, I engaged to manage it for her. Told him that he must let me show him to two people who considered me as the greatest man in the world, and him as the next, for being my friend. Very good-naturedly allowed me to walk him past the windows, and wished to call upon them; but I thought it better thus."

From Dublin the travellers went south, staying in Kilkenny, that town of happy memories, going on to Killarney, and through Kerry. One result of this tour was *Captain Rock*, of which we shall hear more presently. These were busy years. *Fables of the Holy Alliance* appeared under a pseudonym in 1823: the ninth number of the *Irish Melodies*, the second of *Sacred Songs*, and *Captain Rock* in 1824: and the *Life of Sheridan* was completed in 1825. All this time (the engagement lasted to 1828) he was contributing regularly to *The Times*, at a salary of £400 a year. He contributed also to the *Edinburgh Review*, and was offered the joint editorship, but characteristically refused when he found that the offer was part of a scheme to oust Jeffrey.

Moore remained all these years at Sloperton, with occasional trips to London and Dublin, working hard, dallying with politics, sure always of a welcome at Holland House, his position secure, his powers at full maturity. In 1831, he made, in Dublin, his first and last political speech, with immense success. It was an uneventful life, in the sense that nothing very new came into it, but it was full of incident and crowded with personalities. Moore knew everybody, and everybody knew Moore. Entry after entry in the Journal begins "Breakfasted at So and So's", with half a dozen famous names, and goes on "Dined at Such and Such's"—with half a dozen more. It was the life he loved, and the faithful Bessy, if not always by his side, was close behind him.

CHAPTER XIV

RELIGION AND POLITICS

Moore as a Catholic—His view of the Protestants—His religious sense — Politics and principles — Catholic Emancipation — *Captain Rock—Travels of an Irish Gentleman*—Invitations to stand for Parliament—The electors of Limerick—A misunderstanding — Differences with O'Connell — Moore's political importance

THE lives of most writers can be told without any detailed enquiry into their religion. Moore is an exception, for two reasons. He was a man of deep religious sense, which directly influenced his conduct, both public and private; and he has been repeatedly attacked by his own countrymen as one who deserted the faith into which he was baptized.

It is certain that he was never an ardent Catholic. He early gave up going to confession. He married a Protestant, and, instead of following the usual practice, rejoiced in the fact that this gave his children freedom of choice. He showed no liking for the official Catholic Church, though it was never treated to the unvarying hostility with which he regarded the Protestant Church of Ireland. Sydney Smith was once looking over the shoulder of a painter to whom Moore was sitting.

"Could you not contrive," he asked, "to throw into the features a little more hostility to the Establishment?"

The hostility was always breaking out, and it was usually well documented.

"To be ground down by a hard-hearted landlord was galling enough to the poor Catholic; but to have both body and spirit wasted away in thankless labour, in order to support in luxury the ministers of that religion by which his own faith was proscribed, his children tempted to turn traitors, and himself chained down in misery and bondage—this, indeed, was a refinement in misery,—a sort of complicated infliction, which, if ever the art of driving people mad should again become the study of a Christian government, deserves to be remembered among its most efficacious rules." [1]

It was a local and definite hostility, however, rather than a hostility to Protestantism as such. "We then talked", he writes in his Journal, after the death of his father, "of the difference between the two faiths; and they who accuse all Catholics of being intolerantly attached to their own would be either ashamed or surprised (according as they were sincere or not in the accusation) if they had heard the sentiments expressed both by my mother and sisters on the subject." Moore attended a Protestant church, in England, and, while he defended Catholicism against the assaults of outsiders, allowed himself the greatest freedom in criticizing it.

About his general position there is no doubt at all. He was a moral and deeply religious man, with an interest in theology which astounded those who had known him only as a musician and a wit: but he lacked the sacramental sense, and was a lukewarm Catholic, though he always professed the faith and showed no inclination to change it. "They take you for a Catholic," exclaimed Lord Lansdowne, of an article which Moore had written in a magazine: to which Moore replied, "They had but too much right to do so." When his sister Kate thought of turning Protestant, he advised her against the change, and she took his advice. For himself, he proclaimed, "I was born and bred in the faith of my fathers, and in that faith I intend to die."

That he died in it, we have the reported evidence of the Vicar of Bromham, who told an enquirer (Dr Ambrose) that Moore was visited shortly before his death by a priest. The priest, so the Vicar understood, administered to him the last rites of the

[1] From *Captain Rock*.

Church. There is no reason to doubt this, but the Vicar's value as a witness is a little discounted by his statement that Moore never attended service at Bromham.

". . . He used to come to the door with his wife—who was a member of my congregation—and the boys, and then depart."

Doubtless he often did: but he sometimes went inside, and commented afterwards on the sermon.

That his religious sense was deep and genuine is proved by a hundred entries in the Journal, and by the testimony of almost all who knew him. Niagara, as we have seen, moved him to wonder at the power of God. His first act after Bessy's safe delivery was to fall on his knees and give thanks. He prayed for her continually: "Found my darling Bess a little better; but the state of her health gives me many a sad moment. Great God! spare her to me." Any act of kindness, anything which really touched his heart, moved him to thanksgiving. Goethe's *Faust* stirred him in the same way:

"I, before I went to bed, experienced one of those bursts of devotion which, perhaps, are worth all the church-going in the world. Tears came fast from me as I knelt down to adore the only God whom I acknowledge, and poured forth the aspirations of a soul deeply grateful for all his goodness."

He believed in the immortality of the soul. "Whatever may be thought," he writes, in his *Life of Sheridan*, "of particular faiths and sects, a belief in a life beyond this world is the only thing that pierces through the wall of our prison house, and lets hope shine in upon a scene that would otherwise be bewildered and desolate." And, writing to Byron about *Cain*, he reminds him that, while "particular sects and creeds are fair game enough . . . our faith in the Future is a treasure not lightly to be parted with". Shelley, in a tribute to "the character, no less than the genius" of Moore, exempts the "pure doctrines" of his theism from his general condemnation of Christian worship.

Those who wish to go more fully into the matter should

consult Professor W. F. P. Stockley's *Essays in Modern Biography*,
where the question of Moore's religion is thrashed out with great
care and scholarship. The general reader may be satisfied with
the conclusion that he was a Liberal Christian, typical of his
time: that, while his religion was largely emotional, and coloured
by his sensibilities as an artist,[1] he had a respect for theology:
that he was no sectarian: and that he did his best to put his
religion into practice, and do good to his neighbour.

II

The essential point about Moore as a politician is that to him
politics and principle were one and the same thing. As soon as a
party, from expediency or mere laziness, seemed to be forgetting
the principles which had led him to join it, Moore abruptly
withdrew his allegiance: and he was obstinate to the point of
folly, refusing to recognize even reasonable compromise,
wherever he felt his principles were involved.

This characteristic was well known to his friends, and they set
themselves at different times to combat or to modify it. A letter
from Mary Godfrey, written after the disappointment of his
hopes about Lord Moira, puts the whole point clearly:

"And, my dear Moore, as to your political opinions, it was
very fine to indulge in them and act up to them while there was
a distant perspective in so doing of fame or emolument, and at
the same time a feeling that the triumph of such opinions, and
the success of the party you belonged to, might be conducive to
the prosperity of your country. But now when those opinions

---

[1] *Cf.* of hearing Mass at the Church of the Annunziata in Florence:
"Whether it be my popish blood or my poetic feelings, nothing gives me
more delight than the 'pomp and circumstance' of a mass in so grand a church,
accompanied by fine music and surrounded by such statuary and such paint-
ings: it is a most elevating spectacle." And, elsewhere, of a service in Warwick
Chapel, "Music is the true interpreter of religious feelings: nothing written
or spoken is equal to it."

have less and less influence, and that party less and less consideration,—when your family is increasing, and your wants of course
increasing with it,—don't you think prudence should have its
turn? Would not your love for your wife, and anxiety for the
welfare of your children, reconcile you to some little sacrifice of
political opinions? I have a great deal of good reasoning upon
this subject in my own mind for you, but there it must remain
at present, lest I should tire you without convincing you. I wish
we could see you and talk the matter over with you; I should not
then despair of sending you back a complete rat. The time of
Roman virtue, if such a thing ever existed, is gone by; and why
will you remain bolt upright, talking of systems and opinions to
people who are only thinking of places and pensions, and only
trying to get into power that they may have the full enjoyment
of them? Get into place and power whenever you can, and
tell a plausible story how a sudden light from heaven shone
upon you and convinced you. Your wife and children will be
all the better for it, and yourself and your country not a bit the
worse."

This is of the greatest interest. Mary Godfrey, as we have
already seen, was not one to flatter. She was always outspoken
in her criticisms, and did not at all view her correspondent
through rose-coloured spectacles. Her testimony that, at this
early age, he struck his friends as almost quixotically faithful to
his principles is an important piece of evidence, and one which
Moore's detractors—Mr James Joyce makes a character in his
Portrait of the Artist as a Young Man call him "servile"—have been
wise to ignore.

Indeed, unless it be intended to characterize his first pleasure in
the Prince's patronage, it is the last adjective for which there is
any justification. At real risk to his prospects, Moore attacked the
Prince and the Government after their failure to do anything for
the Irish Catholics. He refused a very tempting offer from *The
Times* to write leaders, in order to keep a free hand. Accepting its

subsequent offer of £400 a year to write political satire, he broke off at once when its attitude towards Ireland became unfriendly. It is fair to say that self-interest never deterred him from saying or doing what he thought right, nor impelled him to do or say what he thought wrong.

The political project nearest to Moore's heart was always Catholic Emancipation. It cemented his attachment to Lord Moira. As soon as he saw that the Prince would do nothing for the Catholics, it turned him dead against the Prince. When he went to Ireland in 1818, Lady Donegal, afraid that it would lead him into trouble, warned him against associating with "the Irish democrats". She need not have bothered. Moore could cherish a principle and detest its exponents. As early as 1807, he wrote to his mother:

"Dublin is again, I find, or rather *still*, the seat of wrangle and illiberal contention. The Roman Catholics deserve very little, and even if they merited all that they ask, I cannot see how it is in the nature of things they should get it. They have done much towards the ruin of Ireland, and have been so well assisted by the Protestants throughout, that, between them, Ireland is at this instant as *ruined* as it need be."

About the possibility of their "getting it" he was to modify his opinion. *The Twopenny Postbag*, which first appeared in 1813 under the pseudonym of "Thomas Brown the younger", was largely devoted to mockery of those who opposed Catholic Emancipation; but he continued for a long time to think poorly of his co-religionists (and, needless to say, even worse of the Protestants). ". . . As for the Catholics . . . one would heartily wish them all in their own Purgatory, if it were not for their adversaries, whom one wishes *still further*." "I love Ireland," he told Isaac Corry, "but I hate Dublin": and its inhabitants he elsewhere denounced as a "low, illiberal, puddle-headed, and gross-hearted herd"—obloquies which poets of a subsequent generation have echoed but not bettered.

Thus he was able to reply to Lady Donegal in terms which must have reassured her:

"If there is anything in the world that I have been detesting and despising more than another for this long time past, it has been those very Dublin politicians whom you so fear I should associate with. I do not think a good cause was ever ruined by a more bigoted, brawling, and disgusting set of demagogues; and, though it be the religion of my fathers, I must say that much of this vile, vulgar spirit is to be traced to that wretched faith, which is again polluting Europe with Jesuitism and Inquisitions, and which of all the humbugs that have stultified mankind is the most narrow-minded and mischievous; so much for the danger of my joining Messrs O'Connel, O'Donnel, etc."

This is vigorous enough, and seems on the face of it good grounds for those who charge Moore with desertion of his religion and his country. But he was too clear-headed to confuse the merits of a case with the demerits of its advocates. There was too, it must be admitted, more than sheer aesthetic and moral disapprobation behind his abuse of Dublin and its citizens. His views were undoubtedly coloured by the fact that the city had taken no notice of him to compare with his renown in England. When, in 1818, he went over and was everywhere entertained, his demeanour warmed at once. All the same, it is only fair to record that, whatever views he expressed to his friends, during the time of his neglect by his own countrymen he remained a staunch advocate of the Irish cause, though less effective than he might have been, through having lost touch with what was going on in Irish minds. After 1818, his support became more ardent and more practical, and *The Memoirs of Captain Rock*, written in 1823 after a tour of the country with Lord Lansdowne, was of real help to the cause of Catholic Emancipation.

There was real feeling behind it. Moore had been shocked and angered by the sights he saw on his tour.

"I wrote a pamphlet," he tells Murray, "on my return from

Ireland, to get rid of the bile that was (in Lord Melville's phrase) rolling on my stomach. It will not, however, be printed (if at all) till the meeting of Parliament." [1]

The plain fact is that Moore's relations with his country run side by side with his development as a man. The first fire of patriotism touched him at the dinner when he sat on Napper Tandy's knee. Friendship with Emmet blew up the flame, but for many years—the years that produced the best of the *Melodies*—Moore's love of Ireland was romantic and idealized. It was genuine, and deep-rooted, or the *Melodies* could never have been what they were. He testified to it by many acts of courage and disregard of self, but it remained an ideal, and one which ("Rich and rare were the gems she wore") he was capable of translating into sentimental absurdity. Then, after 1818, as, maturer and wiser, he came into touch with the facts of Irish life, his patriotism took a practical turn, and he was willingly drawn into Irish politics. From this point, it is pertinent to remark, the *Melodies* declined in quality. The old mood had gone. The fanciful figures no longer satisfied his imagination. He worked at them with a dwindling conviction. It was not that he loved Ireland less or better, but that he could no longer express his love in the old way. So, history and irony took the place of romantic lyrics, and he wrote *Captain Rock*.

"Our Irish rulers have always proceeded in proselytism on the principle of a wedge with its wrong side foremost . . . The courteous address of Lancelot to the young Jewess, 'Be of good cheer, for truly I think thou art damned,' seems to have been the model on which the Protestant Church has founded all its conciliatory advances to Catholics."

Captain Rock, which had a great success in Ireland, and made even the maligned Catholics see in Moore a champion of the Irish cause, was followed by a *Life of Lord Edward Fitzgerald*. This Moore undertook instead of the far more profitable life

[1] It appeared in 1824.

of Canning which had been suggested to him. To tackle Fitzgerald was dangerous both to his pocket and to his popularity,
but Moore was anxious at all costs to serve his country,
reserving to himself always the right to choose his methods. *The
Travels of an Irish Gentleman in Search of a Religion*, which
followed, was, it is true, hardly likely to commend itself to the
Irish public at large, being a somewhat left-handed vindication of
Catholic against Protestant, composed, like Mr W. B. Yeats'
senatorial speech on divorce, to give offence rather than to
persuade.

The *Travels* is an ironic work, written in the form of an autobiography. The "Gentleman", on the passing of the Catholic
Emancipation Bill, finds himself no longer tempted by self-
interest to turn Protestant, and no longer constrained by self-
respect to remain a Catholic.

"It was on the evening of the 16th day of April, 1829—the
very day on which the memorable news reached Dublin of the
Royal Assent having been given to the Catholic Relief Bill—
that, as I was sitting alone in my chambers, up two pair of stairs
in Trinity College, being myself one of the everlasting 'Seven
Millions' thus liberated, I started suddenly, after a few moments'
reverie, from my chair, and taking a stride across the room, as
if to make trial of a pair of emancipated legs, exclaimed, 'Thank
God! I may now, if I like, turn Protestant.'"

The operative words were "if I like". Moore was at some
pains to make it clear that the "Gentleman" and he were not
necessarily one and the same man, and that, in expressing gratitude for the opportunity to choose a faith, he is not disparaging
Catholicism.

"My views concerning the superiority of the Roman Catholic
Religion over the Protestant in point of antiquity, authority, and
consistency, agree with those of my hero, and I was induced to
put them so strongly on record from the disgust which I feel, and
have ever felt, at the arrogance with which most Protestant

parsons assume to themselves and their fellows the credit of being
the only true Christians, and the insolence with which weekly
from their pulpits they denounce all Catholics as idolaters and
anti-Christ."

This work greatly increased Moore's reputation in Ireland,
and he was invited to stand for no fewer than three constitu-
encies, Limerick, Carlow, and Dublin University. The invitation
for Carlow was tentative and rather lukewarm, and he can have
had no difficulty in declining it, though he was sufficiently
pleased to file it, with a note in his own handwriting, among his
papers. He refused Limerick, on the ground that he could not
afford to stand. The invitation to represent the University
originated, surprisingly enough, with the Viceroy, Lord
Anglesey. Moore bristled at once. The Government were trying
to get at him, were they? He sat down, and wrote an explicit
refusal, saying that as long as Ireland continued to be governed
in the manner the Government saw fit to use, he could never
allow his name, "however humble", to be coupled with theirs.
More servility!

III

Meanwhile, the electors of Limerick had returned to the
charge. Negotiations were conducted by William Griffin,
brother of Gerald, who wrote *The Collegians*, and they make
interesting reading. Moore had pleaded poverty, and stated, in
very guarded terms, his dislike of Repeal. Griffin replied as
follows:

LIMERICK, 48 GEORGE ST.
October 11 1832.

DEAR SIR,

I was much gratified on receiving your very candid reply to
my late letter and can fully appreciate the difficulties which you
seem to think preclude the possibility of your accepting a seat in

Parliament. I believe however, I only give expression to the feeling of thousands in Ireland in saying it is the interest and desire of the country that no such difficulties should remain, and I have too great reliance on your zeal for her welfare, to imagine any others can eventually occur to you. It should be melancholy indeed, if a nation like ours, could not place in Parliament those most likely to advocate her interests with ability, and still more so, that one who would do her most honor and service should refuse the advocacy.

Under these circumstances, you will not be I hope surprised at the measures taken by the Political Union here yesterday, which are given in the newspaper accompanying this letter.

The "measures" were, first, to relieve Moore of possible embarrassment by keeping him in ignorance of the Local Repealers' plans until he should be their representative, and second, to overcome the monetary difficulty by presenting him with estate worth £400 a year. At this point Moore evidently havered a little. Probably he was flattered, and could not make up his mind to refuse such an offer out of hand. At any rate, Griffin expressed much satisfaction at his reply. A week later, he was becoming impatient.

48 GEORGE ST., LIMERICK.
Nov. 3rd 1832

MY DEAR SIR,

It is very unfortunate that your distance from us precludes the possibility of your understanding the state of political feeling here,—if it was distinctly before you I am quite assured, there could not be a moment's hesitation on your part in acceding to our desires.

Then, crossing his, Moore wrote a letter which plunged the unfortunate man into great consternation. Griffin wrote off at once in the heat of it.

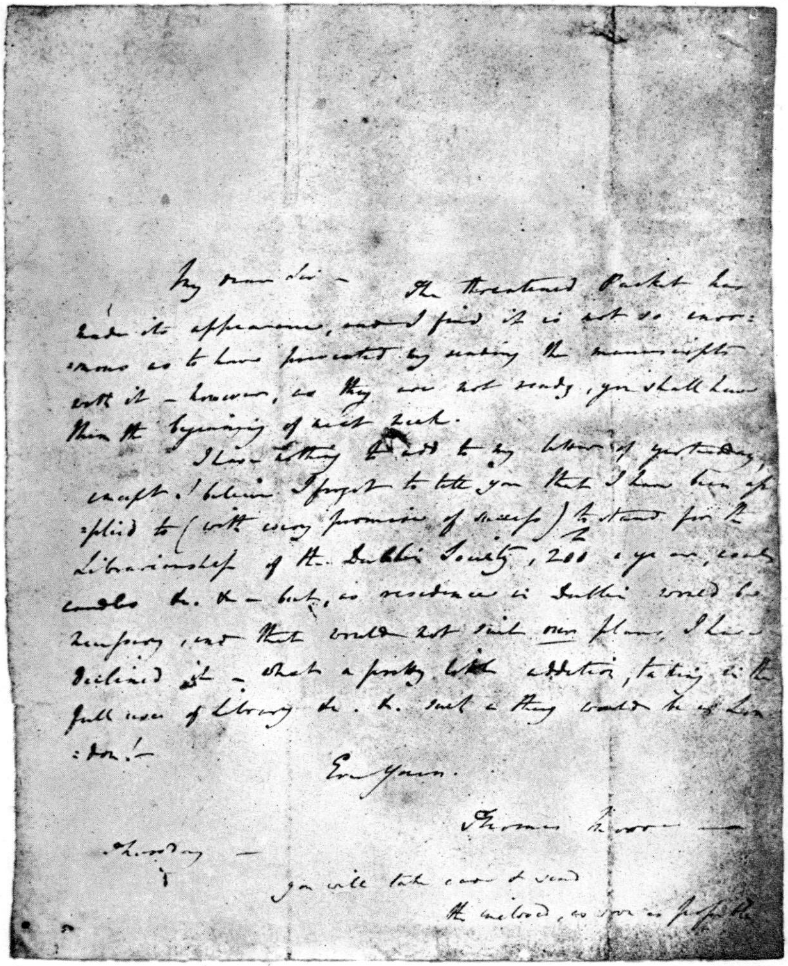
My dear Sir — The threatened Packet has made its appearance, and I find it is not so enormous as to have prevented my sending the manuscripts with it — however, as they are not ready, you shall have them the beginning of next week.

I have nothing to add to my letter of yesterday, except I believe I forgot to tell you that I have been applied to (with every promise of success) to stand for the Librarianship of the Dublin Society, 200 a year, coals, candles &c. &c — but, as residence in Dublin would be necessary, and that would not suit our plans, I have declined it — what a pretty little addition, taking in the full use of Library &c. &c. such a thing would be in London! —

Ever Yours.

Thomas Moore —

Thursday —

you will take care & send the enclosed, as soon as possible

THOMAS MOORE
A facsimile letter

LIMERICK, 48 GEORGE ST.,
Nov. 5th.

MY DEAR SIR,

Your letter of Novemb^r 1st which only arrived to-night has found me in the greatest state of uneasiness and perplexity. I never interfered in the politics of this city before and professionally it was little calculated to serve me to do so now. I was however tempted by your name, and by a letter accidentally falling into my hands in which an acquaintance of yours stated that he was authorized to say you would stand for the representation of Limerick if publicly invited. A subsequent letter from you to that gentleman still countenanced the idea and was in many respects such a one, as would lead us to imagine you could have little hesitation in accepting the offer of any body of electors who were on your side in politics. In your first letter to me, declining a proposal, which though caught up warmly here, originated in the suggestion of your London friend, you expressed the strongest desire to advocate the interests of your country in Parliament, to which you seemed to see but one great obstacle. This we undertook to remove and the manner in which it was proposed to be done was explicitly stated. Your reply was one of, as you say, general expressions of gratitude and of devotion to the people of Ireland, but placed as this last sentiment was in the letter, it seemed to us to mean nothing if it was not an earnest of your future exertions in Parliament and of your thorough sympathy with the feelings of the people. Besides this, there was, after all that had gone before, not one word to arrest the measures which necessarily committed us here to the electors of the city. How my dear Sir could you possibly imagine we would look upon your letter otherwise than as an approval or acceptance. A formal answer was certainly not then expected to the proposal—all we asked or hoped for was an understanding that the object in view and the means were agreeable to you, before we committed ourselves to the public—that in short when the

15

time arrived for sending you a public invitation there could be no danger of your disappointing the city. I can fully comprehend how readily the nature of your feelings at the moment might prevent your considering all the consequences of what we must now regard as so undecided a letter. It has not the less involved us with the electors—Your name has stood in the way of private friendship and private interest, and in the way of other candidates with strong claims for whom many were anxious—We shall not be you may judge readily forgiven for all this. It is however useless now to regret what cannot be remedied—My two brothers left this at 7 o'clock this morning to wait on you with a public requisition from the city—In your refusal, (if it is to be such) I have only to intreat you will so word it as to protect us from the charge of having led the electors astray or relieve us in any other way you please—I did not impress the necessity of this [on m]y brothers at their departure because I really thought [it wa]s merely necessary that they should explain the state of the city and the certainty of your return to induce you to meet the wishes of the electors—

In concluding a correspondence with the hopes of which many pleasing dreams for my country were associated, allow me to assure you, that I feel the present disappointment, not as personally annoying to us but as a national misfortune.

Yours dear Sir,
Very truly
WILLIAM GRIFFIN

A mere admission that you were undecided at first, or that you thought you could have accepted the proposal would in some sort relieve us—no names should be given.

At this point O'Connell himself took a hand. He was exceedingly anxious to secure Moore's candidature, and Gerald Griffin came over to Sloperton in order personally to urge Moore to accept. The next letter from William Griffin is full of apologies, and the whole business concluded amicably, Moore informing the electors that, while he would rather be the people's servant than the Government's, he preferred to devote himself, in his own way, "to that cause which has always been uppermost in my heart, which was my first inspiration, and shall be my last—the cause of Irish freedom".

There is no reason to doubt his sincerity, but other factors, of which he was perhaps hardly conscious, may have contributed to his decision. This all took place in 1832, when he was at an age at which he might easily find good reasons for declining to embark on something new. Yet the refusal produced no such impression on his contemporaries, and they congratulated him upon his independence.

Moore was no believer in Repeal, and must have seen that he would be both embarrassed and useless in a party committed to it. He did not like O'Connell, and probably did not relish the idea of serving under him. It was better to go on, expressing his patriotism in his own way: and his own way was singularly effective.

A couple of years afterwards, he had an open breach with O'Connell, whom he accused of making himself a dictator. O'Connell had taken exception to a lyric in the final number of the *Melodies*.

THE DREAM OF THOSE DAYS

The dream of those days when first I sung thee is o'er,
Thy triumph hath stain'd the charm thy sorrows then wore;
And ev'n of the light which Hope once shed o'er thy chains,
Alas, not a gleam to grace thy freedom remains.
Say, is it that slavery sunk so deep in thy heart,
That still the dark brand is there, though chainless thou art;
And Freedom's sweet fruit, for which thy spirit long burn'd,
Now, reaching at last thy lip, to ashes hath turn'd?
Up Liberty's steep by Truth and Eloquence led,
With eyes on her temple fix'd, how proud was thy tread!
Ah, better thou ne'er had'st liv'd that summit to gain,
Or died in the porch, than thus dishonour the fane.

Moore refused to withdraw or "alleviate" a word of it. He persisted that O'Connell's policy was calculated to lead to an abuse of power. He called him "the mighty unit of a legion of ciphers", and wrote in his Journal that he felt compelled to record "in the only work of mine likely to reach after-times" his dislike of the spirit and manner in which the cause nearest his heart was being conducted. O'Connell retorted that Moore had made patriotism an article of the toilet, and relations between the pair were severed. Two years passed before they were personally reconciled: but the difference remained.

IV

As a political thinker, Moore was unimportant. He had a constitutional abhorrence of violence, which kept him out of the Young Ireland party, and made him intolerant of armed revolution in every form. He was all for persuasion and reform by constitutional means. His one instance of real acumen was his perception that Repeal must ultimately mean separation from Britain, for which he maintained that Ireland would not be ready for very many years. He erred, however, in supposing that it must follow immediately on Repeal. In general, he was, as one would expect from his temperament, a humane Whig, all for religious freedom and the rights of small nations: but that did not prevent him from disapproving heartily of individual Whig governments, even when friends like Lord Lansdowne and Lord John Russell were in power. Some of this disapproval may have been due to the fact that, until late in his life, the Whigs failed to reward him for his services. Much of it was certainly due to the Irish Coercion Act. An attack on Ireland would have turned Moore against the Archangel Gabriel. But, except where Ireland and Catholic Emancipation were concerned, Moore did not feel strongly enough about politics to exclude personal considerations from his thoughts about them.

He refused to write the life of Canning, because it would mean criticizing Lord Grey, who had been kind to him. Anyone could purchase immunity from Moore's pen by a deed of personal friendliness.

This characteristic robbed his political satire of its barb. He could not hate sufficiently to wound. Except for Castlereagh, whom he regarded not only as an enemy of Ireland but as a renegade, he was never pitiless. His satire as a whole was good humoured: as Mr Stephen Gwynn has said, no one was much the better or the worse for it. "No one could be hurt", wrote the *Standard*, "by libels so witty as those of Mr Moore." The Prince, after Moore turned upon him, was not in the least disconcerted, but quoted a satiric couplet to Scott with evident satisfaction.

As he grew older, Moore's political thought did not mature. The Act of Emancipation marked the end of his practical interest in politics. The last number of the *Melodies* and his bickerings with O'Connell were the expressions of personal taste rather than of political conviction. Once Emancipation was a fact, Moore's political mainspring was broken. The following, from a letter to Murray, dated April 17th, 1829, is both explicit and prophetic:

"How peaceable you all are in town after this destructive Bill! I little thought I should live to see the *end* of my politics—but so it is—the Duke has had the merit of exorcising the Devil of rebellion out of me and I am now (at your service) as loyal and well-behaved an author as you could desire. In this feeling, too, I rather think I am the representative of the great mass (or rather mass-*goers*) of my countrymen. All we wanted was fair treatment, and God forgive you and your Quarterly Reviewer who so long grudged it to us."

Moore's pronouncements and forecasts about himself were not always accurate: for instance, early in 1819, he was declaring, stung by a criticism,

". . . I have cut out all that kind of thing, and mean (seriously)

never to attempt another line of humour or satire in my life—
for to have such rackety things laid at one's door is too bad . . ."
but, on this occasion, he spoke truer than he knew.

Lord John Russell once remarked that, had the Reform Bill
never been passed, Moore would have been an ardent Reformer.
With this comment, and all that it implies, we may rest satisfied.
Moore was no politician, but a great and life-long lover of his
country.

V

Contrary to what so many of his Irish admirers have wished to
believe, Moore's influence upon English politics was negligible.
He helped to draw attention to Catholic grievances: *The Times*
sought his services as a leader writer: Canning asked him out to
dine: he was offered a position by the Duke of Wellington. But
he had no real influence. The English are suspicious of versatility.
They like to label a man, and, once they have labelled him, the
label has to cover everything he does. They had labelled Moore
an entertainer, and were duly amused by his satires. Besides, he
was disqualified from English politics by his disposition to rate
cause and principle above party: persons so disposed having
always been regarded in England as politically untrustworthy.

VI

Enough has been said to show that there is more justification
in Moore's case for including religion and politics in the same
chapter than in the case of most writers—and politicians. His
actual religious writings are less explicit than his conduct. The
Sacred Songs, of which there were a great many, might, apart
from their technical skill, have been written by anybody. His
disquisitions on the Early Fathers are more remarkable for being
the work of Moore than in themselves. The primitive church

exercised a strong fascination for him, prompting him to one of his rare lyrical flights in *The Travels of a Young Man*. The hero is made to dream of a service in a third-century church:

"Never shall I forget the effect as it then presented itself to my fancy, of the still and unbreaking silence of that vast multitude of Christians,—till, at the awful moment of Communion, when, as the Priest, raising the Sacred Host, pronounced it 'the Body of Christ', the whole assembly fell prostrate, in adoration, before it, and the word 'Amen', as if with one voice and one soul, burst from all around. It was like a sweet and long-drawn peal of music, a concert of sounds, unbroken by a single breath of dissonance, from every quarter of this earth which the wind visits,—all blending in the belief of an incarnate God, who by his flesh hath redeemed, and with his flesh still feeds his creatures."

This is immediately contrasted with the service in a nineteenth-century Protestant conventicle, at "Ballymudragget".

It is perhaps their enjoyment of passages like these that makes such a number of Catholic authorities (*vide* Professor Stockley) profess themselves satisfied with the temperature of Moore's Catholicism.

BYRON

MOORE's friendship with Byron was the most important of his
whole life, involving him in actions and controversies which will
last as long as Byron's name. Its beginning was inauspicious.
Byron, in *English Bards and Scotch Reviewers*, made a pass at
Moore, in his character of Thomas Little. Byron, who had not at
all relished being called "a young Moore" by those whom his
first early work had shocked, and who was conscious moreover
that "Little's" verse had considerably influenced his own, was
glad of the chance to get in a dig. He wrote accordingly of "the
melodious advocate of lust",

> The young Catullus of his day
> As sweet, but as immoral in his lay.

Moore did not like this, but he was fairly well used to it, and
probably realized by this time (1809) that he had only himself to
blame if people took the Little verses at their face value. Worse,
however, followed.

> Can none remember that eventful day,
> That ever glorious almost fatal fray,
> When Little's leadless pistol met the eye,
> And Bow Street's myrmidons stood laughing by?

As if this were not enough, a note was added to the effect that "on examination, the balls of the pistols were found to have evaporated".

A reference to this unlucky business never failed to draw Moore, but, since the poem was anonymous, he could not at first do anything to express his annoyance. The second edition, however, bore Byron's name, and Moore, forgetting his promise to Lady Donegal, at once challenged him to a duel. Byron was abroad, and Hodgson, reasonably supposing that the letter could bode no good, never forwarded it; so Moore had no answer to his challenge.

Byron did not return for more than a year, by which time Moore was married, little Barbara had arrived, and he looked on the possibility of being killed with less tolerance. All the same, he had been insulted, and, touchy always on a point of honour, he did not intend to let the insult pass. The death of Byron's mother delayed him, but, as soon as he decently could, he wrote a second letter, asking if Byron had received the first, telling him what was in it, and explaining that while he no longer wished to fight, he could not in honour suffer a charge of falsehood to go unchallenged. He therefore invited his Lordship to withdraw it. Should Byron do so, then the writer would be happy in the opportunity of seeking to be numbered among his acquaintances.

Byron's reply was reasonable but not cordial. He said that he had not received the first letter, nor been aware that Moore had ever publicly contradicted the story about the lost bullet. In the circumstances, therefore, he could neither withdraw nor apologize for the "charge of falsehood", since he had never made it. In all other respects, however, he was at Moore's disposal.

Quick to sense a rebuff, Moore fastened at once on the fact that Byron had made no allusion to his suggestion that the two should become acquainted. A second letter expressed his resentment. Byron replied that, since Moore considered himself the injured party, the first overture towards acquaintance should come from him: adding that he himself was ready to receive it.

Moore did not at all fancy being put in the position of a suppliant, and replied stiffly that, as far as he was concerned, the correspondence was closed. To his astonishment, Byron replied with a frank and charming letter, saying that he would be delighted to make Moore's acquaintance when and where he pleased, and that, if the meeting led to any degree of intimacy between them, he would count the whole episode amongst the happiest events of his life.

Rogers, hearing the whole story from the excited and gratified Moore, suggested that the encounter should take place at his house. Accordingly, Byron was bidden there to dinner, with Campbell to make a fourth. There must have been considerable tension to begin with. Rogers asked Moore and Campbell to withdraw on Byron's arrival, thinking it best to receive him alone. But all went well. In spite of the fact that Byron refused everything that was put in front of him, asked for biscuits and soda water, and finally dined off mashed potatoes and vinegar,[1] the dinner was a great success, and Byron formed lasting friendships with Moore and his host.[2] This dinner was his real introduction to literary London, and he proceeded to startle it with *Childe Harold*, which had a success that left his new friends in the shade. Moore, at any rate, did not mind. He had been enthusiastic in his praise before the poem appeared: "the third canto of the Childe is magnificent—no man living can write up to it": and its success delighted him. Jealousy was not in his nature. In any case, Byron's admiration for him and his work was too genuine and too freely expressed for him to be anything but happy in the friendship. For several years, the two were to be frequently together, and to exchange innumerable letters, Byron confiding to his friend almost everything that occupied his mind.

---

[1] It is worth remarking that Byron went round to his club at the end of the evening and ate a "hearty supper".

[2] Moore's lasted the longer. By 1821 Byron was writing very spitefully of Rogers.

One office, that of go-between, Moore declined from the first. Attracted to Byron as he was, and "loving a lord", he was perfectly clear about his character. When Byron sought his good offices in the matter of Lady Adelaide Forbes, a grand-daughter of Lord Moira, with whom he was "amazingly inclined—remember I say but *inclined*—to be seriously enamoured", Moore declined the honour.

"If the lady could have consented to undertake the perilous—but still possible and glorious—achievement of attracting Byron to virtue, I own that, sanguinely as in theory I might have looked to the result, I should have seen not without trembling the happiness of one whom I had known and valued from her childhood risked in the experiment."

The phrasing is cautious and pedantic, but the meaning is clear.

This was by no means the only lady about whom Byron wrote. His confidences often embarrassed Moore, who shook his head, and continued to offer good advice which never seems to have irritated its recipient.   Odd though it may seem, Moore brought out the best in Byron. In his company, Byron was happy and without a care.[1] As free from jealousy as was Moore, and sincere in his admiration of Moore's gifts—"My dear Moore, you strangely underrate yourself. . . . Seriously, what on earth can you, or have you, to dread from any poetical flesh breathing?"—Byron lavished on him an affection which hardly another man called forth. Years afterwards, Byron, in a mood of despondency, said that the two people he cared most for were Lord

---

[1] One night at Rogers's, after supper, Byron and Moore got hold of a presentation copy of Lord Thurlow's poems, and began to ridicule it. Rogers protested. Then they found some lines addressed to Rogers himself:

> "When Rogers o'er this labour bent,
> Their purest fire the Muses lent,
> T'illustrate this sweet argument."

Byron was laughing too much to read them out, and Moore too was incapable. Finally Rogers thawed, and all three collapsed into "a state of inextinguishable laughter".

Clare and Moore. His letters to Moore are more numerous than Moore's to him, and it is obvious that his affection was the deeper of the two. Moore is hardly to be blamed. He was happily married, and had numbers of friends, with whom he carried on a voluminous correspondence. Byron was in a different case.

The peak year of their friendship was 1814, when Byron dedicated *The Corsair*[1] to Moore, and, for the length of his visit to town, the two were in each other's company almost every day. They discussed freely whether Byron should marry, and whom: and perhaps, if Moore's advice had been taken, the stormy life would have run a different course. But Moore entered just as eagerly into his feelings when he did marry. Indeed, he could hardly help it, since Byron was not at all reticent in his confidences. Moore was anxious for the success of the marriage, and his letters reflect his anxiety. ". . . Only do tell me that you are happier than that letter has led me to fear, and I shall be satisfied." When Lady Byron left, through all the vilification and lampooning and general filth that followed, Moore was angrily sympathetic. Byron was grateful. On his departure from London, he wrote the beginning of *My Boat is on the Shore*.

> My boat is on the shore
> And my bark is on the sea;
> But before I go, Tom Moore,
> Here's a double health to thee!
>
> Here's a sigh to those who love me,
> And a smile to those who hate;
> And whatever sky's above me,
> Here's a heart for every fate.

It was completed over a year later, when Moore received it in a letter from Venice.

---

[1] *The Corsair* sold ten thousand copies on the day of publication, and thirty purchasers returned to the shop to express their delight with it. Moore said of it, "Anything more fearfully interesting, more wild, touching, and 'negligently grand', I have never read from *your* pen."

Though the ocean roar around me,
Yet it still shall bear me on;
Though a desert should surround me,
It hath springs that may be won.

Were't the last drop in the well
As I gasped upon the brink,
'Ere my fainting spirit fell,
'Tis to thee that I would drink.

With that water, as this wine,
The libation I would pour
Should be—peace with thine and mine
And a health to thee, Tom Moore.

II

It must be counted as one of Moore's virtues that he somehow
provoked Byron to write some of the best letters in the language.
What could be better than this, written *à propos* of Moore's
projected *Life of Sheridan*:

"I do not know any good model for a life of Sheridan but
that of *Savage*. Recollect, however, that the life of such a man
may be made far more amusing than if he had been a Wilber-
force;—and this without offending the living, or insulting the
dead. The Whigs abuse him; however, he never left them, and
such blunderers deserve neither credit nor compassion.—As for
his creditors,—remember, Sheridan *never had* a shilling, and was
thrown, with great powers and passions, into the thick of the
world, and placed upon the pinnacle of success, with no other
external means to support him in his elevation. Did Fox * * * *pay
his* debts?—or did Sheridan take a subscription? Was the Duke of
Norfolk's drunkenness more excusable than his? Were his intrigues more notorious than those of all his contemporaries? and
is his memory to be blasted, and theirs respected? Don't let your-

self be led away by clamour, but compare him with the coalitioner Fox, and the pensioner Burke, as a man of principle, and with ten hundred thousand in personal views, and with none in talent, for he beat them all *out* and *out*. Without means, without connexion, without character, (which might be false at first, and make him mad afterwards from desperation,) he beat them all, in all he ever attempted."

Or what more pertinent than this:

"The truth is, my dear Moore, you live near the *stove* of society, where you are unavoidably influenced by its heat and its vapours. I did so once—and too much—and enough to give a colour to my whole future existence. As my success in society was *not* inconsiderable, I am surely not a prejudiced judge upon the subject, unless in its favour; but I think it, as now constituted, *fatal* to all great undertakings of every kind. I never courted it *then*, when I was young and high in blood, and one of its 'curled darlings'; and do you think I would do so *now*, when I am living in a clearer atmosphere? One thing *only* might lead me back to it, and that is, to try once more if I could do any good in *politics*; but *not* in the petty politics I see now preying upon our miserable country."

The vigour, the swift, nervous prose, thrust Moore's letters hopelessly into the background: and Moore's are very good in their way.

III

For several years the two corresponded regularly, Byron's letters greatly outnumbering Moore's. They did not meet again till Moore came to La Mira in 1819. Moore's account of the meeting is singularly lacking in enthusiasm, in view of his previous cordiality. The physical change in Byron seems to have put him off at first,[1] and a good deal had happened to modify his original feelings. Moore was not censorious, but his correspondent had occasionally tried him high. A letter to Murray, giving an account of an affair with the young unmarried daughter of a Venetian nobleman, without any attempt to hide her identity, had shocked him. "This is really too gross," he wrote in his Journal. He was, too, unenthusiastic about the Countess Guiccioli, Byron's lady of the moment, though, on a second meeting, he partly revised his estimate.

Byron, as ever, kept nothing back. He showed Moore, on their second day together, a letter from the Count Guiccioli to his wife, suggesting that she should get Byron to lend him a thousand pounds. Moore—one can see his Irish nose wrinkling in distaste—advised Byron to lend the money, on the ground that it might somewhat ease the situation: but Byron did not take his advice.

In spite of these serious interludes, the two spent most of their time together very happily. "Our course was, I am almost ashamed to say, one of uninterrupted merriment and laughter," is Moore's comment, as they reviewed old times. Byron, delighted to see someone belonging to his London days, and particularly his best friend, put forth all his charms, and Moore was not the man to resist him.

So matters went till the end of the visit, when Moore started for Rome. Byron wanted to leave the Countess, and go with him. Some such plan had been mooted, before Moore knew how the land lay at La Mira. Now, however, he protested that such a desertion would be callous and cruel in the extreme, and Byron reluctantly saw the force of his objection.

---

[1] He gave a very damaging account of it to d'Israeli . . . "His facing has swelled out; his hair is grey and his countenance has lost that 'spiritual expression' which he so eminently had. His teeth are getting bad, and when I saw him he said that if he ever came to England it would be to consult Wayte about them . . . I certainly was much struck with an alteration for the worse."

"Lord B. came on with me to Stra, where we parted. He has given me his Memoirs to make what use I please of them."

It was their last meeting, and Byron's farewell gift was destined to cause his friend a peck of troubles, and start a controversy which has smouldered ever since.

IV

The story of the Byron Memoirs is long and complicated. We will keep it as short as we can. Byron, as has been explained already, made Moore an absolute gift of his MS., so that Moore, in want of money to meet the Bermuda claim, might raise as much as the Memoirs would fetch from any publisher to whom he should assign the right of future publication. The MS. received continual additions till 1821, when Moore made a deal with Murray. Murray was to publish the Memoirs after Byron's death, Moore was to edit them, and to add an account of Byron's life from the point reached in the Memoirs. For this Murray was to advance Moore the sum of two thousand guineas. Deeds of assignment were made by both Moore and Byron.

A year later, Byron, hoping that he might possibly become reconciled to his wife, did not like the idea of the Memoirs being no longer under his control. Moore, too, had been worried by comments on the transaction. Lord Holland had expressed dislike of it, on the grounds that the Memoirs might be damaging to the characters of persons mentioned in them. Moore objected that, as editor, he had the power to omit anything he chose:[1] but, sensitive as ever to any possible imputation against his honour, he strove to have the position altered, and an entry in his Journal for April 22nd, 1822, records his success.

". . . I spoke to Murray upon the subject of Lord B's 'Memoirs'; of my wish to redeem them, and cancel the deed of sale; which Murray acceded to with the best grace imaginable.

[1] For his letter on the subject to Lord Holland, see Appendix C.

Accordingly, there is now an agreement making out, by which
I become his debtor for two thousand guineas, leaving the MS.
in his hands, as security, till I am able to pay it. This is, I feel, an
over-delicate deference to the opinions of others; but it is better
than allowing a shadow of suspicion to approach within a mile
of one in any transaction; and I know I shall feel the happier
when rid of the bargain."

By this agreement, finally executed on May 6th of the same
year, Moore or Byron were entitled to redeem the MS. at any
time during Byron's life.

Murray brooded for a while over this document, and became
worried. Finally, in February of the next year, he wrote to
Moore, saying that a clause in the agreement pressed unfairly
upon him, and suggesting an alteration. Moore replied,

"I shall most readily make the alteration in our agreement
which you propose; it not being my wish to do anything which
could for a moment be stigmatized as 'unfair'."

He declined, however, to tear off the part of the agreement to
which Murray objected, asking him to wait till he next came to
town, and added that he hoped soon to be in a position to redeem the MS. altogether. Further correspondence followed, in
which Moore got on his high horse. The word "unfair"
rankled. His honesty and his independence were the only things
on which Moore was touchy, and on them he was as touchy as a
hedgehog. By the end of March, however, the trouble was
over, and Moore was writing in his best magnanimous vein:

"It has been my good fortune to have passed through life
without having had, in either friendship or business, a serious misunderstanding with anyone—and it would have given me great
pain to begin with you, whose real and kindly friendship to me,
on all occasions, I have always acknowledged more warmly to
others than to yourself. But not less new to me than quarreling,
was the having the word 'unfairness' coupled with any transaction in which I was concerned, and I own it startled me into

16

something like indignation. Your explanation, however, is perfectly satisfactory."

In 1824 Murray, deciding that the position was still ambiguous, asked Moore either to redeem the MS. or to destroy the second agreement. Moore said he would redeem the MS., and would come to London to raise the necessary sum. He was going to insure his life, or arrange to get the money from Longmans. Longmans were willing, but, before Moore had done anything definite, he received news of Byron's death.

"Could not believe it, but feared the worst, as his last letter to me about a fortnight since mentioned the severe attack of apoplexy or epilepsy which he had just suffered. Hurried to inquire. Met Lord Lansdowne, who said he feared it was but too true. Recollected then the unfinished state in which my agreement for the redemption of the 'Memoirs' lay. Lord L. said, 'You have nothing but Murray's fairness to depend upon.' Went off to the 'Morning Chronicle' office, and saw the 'Courier', which confirmed this most disastrous news."

Moore hurried round to Murray's, but the publisher was not to be seen, and he had to content himself with leaving a note,[1] in which he asked Murray to complete the arrangement agreed upon. That evening, Douglas Kinnaird, on behalf of Lady Byron and the family, wrote offering to advance the money for the Memoirs, so that they might see whether or no they wished them to be published.

The next morning, Moore went to Kinnaird, and told him how matters stood. He would not even consider Lady Byron's offer.

---

[1] May 14, 1824.

DEAR SIR—I have called in consequence of this melancholy intelligence to know when it will be convenient for you to complete the agreement with respect to the Memoirs which we agreed upon when I was last in London—your answer, as soon as possible, will very much oblige.

Yours truly
THOMAS MOORE

"It is I alone who ought to pay the money for it, and the money was ready for the purpose. I would then submit it (not to Lady Byron) but to a chosen number of persons, and if they, upon examination, pronounced it altogether unfit for publication, I would burn it."

The same day, Moore learned from Hobhouse that negotiations were going on between Murray and Wilmot Horton, who was representing Byron's family, to hand over the Memoirs direct without consulting him. He protested at once that he alone had the right of disposal. Actually, on Byron's death, the MS. had, by the agreement of 1822, become Murray's property: but Moore relied on a clause which he said he had had inserted in the agreement, on the advice of his friend Luttrell, giving him three months' grace after Byron's death in which to redeem the MS.

"This clause I dictated as clearly as possible both to Murray and his solicitor, Mr. Turner, and saw the solicitor interline it in a rough draft of the agreement. Accordingly, in recollecting it now, and finding that Luttrell had a perfect recollection of the circumstance also (i.e. of having suggested the clause to me), I felt, of course, confident in my claim."

On the strength of this, he refused to hand the MS. over to Lady Byron, but said he would deliver it to Mrs Leigh, Byron's sister. Sir John Hobhouse and Douglas Kinnaird were firm that Mrs Leigh

"would and ought to burn the MS. altogether, without any previous perusal or deliberation. I endeavoured to convince them that this would be throwing a stigma on the work, which it did not deserve; and stated, that though the second part of the 'Memoirs' was very full of coarse things, yet that (with the exception of about three or four lines) the first part contained nothing which, on the score of decency, might not be most safely published."

All the same, he agreed to hand the MS. over to Augusta, to

deal with as she might think fit: ". . . my whole wish was to consult the feelings of Lord Byron's dearest friend, his sister."

On the next day, there was a discussion between Moore, Kinnaird, and Hobhouse, at which Moore again protested against the burning of the Memoirs.

The final and historic meeting took place on Monday, May 17th, at Murray's. There were present, besides Moore and Murray, Hobhouse, Horton, and Colonel Doyle. Murray produced the two agreements, and it was clear that Moore had no control over the disposal of the MS.[1] Two alternative proposals, one, that Moore should keep the MS., read it, and issue a discreet selection, the other that it should be deposited in a bank and edited later on, were vetoed by Hobhouse, with Murray's concurrence. Moore for a last time protested against the MS. being burned, and was reminded that he had no voice in the matter. Horton and Doyle tore up both the MS. and a copy which Moore had had made, and put them on the fire.

Moore, hurt and angry, produced the two thousand guineas which he had obtained from the Longmans. Murray very honourably said he could not take it, since the agreement proved that the Memoirs were his property, not Moore's. But Moore's pride was up. He was by no means convinced that he had no control over the MS., and to agree with Murray on the one point would tacitly concede the other: and he was doubly determined to be out of pocket, for fear those present should suspect that his motive for wishing to preserve the Memoirs was financial. So he would take no refusal, and Murray at last unwillingly accepted the money. Moore then left, whereupon Murray put it to the others that it was not right that he should be at so grievous a loss, which he assuredly could not afford. They were unanimous that

---

[1] Both the rough draft and the agreement were brought in, and no trace could be found of the clause which Moore tells us he had inserted. We can only wonder how Moore came to make such a mistake.

Byron's family should make his loss good, and, after some discussion, it was agreed that Augusta and Lady Byron should make
up the sum between them.

Actually, they did not make it up. It was Murray who finally
cleared the debt, but not until 1828, when he arranged with
Moore to write Byron's life. Including the advance to Moore,
and interest on the debt, the agreement cost him no less than
£4,620. It is pleasant to know that he soon got it back, for the
Life developed into a very valuable property indeed.

v

We come now to the two disputed questions, Moore's culpa-
bility, and the value of the lost MS. Moore, as we have seen,
protested against the burning, and was finally proved to have no
legal power to stop it. The MS. had ceased to be his property,
and had become Murray's. Two at least of Byron's biographers,
Miss Ethel Colbourne Mayne and Mr John Drinkwater, acquit
Moore of blame. I find it hard to acquit him altogether. His protest was that the burning was "contrary to Lord Byron's wishes
and unjust to himself". Yet Byron's wishes were not uppermost
in his mind. He had said, a day or so previously, and entered the
fact in his Journal, that his "whole wish was to consult the feelings" of Augusta.   And he was, beyond all doubt, thinking of
himself: not of his profit, but of his honour. If the MS. were
preserved, there was the likelihood that he might edit it and be
the gainer. The thought that the others might suspect him of this
motive for objecting to its destruction struck him in his tenderest
spot. All his pride, his passionately cherished integrity, boiled up
instantly. He thought less of Byron, and more of Moore. It was,
admittedly, a nasty position. The opposition was formidable,
and Murray was taking a very firm line—"by God, I say I will
burn the papers, let what will, come of it . . ." Even so, a
stronger man might have overcome the others—Moore's pro-

tests seem to have been rather in the nature of legal submissions
—and let them impute what motive they liked, provided only
his point was gained, and his friend's testament saved from the
flames.

Moore had half a dozen reasons for acting as he did. His conduct was honourable towards the living, but we may wish that
he had been a little unscrupulous for the sake of the dead. Being
what he was, he could hardly have done otherwise than as he did.
No doubt as to the rightness of his conduct ever assailed him. In
the very same year, he told Hobhouse—according to Hobhouse
—that he had "become a convert to [his] opinion about the propriety of the destruction, and of not making extracts for publication": and to the end of his life he was convinced that, in allowing the burning, he had acted in a high spirit of self-sacrifice. He
was deceived. When all allowance has been made for the more
than awkward position in which Moore was placed, a reproach
remains.

The loss of the Memoirs is tantalizing. True, a number of
people who saw the MS., including Lord John Russell, say that
it was not particularly notable. But they would say this: it is only
natural. Even if the whole were not good, there must have been
first-class things in it. Byron was possessed of an astonishing
genius. The phrases sprang alive from his pen: in prose at any
rate, he could not be dull if he tried. One has only to look at the
letters to marvel at the power and versatility of his mind. We
have certainly lost some excellent prose: and something else
besides.

The autobiography of any great man is valuable, even though
it does not explicitly present an accurate picture of its writer.
The writer gives away more than he intends. Byron was capable
both of great honesty and of wild romancing about himself.
The lost MS. must have provided material of the first importance, and, one imagines, a certain body of new facts.

No: in this matter, although his path was beset with the kind

of difficulties he would feel most cruelly, the conclusion cannot
be resisted that Moore failed his friend.

VI

There remains the last phase of the friendship, Moore's *Life of
Byron*. Nothing could replace the lost papers, but Moore, in this
just and highly-praised piece of writing, did much to make
amends. He was anxious to save Byron's name from the sensa-
tionalism and the obloquy with which it had been smirched, and
the figure he presented to the public, that of the early Byron, the
man he knew, was something very different from the figure of
legend. Byron's death set him, in the Irishman's mind, somewhere beside Emmet and Fitzgerald, as a martyr to the rights of
small nations. Even so, his account is balanced, and by no means
all eulogy.

The preparation and writing of the *Life* caused him more uncertainty and more trouble than anything he ever attempted.
The crippling load of debt under which his pride had placed him
made it essential for him to undertake some profitable work, and
nothing promised so well as the *Life*, but there were several,
including Hobhouse, who thought it should not be written, and
Moore, sensitive on the whole subject, hesitated for a long time
before the persuasions of others decided him to start.

His first negotiations were with the Longmans, but he kept in
close touch with Murray. Byron, in his will, had left a large
number of his papers, letters, etc., to Murray. A recent biographer of Maginn, Miss Miriam M. H. Thrall, asserts that
Murray first of all offered the writing of the *Life* to Maginn, but
was deterred when the editor decided to "publish the letters
entire, with libels, sneers, satires, sarcasms, epigrams, confessions,
and intrigues, unmutilated and unasterisked, and merely prefix to
the work such information as was absolutely indispensable".
This is highly characteristic of Maginn, and it is borne out by his

statement, in 1825 (*Blackwood's Noctes*, no. XV), that he had read Byron's "memoirs and letters".[1] These can hardly have been the papers destroyed at the historic meeting in Albemarle Street, since, in view of the agreements between Murray and Moore, the publisher would have been in the last degree unlikely to consider another editor before Byron's death; and there was no time afterwards. So Maginn, if the offer was made him, must have seen the second set of papers between Byron's death and 1825. I must say, however, that, by the courtesy of the present head of the firm, I have examined the file of Maginn's letters to Murray without finding a reference to any such project, or any mention of Byron at all.

Be that as it may, in February 1827 Murray wrote to Moore, telling him of his decision not to publish or use in any way the papers left him by Byron, and definitely offering him £2,500 to write the *Life* without them. Moore declined, saying that the only reason for taking the work away from the Longmans would have been in order to make use of the extra material in Murray's possession. "I must now," he wrote to Hobhouse, "only make out of it as good and harmless a book as I can. The public will, of course, be disappointed, but better so than wrongly gratified."

Finally, Murray took over the project on the terms mentioned at the end of Section IV, and Moore applied himself to his task. He worked conscientiously and with real energy. A score or more of letters to Murray attest his industry and perseverance in ferreting out everything that might bear upon his subject. There were many difficulties. Augusta was one. "Mrs Leigh is an odd person", he writes, "and if she was not Byron's sister I should be disposed to say something worse of her—but she *is* a very odd person." And, a few weeks later, "Mrs Leigh is a most provoking person."

---

[1] "His memoirs and letters are the only things of his that I have ever seen that gave me, in the least degree, the notion of a fine creature, enjoying the full and unrestrained swing of his faculties."

As time went on, Moore began to take a more hopeful, and somewhat more resolute, view of his task. In 1829 he wrote to Mary Shelley,

". . . I must . . . blink nothing (nothing, that is, but what is *ineffable*), bring what I think *shadows* fairly forward, but in such close juxtaposition with the *lights* that the latter will carry the day. That is the way to do such men real service."

Things looked better: but he was not altogether easy in his mind.

VII

Moore's uneasiness continued all through the preparation of the *Life*, rising almost to a fever just before it appeared, as is shown by his letters to Mary Shelley, to whom he poured out all his doubts and anxieties. His friends all knew how anxious he was: and there is preserved among his papers a note, unsigned, in which someone hastened to inform him that Blackwood's had called it "the best book of Biography in the English language." [1] . Not all the critics were so flattering, and the state of nerves to which Moore had been reduced is shown by his reaction to some comments of Mary Shelley. He tells her that he is glad she likes the book, but that he will not answer her criticism for fear she may produce some more.

". . . You know (or at least, *ought* to know) that there is nothing so fidgetting to me as these little nibbling details after the whole thing's despatched and the fool's bolt shot irrevocably. It is bad enough to run the gauntlet of the *public* criticisms without having also little snug private ones. It is like a man being scolded by his wife at home as well as bullied abroad."

This testiness is unlike Moore: but, as he says at the end of the same letter,

"By all accounts, my Book is doing very well—but I am (as you will divine from the foregoing) still in a twitter about it."

[1] February 1830.

In the *Life*, Moore's prose attained a dignity and a weight it had not hitherto reached. Here is his conclusion:

"The arduous task of being the biographer of Byron is one, at least, on which I have not obtruded myself: the wish of my friend that I should undertake that office having been more than once expressed, at a time when none but boding imagination could have foreseen much chance of the sad honour devolving to me. If in some instances I have consulted rather the spirit than the exact letter of his injunctions, it was with the view solely of doing him more justice than he would have done himself; there being no hands in which his character could have been less safe than his own, nor any greater wrong offered to his memory than the substitution of what he affected to be for what he was. Of any partiality, however, beyond what our mutual friendship accounts for and justifies, I am by no means conscious; nor would it be in the power, indeed, even of the most partial friend to allege anything more convincingly favourable of his character than is contained in the few simple facts with which I shall here conclude—that through life, with all his faults, he never lost a friend;—that those about him in his youth, whether as companions, teachers, or servants, remained attached to him to the last; that the woman, to whom he gave the love of his maturer years, idolizes his name; and that, with a single unhappy exception, scarce an instance is to be found of any one, once brought, however briefly, into relations of amity with him, that did not feel towards him a kind regard in life and retain a fondness for his memory.

"I have now done with the subject, nor shall be easily tempted into a recurrence. Any mistakes or mis-statements I may be proved to have made shall be corrected;—any new facts which it is in the power of others to produce will speak for themselves. To mere opinions I am not called upon to pay attention—and still less to insinuations or mysteries. I have here told what I myself know and think concerning my friend; and now leave his character, moral as well as literary, to the judgment of the world."

So the long chapter is closed. To his life's end, Moore looked back with regret to the day when Byron entrusted to him the first part of the Memoirs. Yet, all things considered, the scores were even. Moore failed to prevent one wrong to Byron's memory, but he did a great deal to preserve and safeguard what remained. On the other side, were it not for Byron, Moore would be less than he is. Among his chief claims to remembrance is his association with one of the most remarkable figures in English literary history.

CHAPTER XVI

MISCELLANEOUS WRITINGS: PROSE AND VERSE

Moore's three Biographies—*Sheridan*—*Byron*—*Fitzgerald*—His
qualities as a biographer—His critical equipment—Judgments
on contemporaries—An evening with Coleridge—*The Loves of
the Angels*—*The Fudge Letters*—*Fables for the Holy Alliance*

MOORE's reputation as a writer of prose depends upon his Lives
of Sheridan, Byron, and Fitzgerald, upon such work as *Captain
Rock* and *The Travels of an Irish Gentleman*, and upon his letters.
His prose is easy, flexible, and unaffected. He wrote directly,
without self-consciousness, and, *The Epicurean* apart, without
attempt at ornament; and, in his letters, he achieved a real
intimacy. He kept his prose for the practical, business side of life,
and for his unbuttoned moments. As a result, it is a faithful index
of his character. He is well outside the first class as a prose writer.
Facility, a mind lacking in distinction, and, except when he was
moved to sarcasm, a want of weight and power, disqualify him:
but he could write excellently on occasion, and, in general, his
prose was a serviceable and smoothly running vehicle for his
thought.

Of the three lives, although his *Byron* was so highly praised
by Blackwood's, the slighter and less-known *Fitzgerald* is as
good. It was written *con amore*—but then, so was the *Sheridan*.
Moore had known and liked and admired "old Sheridan". He
felt his death, and wrote almost savagely upon it. He spent a
long time and took a great deal of trouble in collecting the
material, and his Journal is full of good stories of Sheridan, showing how much he was enjoying his researches. There was, moreover, a striking similarity between the two men. Both were
Irishmen, educated at the same school, and destined for the bar.

Both emigrated early to England and married sixteen-year-old actresses. In rapid success after poverty, in admission to society, in interest in music and the stage, in their politics—both were Whigs, but never "party men", keeping their independence, and steadfast in the Irish cause—in their contacts with the Prince, and subsequent disillusion, their lives ran parallel. Both wrote translations and pasquinades, and both refused stipends in early and middle life. These similarities were strongly felt by Moore: yet the *Life*, when completed, missed something of its subject's character. It is as if Moore had described all the circumference of Sheridan's life without ever getting at the centre. This superficiality was partly due to Moore's temperament, and partly to design. Sheridan had in him just that touch of fire and passion which Moore lacked. It was something the effects of which Moore might observe and chronicle, but which in its essence he could not understand. And there was another obstacle between him and a full treatment of his subject. As he investigated, he found himself obliged in various particulars to modify his view of Sheridan: and for Moore to criticize adversely someone whom he liked was always distasteful. The remedy lay toward vagueness and a tendency to avoid the offending particulars.

"The more I think and the more opinions I receive about the Life of Sheridan, the more I see reason to quake upon the subject. Truth will be deadly, and vague praise will be cowardly— so what am I to do?"

This is not to say that his *Life of Sheridan* is a failure. It is a sympathetic, painstaking, and valuable piece of work, but it does not tell us everything there is to be known about Sheridan.

There is less superficiality about his next biography, although, as we have seen, he was by no means in full sympathy with its subject. It is in sheer knowledge that his *Life* scores. No biographer of Byron has been able or will be able to do without it. It is by no means perfect. Once again, Moore's work suffers from the avoidance of matters he deplored, though in this case the

inability to use Murray's papers, plus discretion and the sus-
ceptibilities of a number of persons still living, were added
handicaps. In so far as Byron went beyond Moore, the *Life*
suffers. It presents the Byron whom Moore knew in England
rather than the Byron of whom he disapproved in Italy. But it
has solid and enduring merits, and the biographer nowhere
comes between the reader and his subject; and it has at least one
modern champion, Mr John Drinkwater, who says that it "ranks
among the best biographies ever given to the world".

The *Life of Fitzgerald* is a paradox. Moore did not know Fitzgerald, had only seen him in the street, yet on this subject,
selected by himself, at his own cost, in preference to a life of
Canning which would have had an assured financial success, he
did his best work as a biographer. The name of Fitzgerald
rekindled all the patriotic enthusiasm of his boyhood. He lost
sight of the Ireland of O'Connell, of all that wearied and dis-
gusted him, in the clear vision of those early days. He recaptured
the spirit that had inspired the *Melodies*, but with the benefits of
a lifetime of experience. The memory of Emmet gleamed once
more, and he paid tribute to the idols of his youth. Moore's *Life
of Fitzgerald* is less read than the other two, because there is so
much less interest in its subject, but it is an admirable piece of
work.

II

The biographies, the *Sheridan* in particular, bring up the question of Moore's critical equipment. Within the limitations of his
temperament, he was a good critic, with an instinct for real
quality, and a judgment founded in sterling common sense. On
the whole, his judgments are much what one would expect of
him. He preferred *The Vicar of Wakefield* (which made him
weep) to *Joseph Andrews*. He could not read through *Moll
Flanders*. *The Heart of Midlothian* he found "fantastic", but Scott
was "our greatest living writer".

His best asset as a critic was a power of seeing what a writer was up to.

"Received this morning Lord Byron's tragedy. Looked again over his letter on Bowles. It is amusing to see through his design in thus depreciating all the present school of poetry. Being quite sure of his own hold upon fame, he contrives to loosen that of all his contemporaries, in order that they may fall away entirely from his side, and leave him unencumbered, even by their floundering. It is like that Methodist preacher who, after sending all his auditory to the devil, thus concluded,—'You may perhaps, on the day of judgment, think to escape by laying hold of my skirts as I go to heaven; but it won't do; I'll trick you all; for I'll wear a spencer, I'll wear a spencer.' So Lord B. willingly surrenders the skirts of his poetical glory, rather than let any of us poor devils stick in them, even for ever so short a time. The best of it is, too, that the wise public all the while turns up its eyes, and exclaims, 'How modest!' "

Moore could be epigrammatic, as in his judgment on Burke:

"There was, in truth, nothing democratic about him but his origin;—his tastes were all on the side of the splendid and the arbitrary. . . . Though doomed to make Whiggism his habitual haunt, he took his perch at all times on its loftiest branches, as far as possible away from popular contact; and, upon most occasions, adopted a sort of baronial view of liberty."

His own limitations he knew exactly. He recognized Wordsworth's genius, and commented in his Journal on the bad taste of the public as evidenced by their preference of himself to Wordsworth. He was shocked by Byron's views on Shakespeare —about whom he said one or two silly things himself. He insisted strongly and repeatedly on the genius of Burns. He shared the popular admiration for Rogers, in whose favour personal friendship had doubtless prejudiced him. He was puzzled by Shelley.

"I have been reading a good deal of Shelley's poetry, but it is,

I confess (always excepting some of the minor gems) *beyond* me, in every sense of the word." [1]

He could not make much of Coleridge, either as a writer or as a man. Keats he does not mention at all. The only reference in the Journal is from a newspaper criticism, copied in one of the last entries. He detected Macaulay's gifts at once, pitching on an anonymous squib in *The Times*, and recommending that the writer be secured as an ally. It was only when he recollected and praised the squib at a dinner when Macaulay was present that he found out who had written it. He thought poorly of Southey, whose opinions he found "bigoted". He admired "the lesser poems, sea-odes etc." of Campbell, and was indignant when Wordsworth and others made fun of them.

Of talkers he gave the palm to Sydney Smith.

". . . Sydney, Sydney is, in his way, inimitable; and, as a conversational wit, beats all the men I have ever met. Curran's fancy went much higher, but also much *lower*. Sydney, in his gayest flights, though boisterous, is never vulgar."

At the other end of the roll he put Crabbe. "I hardly know what to do about Crabbe," he wrote, when asked for his reminiscences of the poet.

"There certainly never was a man of his *calibre* of whose conversation so little remained in one's mind. I remembered having met him, at Longleat, some years since, and I instantly turned to a sort of Journal I kept at that time to see if any 'drop of the immortal Man' had by accident trickled into it. But no—I found that he had been, as usual, as dry as any *land*-crab that ever crawled."

Moore's reviews in the *Edinburgh Review* are full of common sense, and often gracefully written, although he disliked reviewing, and said himself that he always did it badly.

In music, he preferred what he called "the old favourites". He loved especially Haydn and Mozart, to whom he refers

[1] Letter to Mary Shelley.

THOMAS MOORE IN 1832
After Sir T. Lawrence, P.R.A.

often: "a Benedictus of Mozart and the 'Et incarnatus est' of Haydn—both the merum sal of music". He liked Purcell, enjoyed Rossini, and was not interested in Grétry. His Italian journey is full of comments on the music he heard; but, on the whole, music was so much a part of his daily life that he took it for granted, and said little that bears repetition.

There is no doubt that the best of Moore's criticism occurred in conversation. The tributes to his talk, in an age of talkers, are many and unanimous: though he evidently had his limitations.

III

It has been noted already that Moore imperfectly appreciated Coleridge. One or two reasons were obvious, and others we can guess. The author of *The Ancient Mariner* carried too many guns for the Irish singer. This would not have mattered in itself, for there was no pettiness in Moore's nature, and he never resented giving best to anyone whose superiority he could recognize. But he often could not understand Coleridge, whose mind moved on a level that called for more than agility and quickness of wit. Coleridge's metaphysical speculations were beyond him, as indeed they were beyond almost all of his contemporaries: and there were things about the man himself, his manner, his dress, his mode of life, which would not encourage the dapper and normally-living Moore to better acquaintance. Thus we find in the Journal a half-unwilling recognition of Coleridge's genius, a frank record, every now and then, of good things which Coleridge said, and several stories against him, set down without malice but with the relieved, faintly audible sigh of a man reassuring himself by the standards of normal life.

"Drove to Regent's Park; Rogers told of Coleridge riding about in a strange shabby dress, with I forget whom at Keswick, and on some company approaching them, Coleridge offered to fall behind and pass for his companion's servant. 'No,' said the

17

other, 'I am proud of you as a friend; but, I must say, I should be ashamed of you as a servant.' "

There is no trace of hostility in the entry, yet we may be sure that it did Moore good to set it down. His honesty compelled him always to realize something of Coleridge's quality. A few months after the entry above, we read,

"Was too far from Coleridge at dinner, to hear more than the continual drawl of his preachment; moved up to him, however, when the ladies had retired."

He was drawn to listen, whether he liked it or not.

An occasion ten years earlier, when the two men met, also at dinner, is interesting and suggestive. Fortunately, we have another account of it besides Moore's. Moore's runs as follows:

"Dined at Mr Monkhouse's (a gentleman I have never seen before), on Wordsworth's invitation, who lives there whenever he comes to town. A singular party: Coleridge, Rogers, Wordsworth and wife, Charles Lamb (the hero, at present, of the 'London Magazine') and his sister (the poor woman who went mad with him in the diligence on the way to Paris), and a Mr Robinson, one of the *minora sidera* of this constellation of the Lakes, the host himself, a Macaenas of the school, contributing nothing but good dinners and silence. Charles Lamb, a clever fellow certainly; but full of villainous and abortive puns, which he miscarries of every minute. Some excellent things, however, have come from him; and his friend Robinson mentioned to me not a bad one. On Robinson's receiving his first brief, he called upon Lamb to tell him of it. 'I suppose,' said Lamb, 'you addressed that line of Milton's to it, "Thou first best cause, least understood".' Coleridge told some tolerable things. One of a poor author, who, on receiving from his publisher an account of the proceeds (as he expected it to be) of a work he had published, saw among the items, 'Cellerage £3 10s. 6d.' and thought it was a charge for the trouble of selling the 700 copies, which he did not consider unreasonable: but on inquiry he found it was for the cellar-room occupied by his work, not a copy of which had stirred from thence. He told, too, of the servant-maid where he himself had lodged at Ramsgate, coming in to say that he was wanted, there being a person at the door inquiring for a poet; and on his going out, he found it was a pot-boy from the public house, whose cry of 'any pots for the Angel', the girl had mistaken for a demand for a poet. Improbable enough. In talking of Klopstock, he mentioned his description of the Deity's 'head spreading through space', which he said gave one the idea of hydrocephalous affection . . . A good deal of talk with Lamb about De Foe's works, which he praised warmly, particularly *Colonel Jack*, of which he mentioned some striking passages. Is collecting the works of the Dunciad heroes. Coleridge said that Spenser is the poet most remarkable for contrivances of versification: his spelling words differently to suit the music of the line, putting sometimes 'spake', sometimes 'spoke', as it fell best on the ear, etc. To show the difference in the facility of reciting verses, according as they were skilfully or unskilfully constructed, he said he had made the experiment upon Beppo and Whistelcraft (Frere's poem) and found that he could read three stanzas of the latter in the same time as two of the former. This is absurd."

By this account Coleridge certainly would not seem to have shone. But the "one of the minora sidera", later known to the world as Henry Crabb Robinson, the diarist, kept his own record of the occasion; and it does not resemble Moore's.

"On the 4th of April I was one of a party at dinner at Monkhouse's concerning which there is a letter in Talfourd's Letters of Lamb, Vol. II, p. 95, to Bernard Barton. Lamb says of this party: 'I dined in Parnassus with Words, Col., Rogers and Tom Moore: half the poetry of England constellated and clustered in Gloucester Place. Coler(idge) was in his finest vein of talk—had all the talk . . . We did not quaff Hippocrene last night.' The short

letter is in Lamb's charming style. It is a pity indeed to put water
to wine, but there is no help for it. I and Mr Gil(l)man were the
only unpoetical men at table besides the Amphitryon. My
journal says: "Our party consisted of W., Col., L., M. and R.,
5 poets of very unequal worth and most disproportionate
popularity whom the public would arrange probably in the very
inverse order except that it would place Moore above Rogers.
Coler(idge) alone displayed any of his peculiar talent. He talked
much and well. I have not for years seen him in such excellent
health and spirits. His subjects, metaphysical criticisms on words.
He talked chiefly to Wordsw(orth). Rogers occasionally let fall
a remark. Moore seemed conscious of his inferiority. He was
very attentive to Col. but seemed also to relish L. whom he sat
next. L. was in a happy frame: kept himself within bounds and
was only cheerful at last." This seems at variance with his own
letter for he complains of headache and did not go to Ader's
party. I have a very distinct recollection of more than I put in my
journal, as is often the case. For instance I add this with confidence. Lamb sat next Tom Moore and when he was sufficiently
touched with wine to be very amusing, I overheard him say
with a hiccough, 'Mr Moore, let me drink a glass of wine with
you,' suiting the word to the action. 'Hitherto Mr Moore I have
had an antipathy to you: but now that I have seen you I shall
like you ever after.' Some years after I mentioned this to Moore:
he recollected the fact but not Lamb's amusing manner. It
occurred to me at the time that Moore felt, if not his inferiority,
at least that his talent was of another sort. For many years he had
been the most brilliant man of his company. In anecdotes, small
talk and especially in singing, he was supreme; but he was no
match for Coleridge in his vein; as little could he feel Lamb's
humour."

There are two against poor Tom, Robinson and Lamb: and
we must take their verdict. The question remains whether
Moore wrote as he did in malice, because he was conscious of his

inferiority and was anxious to right the balance: or in good faith, because he did not understand. The latter is more probable. Moore was "attentive to" Coleridge, but he was also talking a good deal *tête-à-tête* with Lamb, and so missed part at least of what Coleridge was saying. The rest was, quite simply, over his head. Feeling shut out—he was accustomed to talk and be listened to in the best of company—he remembered, and in unconscious revenge set down, the sillier things that Coleridge said that evening.

We may accept this conclusion without any desire to white-wash Moore or to make excuses for him. No instance of deliberate malice is found in the records of his life, and none of his con-temporaries ever accused him of it, so that this incident is not likely to have been unique. Moore was put in the shade, did not like the experience, and sought to restore his self-respect by an account the bias of which quite escaped him.

IV

The Loves of the Angels does not call for comment. Ornate and amatory, it suffers from the same defects as *Lalla Rookh*, to which it is, on the whole, inferior. Here is the opening:

> 'Twas when the world was in its prime,
>   When the fresh stars had just begun
> Their race of glory, and young Time
>   Told his first birth-days by the sun;
> When, in the light of Nature's dawn
>   Rejoicing, men and angels met
> On the high hill and sunny lawn,—
> Ere sorrow came, or Sin had drawn
>   'Twixt man and heav'n her curtain yet!
> When earth lay nearer to the skies
>   Than in these days of crime and woe,
> And mortals saw, without surprise,
>   In the mid-air, angelic eyes
>   Gazing upon this world below.

Alas, that Passion should profane,
  Ev'n then, the morning of the earth!
That, sadder still, the fatal stain
  Should fall on hearts of heav'nly birth—
And that from Woman's love should fall
  So dark a stain, most sad of all!

The fable of the poem offended a number of worthy souls, including, oddly enough, Lady Donegal. Moore, much disconcerted, made emendations. "What keeps your Quarterly so long?" he wrote to Murray, of the *Review's* failure to notice the poem.

"I am rather in trepidation about it, and shall be not at all sorry to find myself left out, particularly as my angels will all be turned into good Mahometans, which metamorphosis will be a most edifying subject for the succeeding number to dilate upon." [1]

Subsequently he regretted the change, and the angels were restored.

Very much happier were the lighter verses which, under various titles, and sometimes pseudonymously, he poured out for so many years. The *Fudge* collections are not read now, but they are light, skilful, and often, even at this distance, amusing. They are in the form of letters, written by the members of the Fudge family to a number of correspondents, (including Moore's perpetual target, Castlereagh). Miss Biddy Fudge writes from Paris to a girl friend.

But the dancing—ah! parley-moi, Dolly, de ça—
There, indeed, is a treat that charms all but Papa.
Such Beauty—such grace—oh ye sylphs of romance!
  Fly, fly to Titania, and ask her if she has
One light-footed nymph in her train that can dance
  Like divine Bigottini and sweet Fanny Bias!
Fanny Bias in Flora—dear creature!—you'd swear,
  When her delicate feet in the dance twinkle round,
That her steps are of light, that her home is the air,
  And she only *par complaisance* touches the ground.

---

[1] In a letter to J. W. Croker, he lamented that he had not thought of this to begin with.

And when Bigottini in Psyche dishevels
  Her black flowing hair, and by daemons is driven,
Oh! who does not envy those rude little devils,
  That hold her and hug her, and keep her from heaven?
Then, the music—so softly its cadences die,
So divinely—oh, Dolly! between you and I,
It's as well for my peace that there's nobody nigh
To make love to me then—you've a soul, and can judge
What a crisis 'twould be for your friend Biddy Fudge!
The next place (which Bobby has near lost his heart in)
They call it the Play-house—I think—of St Martin;
Quite charming—and very religious—what folly
To say that the French are not pious, dear Dolly,
Where here one beholds, so correctly and rightly,
The Testament turn'd into melo-drames nightly;
And, doubtless, so fond they're of scriptural facts,
They will soon get the Pentateuch up in five acts.
Here Daniel, in pantomime, bids bold defiance
To Nebuchadnezzar and all his stuff'd lions,
While pretty young Israelites dance round the Prophet,
In very thin clothing, and but little of it:—
Here Begrand, who shines in this scriptural path,
  As the lovely Suzanna, without ev'n a relic
Of drapery round her, comes out of her bath
  In a manner that, Bob says, is quite Eve-angelic!
But in short, dear, 'twould take me a month to recite
All the exquisite places we're at, day and night;
And, besides, ere I finish, I think you'll be glad
Just to hear one delightful adventure I've had.

The Fables for the Holy Alliance, dedicated to Byron and published in 1823, find him at the top of his form.

    Methought, upon the Neva's flood
    A beautiful Ice Palace stood,
    A dome of frost-work, on the plan
    Of that once built by Empress Anne,
    Which shone by moonlight—as the tale is—
    Like an Aurora Borealis.

    In this said Palace, furnish'd all
      And lighted as the best on land are,
    I dreamt there was a splendid Ball,
      Given by the Emperor Alexander,

To entertain with all due zeal,
  Those holy gentlemen, who've shown a
Regard so kind for Europe's weal,
  At Troppau, Laybach, and Verona.
The thought was happy—and design'd
To hint how thus the human Mind
May, like the stream imprison'd there,
Be check'd and chill'd, till it can bear
The heaviest Kings, that ode or sonnet
E'er yet be-prais'd, to dance upon it.

And all were pleas'd, and cold, and stately,
  Shivering in grand illumination—
Admir'd the superstructure greatly,
  Nor gave one thought to the foundation.
Much too the Czar himself exulted,
  To all plebeian fears a stranger,
For, Madame Krudener, when consulted,
  Had pledg'd her word there was no danger.
So, on he caper'd, fearless quite,
  Thinking himself extremely clever,
And waltz'd away with all his might,
  As if the Frost would last for ever.

Just fancy how a bard like me,
  Who reverence monarchs, must have trembled
To see that goodly company,
  At such a ticklish sport assembled.

Nor were the fears, that thus astounded
My loyal soul, at all unfounded—
For, lo! ere long, those walls so massy
  Were seiz'd with an ill-omen'd dripping,
And o'er the floors, now growing glassy,
  Their Holinesses took to slipping.
The Czar, half through a Polonaise
  Could scarce get on for downright stumbling;
And Prussia, though to slippery ways
  Well used, was cursedly near tumbling.

It is not a lofty form of verse, but it has been long popular in England, and Moore is among its most varied and skilful practitioners.

PART THREE

THE LAST YEARS

I came when the sun on that beach was declining,
The bark was still there, but the waters were gone.

CHAPTER XVII

WELCOME HOME

A climacteric—O'Connell—Moore's *History of Ireland*—Moore and the Whigs—Visitors to Bowood—An evening with Wordsworth—Young Tom at the Charter House—A pension from the Government—Visit to Ireland—12 Aungier Street again—The Theatre—Avoca—Wexford—Bannow

THE year 1834 was a climacteric in Moore's life. The publication of the last number of the *Melodies*, inferior though it was, marked the real end of his life's work, and cut him off finally from active participation in the march of nationalism in Ireland. When O'Connell protested against the poem already quoted (p. 211) Moore's retort was so outspoken that it made any pretence of further collaboration impossible. "That disgraceful day", "The annual stipend of the begging box", "Mighty Unit of a Legion of Ciphers": none of the phrases was calculated to "alleviate" the burden of the poem or its even more explicit note.[1] O'Connell's reply was that he had nothing to regret, and that Moore had "betrayed great apathy in the Cause of Ireland ever since the measure of Emancipation was effected".

Moore, in turn, pointed out that O'Connell himself had praised his *Fitzgerald*, and that *The Travels of an Irish Gentleman* was "deeply political". It was a pretty quarrel, not improved, in the following year, by the appearance, in the *Quarterly* and elsewhere, of an extract from Willis's book, purporting to give an account of remarks made by Moore about O'Connell at Lady Blessington's. Finally, in 1836, as the result of an instinc-

[1] "Written in one of those moods of hopelessness and disgust which come occasionally over the mind, in contemplating the present state of Irish patriotism."

tive friendly move by O'Connell, the two met at Burke's and were reconciled. But Moore's active work for his country was done.

The same was true of his career as a writer. Nothing which he wrote after this is of real importance. He was past his best. The eighteen years that remained to him did much for his character, but nothing for his reputation, beyond bringing to him the fruits of earlier sowing. In spite of this, they are of intense interest in the study of the man. We have seen him learning how to live; we shall now see him learning how to die. The spectacle is moving, and, except for the few last clouded years, impressive.

II

The beginning of 1834 found Moore at Sloperton. The finishing off of the *Melodies* entailed a "ruinously inconvenient" visit to London, which had its consolations; the usual round of dinners, calls, and amusements, a shake of the hand from Peel at the door of the House, and, not long afterwards, his promise to nominate Moore's second boy, Russell, for the Charter House. Moore saw also Lord Melbourne, Lord John Russell, Rogers, and Hume, who gave Tom a legacy.

Back at Sloperton, he worked hard at his newest project, a *History of Ireland*,[1] but suffered a great deal from eye trouble. He and Bessy celebrated the twenty-third anniversary of their wedding—"we were never more *one* in our lives, which is saying a good deal". Tom came home from school, and Moore's sister Ellen came for a visit. She was still active and well, but Kate (Catherine) had for several years been an invalid.

---

[1] Two copies of the agreement for this survive, dated January 1833. It was originally to have been in two volumes, to be sold outright to Longmans for £1,500. Longmans copy was signed on their behalf by Dionysius Lardner. Moore had not signed his copy, but had struck out various clauses of which he apparently disapproved, and pencilled in emendations to them.

In July, Moore again visited London. He made no secret of his disillusion with the Whigs.

"How rapidly and truly they have confirmed all my worst predictions of them! . . . I have always said that they were like Mazeppa, tied fast to the mad horse they had let loose, and must see its course out."

Throughout these years, he was obsessed with the dread of revolution. "The country is now fairly in for revolution, and stop it who can," he notes gloomily a few months later, when the Government had fallen. "I have never indeed, made any secret to any of them of my feelings of distaste at their being in office, nor of the little concern it would give me to see them out." A month after that he said—characteristically—in a letter, "I was but little disposed to take part with my friends, the Whigs, while in, yet now that they are out, and in their natural position, they would become, I thought, the true rallying point of the country." Lord John Russell's good-natured gibe hit the mark exactly (p. 214). Moore's political thought, like his poetical, was apt to be chilled by the touch of reality.

Meanwhile, he was making the best of summer in town, varying " 'all worky, worky', as the negro says" with parties and visits to the theatre. If there was a suspicion of unreality about his politics, it was not for want of first-hand information. On August 12th he was at Holland House,

"where I found a scene that would rather have alarmed, I think, a Tory of the full dress school. There was the Chancellor (i.e. Brougham) in his black frock coat, black cravat; while upon the sofa lay stretched the Prime Minister, (i.e. Melbourne), also in frock and boots, and with his legs cocked up on one of Lady Holland's fine chairs. Beside him sat Lord Holland, and at some distance from this group was my Lady herself, seated at a table with Talleyrand, and occupying him in conversation to divert his attention from the Ministerial confab at the sofa."

Next day, he forwent such pleasures to take Tom and

Russell to dinner and to the theatre: "I preferred disappointing myself to disappointing them." On the 14th, he took them home for the holidays, returning to work at Sloperton and dinners at Bowood, where he discussed, among other things, "the want of commanding talent that is now perceptible in every walk of intellect and in every country", and "the new and forced style of writing that has become popular both in England and France".

In September, Luttrell and Sydney Smith came to Bowood. Smith was in his best form, making Moore actually cry with laughing. Twice, at breakfast, Moore had "to start up from the table". This type of talk, "sometimes high comedy, sometimes farce; both perfect in their ways", was interspersed with serious discussions: Smith's conversation "as is usually the case in a tête-à-tête, grave and sensible". Smith was replaced by Lord John Russell, who talked politics "with his usual manly frankness", and the rest of the year was spent in hard work on the *History*.

Half-way through December, Kate died. Moore was prepared for her loss, and met it resignedly, since she had been a sufferer for years.

In the beginning of the next year, Moore was getting restive under the continuous work necessary to satisfy the Longmans about his *History*. He complained that, for the first time in his life, he was made to feel a hack, and told Rogers that, if he had realized what he was letting himself in for, he would have seen the publisher further before tying himself to such a task. However, a consultation in town procured a postponement of the volume, and Moore could breathe again and look around him. He went to Brooke's, and the night after to Rogers', where he found Wordsworth, who was "according to his usual fashion, very soliloquacious". Wordsworth told him,

". . . What certainly is no small disgrace to the taste of the English public, of the very limited sale of his works, and the very scanty sum, on the whole, which he had received for them, not more, I think, than about a thousand pounds in all. I dare say I must have made by my writings at least twenty times that sum; but then I have written twenty times as much, such as it is."

Wordsworth went on to discuss his own work at length, to contrast it with Moore's, and to speak of "the immense time it took him to write even the shortest copy of verses,—sometimes whole weeks employed in shaping two or three lines", a state of affairs which he blamed on the English language. He then began to praise Coleridge to such an extent that Moore demurred, but —very properly—Wordsworth took no notice. Finally, Moore became bored, and ceased to listen.

From his account, we can picture the whole scene very vividly: Wordsworth pontificating, Moore sitting forward, gripping the edge of his chair, longing to have his say, then realizing that it was not "possible, indeed, to edge in a word, till he *does* get tired", and resigning himself, "well pleased to be a listener": roused once again to protest about Coleridge, and, in the end, defeated, sinking back in his chair in "a little fit of abstraction". The two poets eventually emerged to find "the night desperate wet", and Wordsworth, who had only to go as far as Jermyn Street, "very goodnaturedly undertook to send a hackney-coach".

There was always good company at Rogers'. On another evening, Moore dined there with Turner the painter, who confessed that he longed to go to Ireland, but was afraid. He went down to the Charter House to see Tom, and tried to let the headmaster see that he could not allow the boy £250 a year to go to college. He was horrified at "the ruinous system of English schools and colleges", and complained that the tutors seemed "to take a sort of vulgar pride in the style of living of their pupils".

The straitness of means, which he shrank from obtruding on the headmaster, was real. His need was known in London, and his name had not the old magic. After his visit to the Charter House, he busied himself (now that his contract with the Powers

was over) in trying to arrange for future musical work. Finally
he reached an agreement with Cramer and Addison's, but it left
a good deal to be desired.

"Our interview ended in my leaving the songs (eleven in
number and one to be added) in his hands, without the price
having been settled; nor any other agreement made except that
I was to draw . . . upon account, for £100 at three months,
leaving the rest to be arranged at some future period. This is
always the fate of poor devils like myself, who, being in want of
an immediate supply, are unable to hold out for good terms. It
made my heart, however, a good deal lighter, to be thus enabled
to meet the demands upon me at home."

The price ultimately fixed was £15 a song—very different
from the £50 for each of the *Melodies*.

Back at Sloperton, he resumed work on the *History* and on a
new Fudge collection, *The Fudges in England*. He resisted further
temptations to London, and mentions that Bowles was pro-
foundly astonished when he showed him a card from the
Duchess of Kent inviting him to meet their Majesties.

"Good God," exclaimed Bowles reverently, "what an
honour! You mean to go up, don't you?"

But Moore, to his surprise, said he had not the slightest notion
of doing so. He had changed since his first visit to London.

III

Then two great pieces of good fortune befell him, a triumphal
visit to Ireland, and a pension from the Government. The latter
was a godsend. In May, Lord John Russell had offered him a
pension for one or both of the boys. Moore replied with joy and
gratitude. He had long since, he said, given up all hope that his
great friends would ever think him worthy of place or office,
and Lord John had chosen the only way of helping him which
he would not instantly decline.

THOMAS MOORE IN LATER YEARS
From a miniature portrait in the National Gallery, Dublin

"I live from hand to mouth, and not always very sure that there will be anything in the *former* for the *latter*. You may have some notion of my means of my going on when I tell you that for my last published volume I received £750, and that I was two years and a half employed upon it. You should not have been annoyed at this view of the interior, but for your own kind consideration of my wants."

Melbourne, however, took the view that whatever was done should be done for Moore himself. On this Lord John offered Moore a Head Clerkship in the State Paper Office, which carried a salary of £300 a year, "with coals, candles, etc.". At the same time he did not advise him to accept it, and Moore had no difficulty in refusing. It would take up his whole time, and bring him in much less than he was making already "in a far more agreeable manner".

Then came a letter from Lansdowne, saying that he had talked with Melbourne about giving him an official pension, which he was convinced Moore ought to accept. Moore agreed to be guided by him entirely, and, after he had crossed to Ireland, he heard that the grant had gone through. Melbourne had mentioned the matter to the King, who made no objection.

The joy of the Moores at this windfall warms the heart. Tom "scribbled a few lines . . . to my sweet Bess, to inform her of this good news". Her letter crossed his.

"Can it *really* be true that you have a pension of £300 a year? . . . At present, I can think of nothing but £300 a year, and dear Russell jumps and claps his hands with joy. Tom is at Devizes. . . . If the story is true of the £300 pray give dear Ellen twenty pounds, and *insist* on her drinking five pounds worth of wine *yearly*, to be paid out of the £300 a year . . . Three hundred a year, how delightful! But I have my fears that it is only a castle in the air. I am sure I shall dream of it: and so I will get to bed, that I may have this pleasure *at least*; for I expect the morning will throw down my castle."

18

And in the morning:

"Is it true? I am in a fever of hope and anxiety, and feel very oddly. No one to talk to but sweet Buss, who says, 'Now Papa will not have to work so hard, and will be able to go out a little.' You say I am so 'nice and comical' about the money. Now you are much more so (leaving out the 'nice') for you have forgotten to send the cheque you promised." And finally, "N.B. If this good news be true, it will make a great difference in my *eating*. I shall indulge in butter to potatoes. *Mind* you do not tell this piece of gluttony to *any* one."

On his return home, Moore was able to describe his Irish visit to Rogers in a letter:

"You have at last heard, with all the world, that while the People were crowning me at Bannow the King was pensioning me at St James's (a concurrence of circumstances, I flatter myself, not common in history); and never, I must add, did golden shower descend upon a gentleman nearer what is called his 'last legs' than I was at the moment when this unasked-for favour lighted upon me. With a little time and a good deal of work, I have now . . . every prospect of surmounting my difficulties."

And he offers to repay Rogers the two hundred pounds owing to his "best of good friends". "With the Longmans I am deeply dipped", but that could be repaid from the profits of the *History*.

IV

The visit to Ireland was one of the happiest experiences in Moore's whole life. He set off by the new railroad, travelling at some twenty miles an hour, and highly approved of it. It was so steady that he could write without difficulty. Arrived in Dublin, he stayed at his sister Nell's, where he found the usual warm welcome and even more than the usual comfort. All was well. Dublin was delighted to see him, and the new *Fudge* book was selling famously. A couple of days after his arrival, he revisited his old house in Aungier Street.

"On accosting the man who stood at the door, and asking whether he was the owner of the house, he looked rather gruffly and suspiciously at me, and answered 'Yes'; but the moment I mentioned who I was . . . his countenance brightened up with the most cordial feeling, and seizing me by the hand he pulled me along to the small room behind the shop (where we used to breakfast in old time), exclaiming to his wife . . . with a voice tremulous with feeling, 'Here's Sir Thomas Moore, who was born in this house, come to ask us to let him see the rooms, and it's proud I am to have him under the old roof.' He then without delay, and entering at once into my feelings, led me through every part of the house, beginning with the small old yard and its appurtenances, then the little dark kitchen where I used to have my bread and milk in the morning before I went to school; from thence to the front and back drawing rooms, the former looking more large and respectable than I could have imagined, and the latter with its little closet, where I remember such gay supper-parties, both room and closet fuller than they could well hold, and Joe Kelly and Wesley Doyle singing away together so sweetly. The bedrooms and garrets were next visited, and the only material alteration I observed in them was the removal of the wooden partition by which a little corner separated off from the back bedroom . . . to form a bedroom for me. The many thoughts that came rushing in upon me in thus visiting for the first time since our family left it, the house in which I passed the first nineteen or twenty years of my life may be more easily conceived than told; and I must say, that if a man had been got up specially to conduct me . . . it could not have been done with more tact, sympathy and intelligent feeling than it was by this plain honest grocer; for as I remarked to Hume, as we entered the shop, 'Only think, a grocer's still.' When we returned to the drawing-room, there was the wife with a decanter

of port, and glasses on the table, begging us to take some refreshment, and I with great pleasure drank her and her good
husband's health. When I say that the shop is still a grocer's, I
must add, for the honour of old times, that it has a good deal
gone down in the world since then, and is of a much inferior
grade of grocery to that of my poor father, who, by the way,
was himself one of nature's gentlemen, having all the repose and
good breeding of manner by which the true gentleman in all
classes is distinguished."

His real triumph was on August 15th, when he went with
Hume to the theatre.

"Found that the audience had been getting rather impatient at
the long delay of my appearance. Shouts of 'Moore!' and rounds
of applause on my first showing myself; but it was evident they
thought the place I had fixed upon too retired: and many comical
hints of this feeling were given to me from the galleries; such as
'Tom, don't be shy!' 'Come, show your Irish face, Tom; you
needn't be ashamed of it!' This latter appeal gave me an opportunity of making what the actors call 'a hit', for I immediately
stretched forth from the box, and, in a very sincere fit of
laughter, bowed round to the whole house, which produced
peals of laughter and plaudits in return. Thinking it was now
time to put myself *en evidence* before them, I went down to the
pit-box taken by the Mearas for themselves and my sister, and
planted myself by the side of Ellen, in the front row. Then came,
indeed, the real thunder of the gods. The people in the pit stood
up and hurrahed; and many of them threw up their hats, trusting
to Providence for their ever returning to them again. I then saw,
to my horror, that there was a general expectation I should make
them a speech; but, thinking it impossible that I could be heard,
I resolved to make *that* my excuse—at least to those near me.
But to my still greater consternation (for I really knew not what
to say) I found, in the very first opening of my lips, that the
whole house, by one common and instantaneous consent,

became as mute as a churchyard. I had nothing for it, however, but to go on, and plead, in the very face of all this silence, the impossibility of my voice being heard through such a space, adding only that they could not doubt how much I felt their kindness, and how much I should *ever* feel it. I then sat down amidst as many and hearty plaudits as ever crowned the most sublime oration. Numbers in the pit crowded towards the box to shake hands with me; and as I was obliged to stoop down to reach their zealous grasps, Ellen was afraid . . . that I should be pulled over by them into the pit. The farce, which had been interrupted all this time, and the actors left standing on the stage, to gape at *our* performance, was now suffered to proceed; and after remaining about ten minutes longer, I thought it as well to take my leave."

From Dublin Moore drove off in a landau and four to the Vale of Avoca and the Meeting of the Waters. He had not been there since the visit which inspired the song, and now, appealed to by his companions to decide where he had sat, and which meeting, the first or the second, he had had in mind, he felt a sense almost of proprietorship as he looked around him. "How wise it was of Scott," he remarks, "to connect his poetry with the beautiful scenery of his country! Even indifferent verses derive from such an association a degree of vitality which nothing else could impart to them."

From Avoca he proceeded to Gorey and Enniscorthy, where he met Mr Boyse, who was responsible for what was to be the climax of the whole trip, a visit to Bannow. Boyse confirmed the favourable impression Moore had formed from his letters. All the same, he was glad to give him the slip and go by himself for "a most delicious walk" by the Slaney. "It was likewise delightful . . . to be *alone* in such a scene, for it is only alone that I can enjoy Nature thoroughly; men and women disturb such scenes dreadfully."

Next day they went on to Wexford, where Moore revived

childhood memories of his visit to old Tom Codd, his grand-father. His strongest memory was of going to a ball one night, and of returning home by himself. This seemed to him a great and manly feat, and it was only in later years that he came to suspect that the Assembly Rooms cannot have been very far from Tom Codd's house. Now the suspicion was proved correct. There was only a door or two between them.

While Moore was inspecting the place, a few people gathered round, and some old women ran before him to the house for which he was seeking. It had come down in the world, and become "a small pothouse".

"Here, sir," cried the old women in chorus. "This is the very house where your grandmother lived. Lord be merciful to her!"

Of his grandmother Moore had no recollection. She died before his visit. His grandfather he remembered very well. There was no trace of the weaving machinery that used to be upstairs, nor of the business of which Moore's mother had told him. She "used to say that he was a provision merchant, which sounded well, and I have no doubt he may have been concerned in that trade, but I suspect that he was also a weaver". Anyway, concluded Moore, he was one of the noblest and kindest of God's creatures, even though he came from so lowly a home.

V

The visit to Bannow was eagerly awaited, and no effort had been spared to make it a success. Affection and solicitude guided every stage of the proceedings, every step of the way.

21 Augt. 35

Dear John,

Our beloved Bard is going to Bannow, take every Earthly care of him.

Yrs sinc^y
M. Scallon

J. Hanlon, Esq.

Boyse was anxious about his guest's first impressions, being at pains to explain to Moore that the harvest season would prevent as large a crowd from assembling as would have come at any other time, and worrying still further, on the day itself, lest uncertainty as to the time of Moore's arrival and the precise road by which he was coming should cause "a dispersion of the multitude". His anxiety was needless.

"We now saw at a distance a party of horsemen on the look-out for us, bearing green banners, and surrounded by people on foot. This party, which turned out to be a mere detachment from the main body, now proceeded in advance of us, and after a short time we came in sight of the great multitude—chiefly on foot, but as we passed along we found numbers of carriages of different kinds, filled with ladies, drawn up on each side of the road, which, after we had passed them, fell into the line and followed in procession. When we arrived at the first triumphal arch, there was the decorated car and my Nine Muses, some of them remarkably pretty girls, particularly the one who placed the crown on my head; and after we had proceeded a little way, seeing how much they were pressed by the crowd, I made her and two of her companions get up on the car behind me. As the whole affair has been described in print (diffusely and enthusiastically enough, Heaven knows!), I shall not here waste time and words upon it, though certainly it would be difficult to say too much of the warmth and cordiality of feeling evinced by the whole assemblage, as well as the quickness and intelligence with which the very lowest of them entered into the whole spirit of the ceremony. In advance of the car was a band of amateur musicians, smart young fellows, in a uniform of blue jackets, caps, and white trowsers, who, whenever we stopped at the arches erected along the road, played some of the most popular Irish Melodies, and likewise more than once, an air that has been adapted to Byron's 'Here's a health to thee, Tom Moore.' As we proceeded slowly along, I said to my pretty

Muse behind me, 'This is a long journey for you.' 'Oh, Sir,' she exclaimed, with a sweetness and kindness of look not to be found in more artificial life, 'I wish it was more than three hundred miles.' It is curious, and not easy, perhaps, to be accounted for, that as I passed along in all this triumph, with so many cordial and sweet faces turned towards me, a feeling of deep sadness came more than once over my heart. Whether it might not have been some of the Irish airs they played that called up mournful associations connected with the reverse of all this smiling picture, I know not, but so it was."

After this, there were speeches and greetings, and Moore retired to spend the night with Boyse, who had given up his own bedroom to him. He exchanged civilities with Boyse's eighty-one-year-old mother, with his sister, and his niece, a girl of fourteen who, never having seen "a bard", could not imagine what such a thing was, and had accordingly been most anxious for his arrival. Next morning there were deputations and addresses, of which the following is a fair sample:

To THOMAS MOORE ESQ.
SIR,

We have been deputed to wait upon you by the Landholders and other Inhabitants of Bannow and its Vicinity to express to you the feelings of unmingled joy with which we received the glad tidings of your approach to this peaceful and happy section of your native Island.

Sir, We have it in special and emphatic command from those on whose behalf we have sought this interview, to say that you are no stranger here; that our geographical position remote and insulated as it is has not precluded us from a familiar knowledge of those transcendent talents, those fascinating accomplishments, but above all of that ardent love of country, which have awakened in the hearts of your admiring countrymen, emotions of no common pride, and filled a delighted world with your praise.

Sir, No sooner was it known that you were coming among us, than all was instant and electric gladness. You saw as you approached our confines the Reaper fling aside his sickle, to join the breathless crowds who flew to offer you the homage of friendly hands and devoted hearts; you saw the shrunken and sinewy arms of our old men, and those alike of our sober matrons and modest maids upraised and open to receive you; and you heard the lisping accents of infancy invoking Heaven to have in its care the life and welfare of our illustrious visitor.

Distinguished, Excellent Sir, We most cordially bid you welcome. We wish for you length of days and store of happiness. We exult and glory in your living fame, we predict its enduring triumphs over Oblivion and Envy and Time itself; we honour your spotless fidelity to the cause of Ireland; we hallow your genius ever ready to do battle in behalf of the oppressed; we pore upon your writings, we quote your sentences, we sing your songs; Oh Sir, when again you "Go where glory waits *you*" in the land of the stranger, let not that be unremembered which has awaited you in this sequestered corner of your own.

We learn with pain that your visit to us will be a short one—May not a second be longer protracted? Let us think so—and if we must give utterance at an early day to the withering word Farewell—Leave with us—Bard, Scholar, Gentleman, Historian, Patriot, Friend! Leave with us the assurance that it will not be for ever

John McBrien	Patrick Corish
Edward Colfer	Richard Reville
James Crane	William Murphy
Samuel Sely	Martin Doyle
Roger Sweetman	Thos. Meylor
Andrew Devereux	Nicholas Ffrench

In his reply, Moore spoke louder and "less Englishly" than the day before. He never had much of a brogue, and his English accent was not always too well received. Then comes a pleasant touch.

"Among other introductions I was presented in form to the reverend president of Peter's College and a number of Catholic clergymen who accompanied him. Just as I was approaching this reverend body, I saw among the groups that lined the way, my pretty Muse of yesterday, and her young companions, still arrayed in their green wreaths and gowns. Flesh and blood could not resist the impulse of stopping a minute to shake hands with a few of them, which I did most heartily, to the great amusement of all around, not excepting the reverend president himself, who had been approaching me with a grave face when I was thus interrupted; and who, immediately joining in the laugh, said, very good-humouredly, 'I like to see character display itself.' "

Then there were dances, Moore taking the floor with his young Muse, and surrendering her "very *unwillingly*" to her former partner. A pretty Quaker asked him for his autograph. A flag, bearing the words "*Erin go bragh*, and Tom Moore for ever", floated over the house. A green balloon inscribed "Welcome, Tom Moore", was released over the dancers' heads.

Before he left, the delighted poet paid a visit to a convent in Wexford, on the pressing invitation of the Mother Superior, who was an old acquaintance of his sister's. Her letter was in such a strain that he could hardly have refused. After expressing her sense of "the *Lustre, your birth* has shed" on Dublin and Wexford, she continued:

"Permit me *then, to beseech of you not* to leave this country without coming to the convent.

"Oh! No not to deprive *us* of the pleasure of seeing you, as from our peculiar situation it may never again be possible to us."

And wound up nobly—

"But I must owe all, and everything to your kind condescension which shall be a source of everlasting happiness to me, and gratitude to you.

"I trust the animation of your presence (so long wished for in this county) has given, will plead my apology.—And I assure you that the beam of your appearance in the convent shall dwell for ever in the proudest, happiest and most fervent recollections of this community.

"Believe me with all the respect and esteem of which I am capable

"Your admiring Friend
"J. M. FRAYNE.

"WEXFORD PRESENTATION CONVENT.
  "*August the 25th,* 1835."

So Moore, of course, went, and was charmed with the lady's appearance and manner. He wondered whether she would like to be complimented on her good looks, but "did not venture it". She asked him to play the organ, which he did, and then conducted him to the garden, where he found he was to plant a myrtle.

" 'Oh, Cupid, Prince of Gods and men!', planting a myrtle in a convent garden! As soon as I had (awkwardly enough) deposited the plant in the hole prepared for it, the gardener while filling in the earth, exclaimed, 'This will not be called *myrtle* any longer, but the Star of Airin!' Where is the English gardener that would have been capable of such a flight?"

On his way home—he crossed to Liverpool—Moore and Hume went to take a look at Mayfield Cottage, which they found altogether neglected and wretched-looking, and then to Alton Towers, to stay with the Shrewsburys. Here there was more ceremony, a harper in full costume playing one of the *Melodies* to greet him, a sprig of ivy from Petrarch's tomb to be planted, and a dahlia which he must choose to bear his name. From Alton he was glad to go to Cooper, his old friend the cotton spinner, and talk of "old times and old recollections, which to me was worth a thousand such pompous days as the two last". Then, back once more to Sloperton, to what Bessy called a "quiet, everyday sort of stillness" broken by occasional visits to Bowood.

The large proportion of the Journal which is devoted to London and parties tends to make us forget that by far the greater part of Moore's time was spent at his country home.

CHAPTER XVIII

TOM AND BESSY

Difficulties with Power—*Collected Poems*—Death of Moore's
mother—His two boys, Tom and Russell—Tom in the army—
He goes to India—Anxieties on his behalf—Russell also goes to
India—Illness and return of Russell—His death at Sloperton—
Tom sells his commission—The Foreign Legion—A cruel hoax
—Death of Ellen—The fatal letter

IT would be pleasant to take leave of Moore there, at Sloperton,
after the return from Bannow, a festivity so much in keeping
with his own temperament: to say good-bye to him at home
with his Bessy, the glow still warm at his heart, and the timely
arrival of the pension promising security. For, after this, the
shades begin to close upon him. Little lay ahead but sorrow and
decline. It was not that he had no further joys and triumphs.
There was another happy visit to Ireland in 1838, when he made
one more speech in a theatre, telling the delighted audience that
there was no title of honour or distinction that he could value
half so much as that of being called the poet of the Irish people.
There was one more literary success, the publishing of his collected poems. The copyright in the *Melodies* belonged to Power.
Moore was no longer on friendly terms with him. It was Moore's
practice to draw money from his publisher on account, as he
needed it, and he was often on the wrong side of the ledger.
Keeping no accounts himself, he did not realize how much he
had drawn, and thus, in the course of the long agreement with
Power—it ran for more than twenty years—there was ample
scope for dispute.

The relations between the two had been cordial to begin with,
and Moore was in the habit of giving Power all manner of com-

missions to execute for him, domestic and otherwise. He wrote from Sloperton, in the summer of 1818:

"If there be any fish you could send us on Saturday that would keep well till Monday (when we have the Bowles's to dine with us) I should be very glad of it—but do not venture unless the weather and the state of the fish is such as to promise certainty in its keeping. If you can get any salt salmon (done like cod) it would be perhaps better."

Small wonder that, on a later occasion, the publisher burst out to Croker: "By God, Mr Croker, I am his banker, bill-acceptor, and fish agent—letter carrier, hotel keeper, and publisher, and now he wants to make me his shoeblack."

When, in 1832, Moore came to look into the accounts, he did not like what he found. Already suspicious that he was being cheated, he proceeded to quarrel with Power over sums paid to Bishop, as arranger, out of the annual £500. Later, he suggested arbitration: and the arbitrators, Longman and Rogers on Moore's side, and Rees on Power's, found that the publisher "had not a leg to stand on".[1] The matter was more or less patched up, and Power raised no objection to the collected edition. Then, in 1836, he died, and the rights passed to his widow; whereupon Longmans purchased them, for the considerable sum of £1,000, and paid as much to Moore for preparing the edition and writing prefaces. By a cruel irony, when the book appeared, in 1841, Moore was too hard hit by misfortune to enjoy its success.

It was his last literary work of any importance. A series of squibs for the *Morning Chronicle*, his *History of Ireland*, and *Alciphron* are the others. The *History*, by far the most ambitious, was a failure. Moore set out to write a history of his country without knowing its language. He worked honestly, and gave

---

[1] Croker says Power was in the right, but his defence is hardly convincing: "While [Moore] declaims, like Shylock, 'I will have my bond,' Mr Power modestly pleads '*lex mercatoris*'—established custom and 'silence gives consent'."

some offence to patriots of a certain familiar type by baldly stating the results of his researches: but the attempt was foredoomed, and the writing is lifeless.

When he had got more than half-way through, he learned that there were several Histories, in Irish, which had long been familiar to scholars.

"Good God!" he exclaimed despairingly, "why did I ever undertake to write a history of Ireland?"

It was a rhetorical question. He knew the answer only too well.

But it was through his family that the worst blows fell. Mrs Moore had died in 1832. Tom, hearing of her illness from Ellen, hurried over, hardly expecting to find her alive: but, by the time he arrived, she was better.

The second day after his arrival, she paid him a great tribute.

"Well, my dear Tom, I can say, with my dying breath, that you have from the first to the last done your duty, and far more, indeed, than your duty, by me and all connected with you."

Her condition improved, and, after a few days, Moore returned, his mind more or less at rest. She lived for a year after that, but he never saw her again. The news of her death plunged Moore into a deep gloom. It was, he said, "like a part of one's life going out of one". When at last he shook the depression off, it was in order to settle down more firmly than ever to the enjoyment of life with Bessy and to hopes for the future of his two boys, Tom and Russell: hopes that were doomed to disappointment and total loss.

II

Of Tom, the elder boy, nothing has so far been recorded except his birth, an illness in infancy, and the fact that, on Peel's recommendation, he was at the Charter House. He was an attractive child, the darling of his mother and of his Aunt Ellen. Ellen had lost her heart to the boy when his parents brought them both over to Dublin. After Anastasia's death, she paid regular visits to Sloperton, and the attachment deepened.

The second boy, Russell, was born in 1823, and grew into a gentle, affectionate child: but he was delicate, and, on this account only, a source of constant anxiety to his parents. Otherwise, he never worried them, as Tom, who was spoilt, began to do quite early.

Moore's chief practical difficulty in life was that he never earned enough to gratify his extravagant tastes, or rather, the style of living to which his friends committed him. Bessy living cheaply at home, Tom cutting a dash in town, was too often the division of labour. It was not altogether Tom's fault. For years he had to visit town, in the terms of his contract with Power, to sing his songs and give them a vogue, and a man who is lavishly entertained in the best houses cannot escape without spending money and doing a little entertaining in return. Young Tom, as he grew up, observed the figure his father cut in town. He talked to his friends at the Charter House, imbibed their ideas of money, and began to think on grand lines, and to be unable to reconcile the life at Sloperton with the life in town. Like many other sons before and since, he did not realize that Moore's carefulness at home was due to real need, and concluded that his father was mean. This point of view was not improved by the celebrated "independence", which made Moore resent very much any effort made by others to lighten the burden, even if it were only by a tip to either of the boys. The effect of this was lost when Tom saw his father tip Sydney Smith's son.

"While I was doing this, Bessy took Tom aside (on whom we have always impressed the propriety of not taking money from any one but ourselves) and endeavoured to explain away the inconsistency of my doing with these boys what I did not choose should be done with him; telling him that some people did not mind their sons taking money, but that he knew *our* feeling on the subject was quite different."

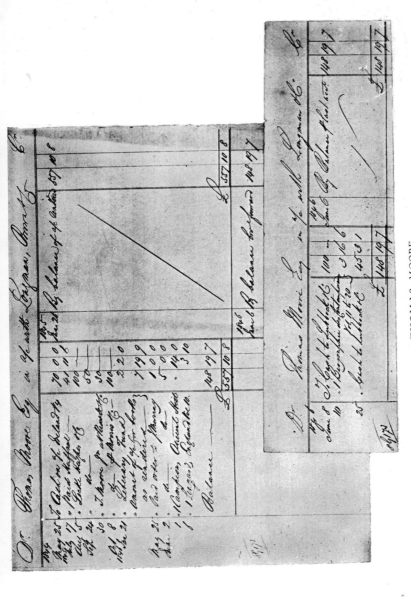

THOMAS MOORE

A facsimile account from his publisher

(Note the two sums for "T. Moore Junior")

It is probable that the explanation failed to satisfy its recipient. Moore was trying to have it both ways, educating the pair above their financial station in life, and expecting them to be wiser than he had been as a young man in a like position. And he could earn, whereas they could not. Small wonder that Tom, who had his father's easy-going nature, but none of his independence and pride, became extravagant, and caused many head-shakings at Sloperton. Russell, level-headed and more perceptive, went his way quietly. His time at home with Bessy, after Tom had gone to school, set the final impress on a thoughtful character.

III

The headmaster of Charter House, as we saw, proposed "college" for Tom, but Tom elected to join the army. Moore, who had been so indignant about the expense of College, was not much better off for the choice. He seems, however, to have believed that Tom would be able to live on his pay; a belief of which Tom soon undeceived him. The boy was gazetted in 1837, and sent to Paris to learn the language, joining his regiment the year after. The first place at which he was stationed was Cork: and the following letter is of interest.

CORK *March* 15th 1838.

MY DEAR SCOTT,

Will you have the goodness to tell Miss Moore, if you should see her, that I dined in company with her nephew yesterday, and found him a most intelligent and agreeable young man. He has just joined the 22nd. Regiment at Cork Barracks, but he expects the route to Dublin in a few weeks. He told me he was most anxious to write to her, but he could not remember her number in Dublin, as he believed she had changed lately. The first person he met in this country was my sister, at a Ball, and though he tried to pass incog., yet she soon found him out, and he became

forthwith the young Lion of the day. Our family have made it
their duty to pay him every attention and he has come in for a
good round of fun since he came here. He is a very handsome
young man, and the officers tell me very likely to be a favourite
with his corps.

If you see the 'Illustrious,' before he leaves town, tell him this,
as it will please him greatly. Kindest respects to Miss Molloy and
believe me ever Truly yours

EDWARD BULLEN.

82 SOUTH MALL
   To JAMES SCOTT MOLLOY ESQ.

The "Illustrious" must have been as greatly pleased as Mr
Bullen expected, for he kept the letter.

Miss Moore was, of course, Ellen, and soon, to her joy, young
Tom was moved to Dublin. When Moore crossed in the summer
of 1838, father and son went about a good deal together, and it
is probable, as Mr Gwynn has suggested, that, seeing his father
courted by the greatest in the land, young Tom was encouraged
in his exaggerated ideas of the family resources, and felt even
surer that it was nothing but meanness that kept him so short.
The boy had his good points, but everyone conspired to spoil
him, and he lacked staying power. He was courageous enough.
When, at his first school, he received an undeservedly severe
beating, he said nothing to his parents until the master had confessed, and, on being questioned, was "very manly and sensible"
about it.

Then his regiment was ordered to India. The hot climate completed his demoralization. Soon after his arrival, he drew a bill on
his father for £112. Moore was away when the bill came, and it
was Bessy who opened it. Horror-struck, she enclosed it in a
letter to Tom.

"I can hardly bring myself to send you the enclosed. It has
caused me tears and sad thoughts, but to you it will bring these

and hard hard work. Why do people sigh for children? They know not what sorrow will come with them. How can you arrange for the payment? And what could have caused him to require such a sum? Take care of yourself; and if you write to him, for God's sake let him know that it is the very last sum you will or can pay for him. My heart is sick when I think of you, and the fatigue of mind and body you are always kept in. Let me know how you think you can arrange this."

"I have already mentioned the difficulties," Moore writes in his Journal, some days later, "to which this bill of Tom's reduced me."

"I had not been more than a week or two at home, when another bill of his, drawn upon me at three months, for £100, was sent to me for acceptance. This blow coming so quick after the other, was, indeed most overwhelming. It seems on his arrival at Bombay, he found that his regiment had been ordered on active service, and he was accordingly obliged to provide such an outfit as would enable him to join it. I could not do otherwise, of course, than accept the bill; but how I am to pay it, when due, Heaven only knows."

Tom answered forgiveness by falling ill in "that wretched place, Lower Scinde". Under stress of the illness, he wrote a letter in which the better side of his nature, and his love of home associations, came uppermost. His parents were greatly cheered. "He will, I trust in God," writes his father, "be yet a pride and blessing to us."

IV

Meanwhile, Russell began to cause an even more serious anxiety. Like Tom, he wanted to go to India, and a cadetship in the Company's army was secured for him. But his health could not stand the climate. Lord Auckland, who had been kindness itself in welcoming the boy and smoothing his path, met him one day out driving, and, shocked at his appearance, took him straight to Government House, where he was put to bed and tended. A serious illness followed, from which the boy recovered: but the doctors warned him that he could not stay.

The next news was that Tom was coming home on sick leave. This was a heavy blow.

". . . how on earth", Moore writes, "am I to meet the additional expenses which the return of both boys will now entail, while still I am in debt too for most of the money which their first outfit, passage, etc. required? I am still willing, and thank God, able to work; but the power comes slower, and the effort is therefore more wearing."

The next letter brought relief. Russell was so much better that he had been able to attend a dinner-party, and the Company was going to pay his passage home. Still, Moore was in a tight corner.

"The difficulty as to how I can raise the £100 to meet Russell's draft, still haunts me most worryingly; there being, in addition to this, the yet unpaid bills for the outfits both of him and Tom."

Hume, however, good friend that he was, came to the rescue with a loan, and the immediate trouble was met. "Couldn't help remarking a little", says Moore, noting the fact, "on the essential difference there is between useful and merely ornamental friends. But one mustn't grumble: both are good in their different ways."

A few months later, Russell came home. The parents waited eagerly, and at last heard the rumble of wheels, and his voice, telling the driver not to drive in at the gate. He was afraid of spoiling the neat little gravel drive. Tom and Bessy looked at one another, their eyes alight at this typical instance of his thoughtfulness. Then all other considerations were banished by the sight of the boy himself, emaciated, white as death, clambering slowly down from the fly. They rushed to him and embraced him, speechless. The only calm one was Russell himself: but, even in that moment of anguish, Moore's first concern was for his Bessy, and the effect this might have upon her.

The doctor (Brabant) confirmed their fears. The boy was suffering from consumption, and was in real danger. Bessy put him in her own bed, and watched over him night and day, springing up every time he coughed to run to his side. "It is for *her* I most fear," Moore reports sadly in his Journal.

To the joy of them both, the rest and nursing produced a visible improvement, as even Brabant allowed. Moore was so far relieved as to go up to town for a few days. Then came a frightful blow. Tom was not simply coming home on sick leave: he had sold his commission. Thus, after costing his father £1,500 to establish him in a profession, he was coming back, without resources, in no better position than when he started.

Now was the moment for Moore to give his influential friends the chance to be useful as well as ornamental: but, probably because, having got his pension, he was ashamed to appear again in need, he did not tell them. All that was needed to buy back the commission was £400, which Moore could have had easily enough. Instead, borrowing a smaller amount from Mr Boyse of Wexford, he set about trying to get Tom a commission in the Austrian army. Tom was in France. He had not dared come home. Presently he wrote with the suggestion that he should join the Foreign Legion. Moore had plenty of friends in France, who used their influence at once, and made much of the prodigal. A hundred pounds or so was raised by another draft, to equip him for this new venture.

Meanwhile, Russell's improvement was not maintained. He was slowly sinking, and Moore was told to prepare for the worst. The boy felt no pain, and, in his quiet way, was happy. Sometimes he sang a little, and, one evening towards the end, asked his father to sing to him. Moore began, but after a few notes burst into tears.

Russell died in November.

"All is over. Our dear boy expired on the 23rd of last month, and the calmness, sweetness, and manliness of his last moments

were such as to leave, even in the mother's heart, not only comfort, but almost pleasure. He suffered but little indeed of actual
pain throughout the whole illness, nor was it till two or three
days before his death that he became aware of his danger. His
mother then, I think, suggested his taking the Sacrament, but he
declined doing so. On the morning of the 23rd, he asked his
mother to bring pen and ink, and make memorandums of some
little gifts he wished to leave. After inquiring about a bequest of
£100 left by Betty Starkie, which was to fall at some distant
period, he said, 'Very well,' and thus proceeded: 'Mrs Hughes
may have the chain; she will like that.' 'And your seal ring,'
asked his mother; 'there's your papa.' 'Papa won't wear it.' 'But
he will use it.' 'Yes, my ring then, to papa.' 'Your dressing case;
shall Tom have your dressing case?' 'He wouldn't like it. Let
Herbert Brabant have my dressing case.' He then proceeded, 'I
should like to give something to Annie' (the daughter of our
neighbour, Mrs Schomberg, with whom the poor fellow, before
he went to India, was rather in love); 'let Annie have the little
seal.' 'What for Ellen? Would you like her to have the little lip-
salve box, and Rogers's Italy?' 'Yes; send my hunting-whip to
Mr Schomberg. Polly Hughes my blue purse. Mr Hughes, of
Buckhill, would like my pencil.' 'And what for Tom?' asked his
mother again. 'I have nothing to leave that he would like. Give
him my dying love, and Campbell's poems.' He then stopped, as
if to rest. 'You haven't said anything for Mr Starkie?' To this he
made no reply. Turning to Ruth, our good-natured housemaid,
he thanked her for her kind attention to him during his illness,
adding, 'I suppose you'll soon be married, Ruth?' (the girl being,
he knew, engaged). 'Yes, sir, please God, some time.' He then
spoke of his clothes, and desired that such as his brother Tom did
not like should be sold or given to the poor. After he had rested
a little while, his mother asked whether she could do anything to
make him comfortable. 'Read to me,' he replied. 'What shall it
be?' 'Read to me about the Communion.' After she had read

some time he said, 'I think I shall take it.' His mother read a little more, and then said, 'Should you like Mr Drury sent for?' 'Yes, but not now.' The poor mother then read on until her feelings became too much for her, and she was obliged to stop. After an interval, she asked, 'Would you like to see Mr Drury to-day?' 'Yes.' He became then composed, and his mother, as usual, washed him, brushed his hair and teeth, and scented his pocket handkerchief. Drury came, and, after having talked with him for a short time, said that he did not hesitate to give him the Sacra-ment as soon as he liked. 'Now, or to-morrow?' 'Now,' answered the dear boy, and, turning to his mother, asked, 'Will you take it too?' 'Yes.' 'Very good.' He then attentively watched Drury's preparations for the Communion; and having before said that he feared Drury would find the room rather offensive, held out his handkerchief for him to smell to. He swallowed the consecrated bread with much difficulty; but when the ceremony was over, Bessy asked him how he felt, and he said, 'Better, and more comfortable.' 'Should you like Mr Drury to come again to-morrow?' said his mother. 'Yes, if I'm alive.' All this, which I have taken down from the poor mother's lips (not being able, myself, to stand the scene), took place on the morning of the 23rd, about eleven o'clock; and within three hours after our beloved child was a corpse."

Characteristically, Moore had once more absented himself from a scene which he felt he could not bear.

v

Moore had written to Tom, urging him to come and see his brother, but Tom could not, or at any rate did not, come. Nor did he come afterwards.

"A letter from Tom, which affected Bessy most sadly, telling us that he cannot come to us before his departure for Algiers. Bessy had counted upon seeing him most sanguinely, though (foreboding the difficulties that might arise) I endeavoured to prepare her for such a disappointment. The reasons he assigns for not applying for a furlough under the circumstances in which he is placed seem all right and prudent, but, not the less for that, disappointing and saddening."

The Moores were somewhat cheered to hear good news of him from Paris, and to be told that he was the first Englishman (*sic*) to obtain a commission in the Foreign Legion. But in less than two months, Tom was writing to say that he was "twenty times worse off than he was in India". Moore sighed. He knew the pay was poor, and the service rough and dangerous, but the boy had been *"suae fortunae faber"*. "However," he concludes, "(hard driven as I am), some further effort must be made to save him."

It was necessary. Almost the next communication from Tom was an appeal for £50 to save him from prison. Not knowing the ways of the place, he told his father, he had been led to incur some expenses which "weren't quite necessary". Moore sent him £30, the rest to follow.

Then someone played a cruel joke upon the needy poet. A letter came from Macroom, near Cork, announcing that a legacy of £300 had been left him. Moore was sceptical, but Bessy, delighted, began to build castles in the air. Soon they discovered that the whole thing was a hoax. "Alas, alas!" Moore wrote, "I wish no worse to the ingenious gentleman who penned the letter than an exactly similar disappointment."

"A strange life mine: but the best as well as pleasantest part of it lies at home. I told my dear Bessy, this morning, that while I stood at my study window, looking out at her, as she crossed the field, I sent a blessing after her. 'Thank you, bird,' she replied, 'that's better than money'; and so it is. 'Bird' is a pet name she gave me in our younger days."

VI

Ellen, from her yearly visits to Sloperton, had become almost
as dear to Bessy as she was to her brother. In February of 1846 a
letter came from her, to say she had not been well, and was going
to Blackrock for a change of air. She promised to write again,
and let them know "how she was coming on, or going off".
Evidently she expected the former process rather than the latter,
for she added a list of concerts and other engagements which she
had in prospect. She was to have written on Sunday, and when,
by Tuesday, no letter had come, Bessy expressed the fear that she
must be worse. On Wednesday, Bessy, down first to breakfast,
found a letter to say that her fears were realized. The Moores
were expecting friends to dinner—"a rare occurrence with us
now"—and Bessy, fearing Tom would be upset, thought it best
not to tell him, but to let the dinner take place. Evidently she had
some extra sense, for, during breakfast, she became violently
agitated, and had to get up from the table.

"I fear Ellen must be worse," she said, when Moore looked up
in quick concern.

He shook his head. "I assure you I think she will outlive us all."

At eleven o'clock a neighbour named Susan Hughes came to
the house. Her face was pale and troubled, and Bessy anxiously
asked what was the matter.

"Have you not heard, then, from Dublin?" asked the neighbour. "Is not Ellen ill?"

Bessy looked hard into her face, and read the truth.

"Then Ellen is dead?"

"She is."

In spite of her fears, the shock hit Bessy hard. As soon as she
recovered, a fresh problem confronted her. How should she
break the news to Tom? She went into the study where he was
working, and for a long time could not bring herself to tell him.
Then, in a roundabout way, she led up to it. Ellen was very ill.

Mrs Meara had written to Susan, asking her to break the news as best she could. Then, when Tom had grasped the truth, she told him how it had happened. As Ellen was getting into bed, the maid went out of the room, only for a few minutes. When she came back, she found her mistress dead. She had died suddenly, and without suffering.

The blow came at a bad time, for the Moores were already sadly worried about young Tom. This was the middle of February, and his last letter home had been written in November. They did not dare write to tell him of the death of his aunt, to whom he was most warmly attached, for fear of depressing him further.

Then, in the middle of March, came a strange and ominous-looking letter, which the old couple opened with trembling hands. It was to say that Tom had died in Africa. Stunned, they could not believe it, and sent off post haste to London and Paris for confirmation or denial. The news was true. "The last of our five children is now gone," Moore wrote, "and we are left desolate and alone. Not a single relative have I now left in the world!"

Some little time afterwards, they received Tom's last letter. Written in hospital, it told of the hardships he had undergone.

"You can easily conceive that exposing myself constantly through that period to the night air and penetrating dew was very unfit for one already so much weakened by illness. During a long time, indeed, I slept on the stones of the Court Gateway, where there was only a cheval-de-frise, as I had the command of the guard; and the Arabs continually fired through the gateway on our sentries. During all this time, I had violent cold 'night-sweats', which ended by bringing on a cough that eventually fell upon the chest; and it now appears that those doctors did not perfectly understand my complaint."

He went on to say how much he longed to come home, and to calculate how his means would allow for the journey.

"The Government stops fifty francs a month for the expenses. This leaves sufficient of my pay for the daily necessities; so that after having drawn what is necessary to pay my debts (from the sum you so kindly sent me), I trust I shall be able to save the remainder intact until my departure for Paris, from whence, when fully restored to health, I shall be able to reach Sloperton. . . . You would really laugh to see me; I am only skin and bone, and might be easily mistaken for Don Quixote's eldest son."

VII

An interesting relic of young Tom has recently been acquired for the Library of Moore's old University. It is a cardboard-covered exercise book, filled with his writing. Stuck on the front is "A Note Book of Young Tom's see Mrs Moore's Note": and below, in Bessy's hand, "Another proof of my poor Tom's industry this Book coming with other papers from Africa. B. M." The poor woman treasured with pathetic care anything that could reflect to her boy's credit.

The writing is neat, and surprisingly like Moore's own. Young Tom writes rather touching notes at the beginning and at the end, about good resolutions, and making a profitable use of his time. The contents are geographical and entomological notes, and there is a large map of the world. To the best of my knowledge, this is the only relic of him which has survived.

CHAPTER XIX

THE MEETING OF THE WATERS

Moore plays Bessy a trick—An evening at the Haymarket—
Certificates from Arcadia—Kingstown—The Order of Merit—
Failing powers—The *History of Ireland* finished—Trouble with
his eyes—Elected to Royal Irish Academy—A last visit to
Rogers—Twilight—Bessy survives her husband

MOORE's last years were not without their happy moments. He
had a temperament which no misfortune could crush, but his
Journal, in quantity alone, shows how swiftly his life sank.
Begun in 1818, it occupies roughly six and a half of the eight
volumes that make up Lord John Russell's Memoir. By the
end of Moore's fifth volume (Volume VI of the Memoir), it
has only got as far as 1833. The next volume covers eleven years,
and the last eight years of Moore's life are represented by a bare
thirty-two pages. After October 1847 he never made another
entry.

A note in 1839 shows one way at least in which Moore could
still find happiness.

"Have again played the same trick upon Bessy, with respect to
her supplies for the poor, as I have done more than once before,
—have confidentially got Boyse to send her a five-pound note,
as if from himself, for the poor of Bromham. It makes her happy
without the drawback of knowing it comes from my small
means, and, in the way she manages it, does a world of
good."

In the same year, he was delighted by a burlesque at the Haymarket, *Tim Moore*, in which several of the *Melodies* were sung.

The scene showed a hostess all agog to receive "the supposed poet". An old dandy was to cry "Dem'd foine" at everything he said. The poet arrived and wrote in their albums, and the lady sang him a medley made up of the first lines of different *Irish Melodies*. The audience vociferously encored this, whereupon the lady sang a second medley. "Altogether," wrote Moore, "between the fun of the thing, and the flattering proofs it gave of the intimate acquaintance of the public with me and my country's songs, I was kept in a state between laughing and crying the whole time. The best of it all, too, was that I enjoyed it completely *incog.*, being in a little nook of a box where nobody could get a glimpse of me."

He rushed off afterwards to Bedford Square, where he was expected, to sing himself.

This same summer, after a certain amount of correspondence, Moore received a certificate of admission to the Arcadian Academy. This was a curious survival of the back-to-nature cult that flourished in Italy in the last years of the seventeenth century. It was a society with pastoral ambitions and conventions, which met (weather permitting) in the open air, and bestowed upon its members the names of Greek shepherds and shepherdesses. Its productions had, needless to say, little in common with the Nature to which they were supposed to return. The members were recruited from the most fashionable circles, built themselves a theatre, and enjoyed a vogue which lasted for many years. By Moore's time, the "College" was moribund: but it sent him very pretty certificates, one to admit him, and a second running as follows:

The learned College of Arcadia, as a greater testimony of its esteem, most gentle and valorous *Lisimenes*, notwithstanding any law to the contrary, has decreed that on the very day on which you have been admitted to the Arcadians, there be transferred to your possession the vacant *Marathean* lands, after which you shall

in future be styled among us *Marathean Lisimenes*, being declared
an Arcadian shepherd of our number.

> Given at the Tabernacle of the Archives,
> under our official seal of guardianship,
> this 20th day of June, 1839.
> FILANDRO GERANTEO (President)
> FILENO ANTIGONIO (Vice-President)

What Moore thought does not appear. He made no comment
in his Journal, but he kept the certificates.

One day in 1841 Moore called upon Miss Berry, the lady who
had found him too well pleased with himself as a young man.
"I didn't so much like you in those days," she told him, taking
a hold of his "grizzly locks". "I like you better since you have got
these."

And, as he left her, he overheard her saying, "That's as good a
creature as ever lived."

That August, he crossed to Dublin, and paid a visit to Kingstown, as it then was.

"Went . . . to the jetty, the great promenade of a Sunday, and
was almost stared off my legs; my companions being Leigh and
Finlay. Shall not easily forget the hearty hug I got from an honest
fellow, who, on my dropping my umbrella, picked it up, and
giving it to me, threw his arms round my neck, ejaculating, 'My
sweet fellow!' Find he is the proprietor of a great glass-shop in
Dublin; and Finlay said that nothing would make him more
happy than my leaving my card at his house; so resolved to do it.
Went from the jetty to Lord Fortescue's, where I dined. After I
had dressed, sat looking out of the window at the beautiful bay
and the solitary light on Howth, and quite forgot how the time
went, till the servant came to tell me that the company were not
only all arrived, but were then going in to dinner. Found to my
shame that it was so."

II

Sydney Smith was all the time his kind and constant friend, coming to see him, and inviting him continually to his house.

DEAR MOORE,

I have a breakfast of philosophers to-morrow at ten *punctually*. Muffins and metaphysics; crumpets and contradiction. Will you come?

And again, a little later:

August 7th, 1843.

DEAR MOORE,—The following articles have been found in your room and forwarded by the Great Western! A right-hand glove, an odd stocking, a sheet of music paper, a missal, several letters, apparently from ladies, an Elegy on Phelim O'Neil. There is also a bottle of eau de Cologne. What a careless mortal you are.

God bless you.

This roused the careless mortal to reply with a set of doggerel verses. It was a novelty for him now to send verses to others. He received shoals of them, as before, and letters of every kind.

"Among my letters lately was one from a zealous teetotaller, who is about to publish a book on the subject; and, after saying that he does not recollect having ever seen any published opinions of mine on the subject, begs that I will favour him with a few sentences in favour of the cause. Wrote back to him to say that I thought no man had a right to preach what he does not practise, and that my own habits at table, though certainly not intemperate, extended to a freer use of wine than would author-ize me with a grave face to recommend abstinence to others."

An incident of the kind Moore loved best happened as he came out of a dinner with Washington Irving.

"The best thing of the evening (as far as *I* was concerned), occurred after the whole grand show was over. Irving and I came away together, and we had hardly got into the street, when a most pelting shower came on, and cabs and umbrellas were in requisition in all directions. As we were provided with neither, our plight was becoming serious, when a common cad ran up to me, and said, 'Shall I get you a cab, Mr Moore? Sure, ain't *I* the man that patronizes your Melodies?' He then ran off in search of a vehicle, while Irving and I stood close up, like a pair of male caryatides, under the very narrow projection of a hall-door ledge, and thought at last that we were quite forgotten by my patron. But he came faithfully back, and, while putting me into the cab (without minding at all the trifle I gave him for his trouble) he said confidentially in my ear, 'Now, mind, whenever you want a cab, Misthur Moore, just call for Tim Flaherty, and I'm your man.' Now, this I call *fame*, and of somewhat a more agreeable kind than that of Dante, when the women in the street found him out by the marks of hell-fire on his beard."

All the tokens of his fame that impressed Moore most, from the watchmaker in America to this, came from humble people.

In 1842 he received a tribute from the other extreme of society, the Order of Merit from Frederick the Great of Prussia, an award which he shared with Herschel the astronomer, and the great Faraday. This cheered him, and he needed cheering, for it came at the time of his greatest anxiety about Russell's health and Tom's lost commission. "Work and worry, my daily portion," an entry in his diary begins: but it was soon followed by something more spirited, when, on a visit to town, he met Lady Holland in her carriage in St James's Street, and was "of course" asked to dinner. He accepted gladly. "I had now dined two successive days at my own expense, which in London is a sort of monstrosity. 'Base is the slave that pays,' says ancient Pistol, and I feel deeply the truth of this aphorism when paying for a dinner for myself in London."

On September 15th, he sang for the first time since the time when he broke down in front of Russell, and was relieved to find his voice much the same as ever. He was able to charm an audience for several years yet, and kept something of his voice to the end.

For some time his literary powers had been flagging, and now his memory began to go.

"Shocked to find that I had promised myself yesterday to Sir Charles Lemon as well as to Bunbury; but if people will not send reminders, what is a many-dinnered gentleman to do? Found myself in another scrape to-day, having promised my company to *some* Amphytrion or other, but couldn't in the least remember *who*."

After this, the Journal shows many signs of failing powers. In 1844, he was laid low by a severe attack of influenza, but made a good recovery, and went to town, where, among other things, he called on Sydney Smith and found him laid up with gout and teaching himself French, "with all the verbs and their moods and tenses, etc., written out as neatly by his own hand as any young boarding-school Miss could have done it". It was his last sight of the famous wit, who died a year afterwards. Longmans at once wrote to Moore, suggesting that he should write a life of his friend: but Moore (with good reason) doubted his ability to do the theme justice.

III

Moore never recovered, mentally or physically, from the blow of Tom's death. He had already suffered from attacks of giddiness, and, as early as the year his father died, had been attacked with fits of violent, almost hysterical emotion, upon which he would have to run from the room and recover himself as best he might. These were most often brought on by singing. His feelings would rise to such a pitch that, as he himself put it, he thought his chest must burst asunder with the strain. Soon

20

after Tom died, he fell seriously ill, and his recovery was only nominal. All his former weaknesses were doubled. His memory became altogether untrustworthy, and, worst of all, his wit and his flow of talk dried up almost altogether. "When he did appear", writes Lord John Russell, "his gay flow of spirits, happy application of humorous stories, and constant and congenial ease were all wanting. The brilliant hues of his varied conversation had failed, and the strong powers of his intellect had manifestly sunk."

Even so, the stricken poet rallied such powers as were left to him to finish his *History*. All interest and pleasure had long gone from the task. "Thank God," he wrote to Bessy, "I feel *now* as if I should survive this dreary task. But often, while employed upon it, I have felt a sort of presentiment that both the work and its weary writer would fall into oblivion together." Happily, only half of the presentiment was justified. Longmans asked for a preface, but this Moore could not write, and at last, in despair, he left it to them to finish as best they might.

A letter from the firm, kind and forbearing, is evidence of the state to which he had been reduced.

LONDON *June* 12
1846

MY DEAR MR MOORE,

The recording angel has blotted out all omissions and commissions on your part regarding books borrowed and apparently not returned, as well as a loss of £11 . 17 . 6¾ (!) on those last sent back. So give yourself no further trouble about the books.

If you like to dispatch the Delphin classics, I will do my best for you, and the same spirit shall place to your account of good works, whatever can be allowed.

That Peel's Cabinet, and our own, should have had some difficulties about Ireland is not wonderful. We have the best of it how ever after all, for we are complete, and his will very soon be broken up.

Title, dedication, and preface will be all as you wish, and like my paper all is now couleur de rose, so here is one cheer for auld Ireland, and with one more for the last of its Bards, we shall as you say "row" along merrily at last.

I shall send you some complete copies and, if you will tell me how many, I shall be obliged.

Hoping you are recovering from London racket and [word illegible]

Believe me,
ever truly yours,
THOMAS LONGMAN.

The poet was lucky in his publishers. He had little money sense, and was for the greater part of his life a difficult man with whom to do business. His dealings with both Longman and Murray are one long record of direct requests for money, requests to cash bills, etc., occurring year in and year out with unfailing regularity. It was not that he tried to get more than was his due. It was that he could not realize that a number of small sums added up to make a single big sum. His resolutions were of the best.

"The remaining five hundred guineas I mean to leave for you to lay out, at your own time, in some advantageous way for my little boy, to whom I mean to make it over."

That was written in 1818, to Murray, but even then Moore failed to live up to his intention. In his later years, he was always in difficulties—pulling the devil by the tail, as his countrymen call it—and tried his publishers hard. Be it set down to their honour that both treated him throughout with magnanimity and forbearance. [1]

[1] Moore wrote to Power, in June 1818: "The Longmans have behaved with uncommon generosity to me about the Fudges—they have added two hundred pounds to my share of the profits from their own, which is a thing, of course, I could never have dreamt of."

Still, financially troublesome though he was, Moore kept with the utmost scrupulousness to his bargains. The letter following, written to Godwin in 1811, illustrates his anxiety not to transgress in the least degree.

My dear Sir,

I ought to have answered you much sooner, but I left town immediately after seeing you, and as I expected to return every day I thought the kind of answer which, unfortunately, I am forced to give could be more graciously delivered in person than by letter—however as you have taken the trouble of writing to me, I must explain to you in this way my reason for refusing such a very simple and agreeable task as you proposed to me— and the truth is (which I ought to have recollected and told you at the time you asked me) that I am bound not to give a note of Music or a line of poetry connected with music to any house except *Powers* in the Strand. . . . The triflingness of the request you made of me, and the idea of the obscure and innocent medium through which the song was to circulate, made me forget at the time that it would in the least interfere with the terms of my general engagement to Power—but a very little thought convinced me that it would be a manifest violation of them and all I have to ask your pardon for is the delay which has taken place in my answer to your application. . . .

Later in the same year, 1846, a report of Moore's death was spread. It was contradicted, in optimistic terms, which stated that he was in the best of health, and that his letters "to his old friends have been such as they were for the last forty years".

IV

In the autumn of 1846, Moore consulted Brodie about the state of his eyes. He had had trouble with them, on and off, for many years. As early as 1814, he complained in a letter to Murray of a violent headache and inflamed eyes. Twenty years later, he told Mary Shelley that his eyesight was failing.

"I often say I know not which are the more precious things, a pretty woman's eyes or a poor author's. *You* who have tried them in both capacities can best decide."

Bessy had been up to London already, to see Brodie about hers. The famous physician was at his country house in Surrey, and consented to treat Moore on condition that he came and spent a few days with him. Moore was only too glad; he had for the past six months been "almost entirely a recluse". Brodie, walking with him in the garden, told him that, of all the dying patients he had attended, he hardly ever met one that was afraid to die. "Let us hope", wrote Moore, "that this picture of deathbeds, drawn as it is by one who had often studied them, is as true as it is consolatory and even cheering."

The visit to Brodie did him good, and soon afterwards he allowed a neighbour, the Reverend Mr Brown, to take him down to Bath to call on Wordsworth, whom he had not seen for many years. (Moore, forgetting the Paris meeting, and the dinner at Monkhouse's, says that he had not seen the poet since the evening they first met at Rogers'.) He kept no record of the Bath encounter, beyond saying that he had "done the honours". He had also been to see the Mount-Edgcumbes, and reports with evident pleasure that his host, who was ill in bed, was all the better for seeing him.

The end of the year brought an honour from Dublin.

Royal Irish Academy
8th Decr. 1846.

Sir,

I herewith beg to forward the certificate of your election as an Honorary member of this Institution which took place at the last stated meeting held on 30th Nov. The meeting of Council held yesterday was the earliest occasion that presented for maling [*sic*] the document, otherwise it should have been forwarded earlier to Thomas Moore Esqr.

I am Sir

Your obedient Servant
EDWARD CLIBBORN
Assnt. Secty.

Possibly the illiteracy of the document discounted its value in Moore's eyes, for he makes no mention of it in his Journal.

In the spring of 1847, he had the happiness of seeing two very old friends, and recalling many pleasant memories. Corry, the chief comedian of the old Kilkenny troupe, was living in retirement at Cheltenham. He invited Moore to come and see him, and the poet, complying, had the additional joy of meeting the Atkinsons: not, of course, Joe, who was long since dead, but his family. Their voices and faces had changed little, Moore records, and took him freshly back into old times.

Fortified with this visit, he invited himself to stay with Rogers. "I had set my heart, my dear old friend," he wrote, "on having a few more breakfasts with you (to say nothing of dinners) before 'time and the hour has quite run out our day' ": and added as a postscript, "I am sinking here into a mere vegetable." Rogers wrote back most cordially, and begged him to persuade Bessy to come too. For some reason, however, she stayed at home.

Moore had a very happy week with his old friend. The carriage was at his disposal, Rogers suggested to him whom he should call upon (he could hardly remember for himself), and there were several "young people of Holland House", whose society he hankered after. The manager of the opera placed a box at his service, so that he might hear Jenny Lind, but Moore was overcome by the heat and by his round of unaccustomed gaiety. He went another night, and heard Grisi instead.

He wrote, on his return, a happy letter of thanks to Rogers, which is the last included by Russell in his edition of the Memoirs.

The expedition was not repeated. Moore remained at home, steadily losing touch with all but his immediate surroundings. The pension, under Bessy's careful management, sufficed for the needs of both: and, in 1850, a further £100, bestowed on Bessy herself, was added to their joint resources. Moore was not unhappy. He did not suffer, but sank into a state of peace, a dream from which little roused him, secure in the love of his Bessy, with no wants other than those of food and warmth. His faith, always strong, comforted him. "Lean upon God, Bessy, lean upon God," he would say, when she was troubled: and he himself leaned more and more upon the unseen, as the visible world faded from his sight.

The landscape-painter Creswick called to see him, and found him, much aged, pottering about his garden. It was planted with laurels, which inspired Moore to his one attempt at a joke. "You find me," he said, "reposing upon, or among, my laurels." Creswick asked him if he was busy on a prose work. "No," replied Moore tremulously. "I have done with prose, and, what is worse, with poetry too."

In December 1849 he received a visit from Lord John Russell and Lord Lansdowne, to whom he "talked freely and agreeably". The same evening, he was seized with a fit, after which his memory seemed to fail entirely.

In the last year or two, he sank into an apathy, doing little more than breathe: though his condition was "occasionally relieved by flashes which showed that, though the exercise of the mental powers was impeded, the powers themselves were not destroyed". Something of habit remained. To the end, he would ask anxiously after the health of his friends.

He lived on till 1852. On the 25th of February, he sang to himself some of the old favourite airs. The next day he faded peacefully out of life. The "consolatory and even cheering" reflection of Brodie had proved true. Far from fearing death, he did not know when it came to him.

V

Moore was buried in Bromham Churchyard, in a vault on the north side of the church. His will, made in 1828,[1] left everything to Bessy. When he died, he had hardly a penny. His civil list pension, however, was continued to Bessy, and Longmans came forward with an offer of £3,000 for his Journal, provided Lord John Russell would edit it. Lord John was a busy man, and unable to give much of his time, but he at once agreed; and, with the money, an annuity was purchased which kept Bessy to the end of her days. She lived till 1865, gentle, quiet, and universally beloved. It was typical of her that, instead of selling Tom's library, which would have fetched a handsome price, she made a gift of it to the Academy which had honoured him in his declining years.

The *Gentleman's Magazine* for October 1865 recorded her death.

Sept. 4. . . . "At Sloperton Cottage, Mrs Moore, widow of Thomas Moore, esq., author of 'Lalla Rookh'. The respect and esteem which accompanied Mrs Moore to the grave were eminently deserved, and there are few chapters in literary history more interesting than the story of her wedded life."

After describing how Moore met and married her, and how Lord Lansdowne gave them the cottage at Sloperton, the writer continues:—

"It is very true that he mixed in the fashionable world without her, and that to some extent she felt his absence; but whoever might be his Lesbias, and Chloes, and Sapphos, 'Bessy' was the sole object of his affections, 'Bessy' alone possessed his heart."

[1] A former will, to the same effect but even simpler, was made in 1819.

CHAPTER XX

CONCLUSION

Survey of Moore's character and achievements

THE private lives of writers often add little lustre to their reputations, or are, at best, irrelevant. Moore was a happy exception. There was, except in the financial sense, no conflict between his private and his public life. His character was expressed in both alike. He had no vice. His worst fault was the weakness that limited his art to sentiment and his conduct to the avoidance, wherever possible, of painful emotion. He had, in early years, his share of vanity, but it led him neither to jealousy nor rancour. The only note of bitterness that creeps in was sounded when, in the late eighteen-twenties, he found that no political preferment or office was to come his way. His love of a lord had let him down. That he did love a lord, that he was proud of his distinguished friends and acquaintances, is undeniable: but we have no evidence that he was therefore inconsiderate to humble folk, or valued them less: rather the contrary.

Moore had high principles, and was faithful to them without being a prig or a bore. A good Christian, he turned to God as naturally in joy as in grief. He was generous, humane, and kind. He loved good talk and good victuals. He had both wit and humour. Money burned a hole in his pocket, and his charity was out of proportion to his means. He was proud—the nearest approach to ferocity he could show was when anything threatened his pride—but never so as to be uncouth or hurt a friend. And, if a man be judged by his friends, Moore approached greatness. "A man", wrote Lord John Russell, "who was courted and esteemed by Lord Lansdowne, Mr Canning, Sir Robert Peele, Mr Rogers, Mr Sydney Smith, and Lord Byron, must have had social as well as literary merits of no common order." Russell continues, "It was part of his nature to prize the tributes he received from such men, but likewise to doubt whether he was worthy of so much admiration." He repaid it with an extreme loyalty which made it difficult for him to criticize anyone who had used him well. He refused a profitable offer because it would mean criticizing Canning. He avoided, in his *Sheridan* and *Byron*, what he could not approve—grave fault in a biographer, but likeable weakness in a friend.

His friendliness was noted by all. "I was at my ease with him in a minute," wrote Charles MacFarlane, of their first meeting; "and before we parted, after a talk of nearly two hours, I felt as if we had been old familiar friends." To a quick sympathy he added laughter and high spirits,

"Moore's spirit," MacFarlane goes on, "was most hilarious. It was impossible to be with him and not be caught by it. His hearty, though not very loud laugh, was irresistibly catching. I have been in his company at times when I was beginning to feel, like himself, the heavy weight of family anxieties and worldly cares, disappointments, and troubles, but I never could hear that laugh without joining in it."

Politically, Moore was negligible. His position in politics was the paradoxical one of an adventurer with principles. Catholic Emancipation was the only issue upon which he was effective, probably because it was the one principle he held which was also practical politics. He was a shrewd observer, drawn to politics by a mixture of patriotism, self-interest, and moral zeal. The patriotism, with the exception above, was best exercised in other ways. The self-interest was disappointed: none of those he sought to serve rewarded him with preferment, until he got his insignificant and belated pension. The moral zeal was inconvenient: no leader could depend on his support.

As a husband, he was loving, faithful, and single-hearted. With a wife who effaced herself and always put him first, he was far less selfish than nine men out of ten. What would ruin so many hardly corrupted him at all. As a father, he was less happy. Affectionate and indulgent, he sought suddenly and too late to use the curb. Young Tom was never able to understand his father's strictness about money, and indeed, springing as it did from an inconsistent attitude, nothing but mutual sympathy could enforce it. In entering both his boys for the army, Moore showed a want of perception. It was natural that he should wish to launch them as "gentlemen", but he should have reckoned the cost, and cut their coats according to his cloth. By refusing to buy back Tom's commission, he sent him (indirectly) to the Foreign Legion and to the hardships which brought his death. Yet it is not fair to blame him. Had he bought the commission back, there was no guarantee that a similar thing might not happen again. And, whatever faults Moore committed towards his children, he paid for them to the full.

Moore's poetry lacks subtlety and depth of imagination. It comes rather from fancy—but not in Coleridge's sense of the word, which is Freudian, that is, which draws its images from the individual memory; for Moore worked best when he had no previous experience to fetter him. He had, as he said himself, "that kind of imagination which is chilled by the real scene and can best describe what it has not seen, merely taking it from the description of others". It glows at no great heat, excelling at a gentle after-dinner melancholy, and a dexterous lightness. "He ought," growled Hazlitt, "to write with a crystal pen on silver paper." And what gave excellence to his songs, the clarity, the simplicity, and the terseness, was a handicap to his longer poems. He had learned habits, appropriate to his peculiar gifts, which he could not shed.

But, in his songs, he is unrivalled. The "particularity of talent, or rather, talents" of which Byron spoke was indeed "all his own".

Even Bagehot, who complained that there was "a little falsetto in the tone", allowed them to be "the best of this sort we have". The best of the *Melodies*, air and verse together, are perfect of their kind, and a kind rare in the English language.

What is more, they transcended the audience at whom they were aimed, and inspired the soul of a people. If it be a test of great art that it appeals to the untutored, Moore's *Melodies* have at least a title to greatness. They caught something that was struggling to be born, and gave it birth. The baby was a girl instead of a boy, but the Irish people took it passionately to their hearts. The *Melodies* became hymns and rallying-cries, and it is an irony, not unpleasing, that the cause of Irish nationalism owes as much to the little dapper poet as to the Liberator: maybe more. Moore has been under a cloud, but it is dispersing, and we shall soon see him in his true places, his high seat of honour in Ireland, and his modest but permanent cottage on Parnassus.

So, in one way and another, he is safe: and the world will be in a bad way when he and Bessy can no longer win our liking.

APPENDIX A

ON the general subject of Moore's relations with women, the following excerpt from *Traits of Character*, by "A Contemporary" (Elizabeth Rennie) is worth quoting:

"He said nearly all the heroines of his lays and melodies were flesh and blood, repeating several of their names, and where they lived, many of them merged into honoured wives and mothers. Though it would be doing him gross injustice to assert that he boasted of his successes with women, still he was very content you should guess and divine he was the admired of many. I believe that was quite the truth. He told us of one young lady who laid regular siege to him; not content with meeting him in society at the houses of friends, whom they mutually visited, she used to wait for him in a carriage, accompanied by a female companion, in sight of the house where he was lodging, in Bury Street, St. James, watching his return from his evening round of parties, frequently till two or three o'clock in the morning, and then pounce on him.

I naturally inquired

'And what then? Surely, if, as you say, she is a girl of character and in a good position, she does not enter your apartment, even with a friend, at that unseemly hour?'

'Oh dear, no,' he plaintively and naïvely answered, 'she makes me get into the carriage with her.'

'And what then?'

'Why, she tells me—but I must not repeat it—she tells me how much she admires my writings.'

'And yourself also, I presume?'

'Indeed, I am afraid so.'

'And do you not reprove her, and point out how wrong all this is, as you are a married man?'

'Indeed I do, and beg and implore her not to come again; but she begins to cry, and what can a man do or say then?' Of course, I was silent; what argument can one oppose to woman's invincible weapon —tears? 'The other night,' continued Moore, 'she cried so dreadfully, I was afraid she was going to have hysterics, and that I should have to go into my room for Eau de Cologne. I was quite in agony.'"

Elizabeth Rennie reports that she saw the girl at a dance a little later.

"She was a very pretty girl; and, considering how much distressed and annoyed he had expressed himself as being at her nocturnal visitations to Bury Street, he certainly lavished on her no small share of gentle and assiduous attention."

The instance was typical. Moore was a charmer, and he meant no harm.

APPENDIX B

*An Attempt to Vindicate the American
Character, being principally a Reply
to the Intemperate Animadversion of
Thomas Moore Esq. Philadelphia 1806.*

This is an anonymous work, written in verse, with a prose preface
and notes. The verse is undistinguished. "You," cries the poet,
apostrophizing Moore,

> "The smallest speck in trifling works espy [1]
> View naught save ruins with the naked eye
> O'er stately edifices scorn to pore,
> But in one town five mouldering walls explore . . ."

Here are points from the notes:

[1] "Nothing can prove more the perversion of his sight while in this
country than the trivial objects which he suffers to engage it, and
which he views with all the scrutiny of an entomologist; while anything large that is not in a lamentable, or what he considers a lamentable, condition entirely escapes his notice."

Further,

"In the preface I have allowed Mr Moore credit for his very uncommon talents, but at the same time lamented his deficiency in the
powers of ordinary perception, or, in other words, his want of a clear
unbiassed judgment. This defect is perceptible in almost every line he
has written on America: if in one state he passes over a rough road he
immediately notes it in his memory for a reflection upon all, and were
he to be borne through every other over turnpikes paved with gold,
it is with me a question if they would be equal to a removal of his
first impression."

APPENDIX C

THOMAS MOORE TO LORD HOLLAND

Monday, November 5, 1821.

DEAR LORD HOLLAND,

What you said yesterday about the sale of Lord B.'s Memoirs made so strong an impression upon me that my thoughts have been, ever since, occupied upon the subject; and it was my resolution—if, after an honest consideration of the transaction, it appeared to me that I could be fairly thought to have done anything wrong or unworthy in thus disposing of these papers—to prevail upon Murray (which I could easily have done) to cancel the deed between us and take back the money he had paid, having it in my power from the kindness of Lord Lansdowne and Lord John Russell to refund nearly the whole of the sum without much inconvenience to me. After the most anxious consideration, however, I see so little change effected in the original state of the case by my late arrangement with Murray, that I cannot perceive any necessity for retracing the steps I have taken. In the first place, my depositing the MS. in Murray's hands neither increases the certainty of publication nor hastens the time of it, and in the next place, I had already pledged myself to Lord Byron to be the Editor, in case I should survive, of these papers, leaving a part of them in their present state and exercising my discretion over the rest. With respect to the portion of them that is to remain unaltered—except the passage about Madame de Staël and an indecent circumstance alluded to in his last interview with Lady Byron (which, however, interpreting my pledge to extend to facts rather than phrases I shall feel no hesitation whatever in softening down) I know but little in the responsibility which I have incurred, to shrink from. The alleged mis-statement of Sir S. Romilly's conduct may be easily remedied by furnishing me with the means of contradicting it, and with respect to any charge against Mr. Brougham (though I do not remember that any such exists in the work) I can answer for his seeing all that is said about him and thereby having an opportunity of correcting any misrepresentation.

What Lady Holland yesterday remarked about Mrs. *L.* is, I find upon recollection, founded entirely on her own suspicions, as Lord B.

merely mentions a nameless person whom he calls his "love of loves" and I never met with but one individual, besides Lady H., who supposed it to allude to the lady in question. The slighting passage about Rogers' Human Life is in the part over which I have discretionary power, and, at all events, is fully atoned for by the estimation which Lord B., on all other occasions, shows for his works, ranking him indeed, at the very head of all the poets of the present day. The allusion to Lady Holland herself deserves no further notice than her own excellent sense bestows upon it, and would, from the present state of his feelings to her be most easily relinquished. Altogether, indeed, as far as concerns those I care for, or who, I think, *ought* to be cared for, there is nothing besides the usual difficulties attending all such responsibilities to make me regret or wish to alter the arrangement I have made.

There is one suggestion, however, which I owe to my conversation with your Lordship, and that is the necessity of exercising the discretion given me as soon as possible and not leaving the passages which I think ought to be omitted to the chances of a future time or the taste of a less scrupulous Editor.

May I ask you to show this letter to Lord Lansdowne on his arrival? To him, above most of the persons of this world, I should wish my conduct on every occasion to appear free from suspicion or reproach.

Ever, my dear Lord, yours most faithfully,

THOMAS MOORE.

APPENDIX D

MOORE considered all portraits of him unsatisfactory.

"In talking of the attempt that had been made to take my portrait, Phillips [the painter] said, that what the public naturally expected to see in a portrait of me was the gay fancy and wit which they had been accustomed to associate with my writings, and that it was the effort to give this which made my portraits unlike me; whereas the character of my head was deep thoughtfulness."

Memoirs, vii. 43–4.

"Having nothing in my round potato face but what they cannot catch,—i.e. mobility of character,—the consequence is that a portrait of me can be only one or other of two very disagreeable things,—a *caput mortuum*, or a caricature."

Memoirs, vii. 122.

Yet another description of Moore's appearance is provided by Elizabeth Rennie:

"He was a very well-dressed, bright, sparkling-looking little man. It is a disenchanting phrase to apply to a sentimental poet; but I must say in his general appearance there was something that very nearly approximated to what is now denominated as 'jolly'. He had dark and most vivacious eyes, hair of the same colour, and in sufficient abundance, glossy, and nicely arranged; a broad, commanding forehead; a complexion fresh, clear, and ruddy; small, but well-defined, features; a mouth which seemed made alone for mirth and brimming smiles; an extraordinary play and expression of countenance, whose changeful variety yet ever betrayed the genius within; a quick, brisk, active gait; a merry, joyous laugh; and the generally-diffused impress of a happy, healthy, easy man—one contented quite with the lot he had drawn in life, and in perfect amity and peace with those about him."

AUTHORITIES

THE prime source of information about Moore is the eight volume edition of his Letters and Journal, edited with a brief memoir and notes by Lord John Russell, and published by Longman, Brown, Green, and Longmans in 1853-6. The Journal proper begins in August 1818, and continues till 1848. The earlier years are covered by Moore's own Memoir, "begun many years since, but never, I fear, to be completed," and dated 1833. This takes him from his birth to 1799, with an additional few pages for 1806, and is supplemented by a number of letters written by and to Moore from 1793 to 1818. The last volume was filled out with a selection of letters which had come to the editor's hand since he began his task.

Lord John Russell, a busy man, made rather a summary job of the editing, and came in for sharp criticism. He appears to have expurgated the Journal pretty freely, particularly in the years 1828-9. Still, failing the MS., which is not available, he is our best authority: and Moore was such a copious letter-writer that we can check the Journal on almost all the crucial passages of his life. (He wrote over twelve hundred letters to James Power, his music publisher, of which Russell used only fifty-seven.)

Besides the published letters, I have had access to more than two hundred unpublished letters of Moore, in various places, and to a large collection of letters received by him, and documents relating to him, preserved by his wife after his death.

The books, pamphlets, etc., which I have consulted include:
Holland House. Princess Marie Liechtenstein. 1874.
The Pope of Holland House. Lady Elizabeth Seymour. 1906.
Letters of Lord Byron. R. G. Howarth. 1936.
Byron. Ethel Colburn Mayne. 1924.

Byron. A. Maurois. 1930.

Life and Letters of Lady Byron. 1929.

Lady Byron: A Letter to Thomas Moore Esq, occasioned by his Notices of the Life of the late Rt. Hon. Lord Byron. 1830.

Life, Letters and Journals of George Ticknor. 1876.

The Creevey Papers. Rt. Hon. Sir Herbert Maxwell, Bart. 1905.

Diary, Reminiscences and Correspondence of Henry Crabb Robinson. 1872.

Memoirs of the Life of Sir Walter Scott. J. G. Lockhart. 1836.

Traits of Character. "A Contemporary." (Elizabeth Rennie.) 1860.

Reminiscences of a Literary Life. Charles MacFarlane. 1917.

Essay on Moore's Life of Lord Byron. Macaulay.

Correspondence between the Rt. Hon. J. W. Croker and the Rt. Hon. Lord John Russell on some Passages of Moore's Diary. 1854.

Notes from the Letters of Thomas Moore to his Music Publisher, James Power. Thomas Crofton Croker. 1854.[1]

Life of Thomas Moore. James Burke. 1852.

Tom Moore in Bermuda. J. C. L. Clark. 1897.

Moore, Poet and Patriot. J. P. Gunning. 1900.

Thomas Moore and His First Editions. Andrew Gibson. 1904.

Moore en France. Allen B. Thomas. 1911.

Summer in Bermuda. M. A. Bosworth. 1912.

Thomas Moore. Stephen Gwynn. 1904.

Tom Moore. W. F. Trench. 1934.

Thomas Moore. Seamus MacCall. 1936.

Essays in Irish Biography. W. F. P. Stockley. 1933.

Samuel Rogers and his Circle. R. Ellis Roberts. 1911.

The Smith of Smiths. Hesketh Pearson. 1934.

Rebellious Frasers. Miriam M. H. Thrall. 1933.

The Wild Irish Girl. Lionel Stevenson. 1936.

Dublin under the Georges. Constantia Maxwell. 1936.

Dublin. Lady Longford. 1936.

[1] New York: publication suppressed in London.

Irish Literature and Drama. Stephen Gwynn. 1936.
The Cambridge History of English Literature. 1932.
Gentleman's Magazine. (*passim.*)
Edinburgh Review. (*passim.*)
Quarterly Review. (*passim.*)

INDEX

Macklin, Hugh George, 36
McMahon, 65
Magee (later Archbishop), 34
Maginn, William, 181, 231
Mahony, Captain, 11
Malone, T. S., 12
Marryat, Captain, 168
Masterson, Mr, 63–5
Masterson, Sally, 41, 65
Mayne, Ethel Colbourne, 229
Meara, Mrs, 260, 282
Melbourne, Lord, 252, 253, 257
Melville, Lord, 205
Mercier, 26
Merry, Mr and Mrs, 91, 93, 96
Metternich, 187
Moira, Lord, 52, 66, 70, 75, 78–80, 81,
84, 88, 89, 93, 101, 108, 117, 144,
147–50, 187, 201, 297
Molloy, James Scott, 274
Monkhouse, 242, 293
Montpensier, Duc de, 83, 187
Moore, Anastasia, 6–12, 14, 16–18, 22,
23, 29, 34, 46–7, 51, 53–4, 60, 61,
67, 68, 70, 73, 74–6, 78, 79, 89,
90, 91, 92, 101, 105, 143, 152,
178, 190, 196, 199, 262, 271
Moore, Anastasia Mary, 151, 154–9
Moore, Anne Jane Barbara, 151, 153,
168, 217
Moore, Bessy, 5, 39, 40, 105, 107,
142–7, 149, 150, 151–61, 169,
173–4, 177, 180, 196, 197, 200,
252, 257–8, 268, 269, 272–83,
284, 293–6, 299, 300
Moore, Catherine, 14 (note), 17, 19,
40, 89, 90, 96, 199, 252, 254
Moore, Ellen, 14 (note), 88, 197, 199,
252, 257, 258, 260, 261, 271, 273–
4, 281
Moore, John, 6, 7, 23, 24, 28, 53, 68,
76, 88–91, 108, 143, 149, 153–4,
159, 167, 196
Moore, John Russell, 161, 252, 254,
257, 271–3, 275–9, 288, 289
Moore, 3rd daughter, Olivia, 152

Moore, Tom, birth and parentage, 6; his mother's influence, 7; happy childhood and youth, 9; lack of passion in his poetry, 10; gift for reciting, 11; schooldays, 12; theatricals and early rhymes, 13; love of music, 17; confession, 23; political influences, 23; literary and debating society, 25; first appearances in print, 26; entry on Trinity Register, 28; holiday at Blackrock, 31; Moore as a poet, 32; Trinity successes, 33; friends at Trinity, 35; love affairs, 37; introduction to Irish music, 42; influence of Hudson and Emmet, 42; letter in "The Press", 47; the Trinity Inquisition, 52; lyrics inspired by Emmet's death, 56; recent disparagement of Moore, 57; begins translation of *Anacreon*, 60; graduates B.A. and leaves Trinity, 61; first journey to England, 62; lodging at George Street, Portman Square, 64; initiation at the Middle Temple, 65; homesickness, 65; introduction to Lord Moira, 66; summer in Ireland, 67; progress of *Anacreon*, 71; début as a singer, 72; serious illness, 73; dedication of *Anacreon*, 74; introduction to the Prince, 75; visit to Dublin, 77; singing improved, 77; first visit to Donington Park, 78; social success, 79; swindled by Carpenter, 81; "The Gipsy Prince", 83; financial worries, 84; the "Thomas Little" poems, 85; refuses Irish Laureateship, 89; departure for Bermuda, 91; stays with the Hamiltons, in Virginia, 93; lack of visual sense, 94; finds Bermuda disappointing, 95; travels in America, 96; meeting with Hudson, 97; impressions of